2021 INTERNATIONAL COMPARISON
PROGRAM FOR ASIA AND THE PACIFIC

PURCHASING POWER PARITIES AND REAL EXPENDITURES

A SUMMARY REPORT

AUGUST 2024

ASIAN DEVELOPMENT BANK

Notes:
In this publication, "$" refers to United States dollars, "₹" refers to Indian rupees, "B" refers to baht, "CNY" refers to yuan, "HK$" refers to Hong Kong dollars, "Rp" refers to rupiah, "S$" refers to Singapore dollars, and "Tk" refers to taka. ADB recognizes "China" as the People's Republic of China, and "Hong Kong" as Hong Kong, China.

On the cover: From left to right — **Women buying their daily supplies at Tekka Market in Little India**. Although Singapore has a more progressive society, housekeeping remains mostly a female responsibility (photo by Lester Ledesma, ADB). **Fruit Seller in Bangladesh.** A vendor is busy selling a variety of fruits at a market in Bangladesh (photo by Eric Sales, ADB).

Cover design by Rhommel Rico.

Contents

Tables, Figures, and Boxes v
Foreword vii
Acknowledgments ix
Abbreviations xi

1   Introduction to the International Comparison Program in Asia and the Pacific 1
    2021 International Comparison Program in Asia and the Pacific 2
    Participating Economies in Asia and the Pacific 2
    Structure of the Report 3

2   Macroeconomic Measures and Intereconomy Comparisons 4
    International Comparisons: Exchange Rates or Purchasing Power Parities? 4
    Exchange Rates: Why Are They Inappropriate? 5
    Purchasing Power Parities of Currencies 5
    Purchasing Power Parities and Price Levels 7
    Nominal and Real Expenditures 7
    Uses and Applications of Purchasing Power Parities 9

3   Summary Results from the 2021 International Comparison Program in Asia and the Pacific 11
    Gross Domestic Product: Size and Shares of Economies of the Asia and Pacific Region 13
    Per Capita Real Gross Domestic Product and Standards of Living 16
    Purchasing Power Parities and Price Levels of Economies for Gross Domestic Product 19
        in Asia and the Pacific
    Household Final Consumption Expenditure 21
    Per Capita Income and Household Expenditure 21
    Per Capita Expenditures for Selected Aggregates 24
    General Government Final Consumption Expenditure 25
    Gross Fixed Capital Formation 28
    Price Level Indexes for Gross Domestic Products and Its Major Components 32

4   Comparative Analysis of Results from 2017 and 2021 International Comparison Program 34
        in Asia and the Pacific
    Revisions to the 2017 International Comparison Program in Asia and the Pacific 34
    Consistency between the 2017 and 2021 Results 35
    Size and Relative Shares of Economies, 2017 and 2021 38
    Interpreting and Decomposing Changes in the Size (Real) of Economies in Asia and the Pacific 39

5   Governance and Methodology 43
    Governance and Structure 43
    Methodology for the International Comparison Program in Asia and the Pacific 45
    Survey Framework 49
    Data Editing and Validation 49
    New Approach for Housing Comparisons in Asia and the Pacific 50
    Aggregation of Price Data and Compilation of Purchasing Power Parities 53
    Reference Purchasing Power Parities 54

6   **Summary and Conclusions**   55
      COVID-19 Challenges and Opportunities   55
      Methodological Developments   56
      Key Results   56
      Uses and Limitation of Purchasing Power Parities in Policy Making and Intereconomy Comparisons   57

Appendixes
1   Statistical Tables on Purchasing Power Parities and Real Expenditures, 2021   60
2   Statistical Tables on Purchasing Power Parities and Real Expenditures, 2017 Revised   77
3   Scope and Coverage of Main Gross Domestic Product Aggregates—2017 and 2021 Cycles   94
4   List of Reference Purchasing Power Parities   95
5   Deriving Price Level Indexes and Per Capita Real Expenditure Indexes with   98
         Asia and the Pacific = 100
6   Participating Economies—Implementing Agencies and Local Currency Units   100
7   Membership of the Regional Advisory Board in the International Comparison Program   101
         for Asia and the Pacific

Glossary   102
References   110

Tables, Figures, and Boxes

TABLES

2.1	Purchasing Power Parities, Exchange Rates, and Price Levels—An Illustrative Example, 2021	6
2.2	Purchasing Power Parities for Gross Domestic Product, Individual Consumption Expenditure by Households, and Gross Fixed Capital Formation for Selected Economies, 2021	8
2.3	Exchange Rate-Based and Purchasing Power Parity-Based Indicators	9
3.1	Summary Results for Gross Domestic Product, 2021	14
3.2	Summary Results for Individual Consumption Expenditure by Households, 2021	22
3.3	Per Capita Real Gross Domestic Product, Actual Individual Consumption by Households, and Individual Consumption Expenditure by Households, 2021	23
3.4	Per Capita Real Expenditure Indexes for Actual Individual Consumption by Households and its Selected Components, 2021	25
3.5	Summary Results for Government Final Consumption Expenditure, 2021	26
3.6	Summary Results for Gross Fixed Capital Formation, 2021	29
3.7	Price Level Indexes for Gross Domestic Product and its Major Components, 2021	33
4.1	Economy-Level Decomposition of Change in Real Gross Domestic Product, 2017–2021	41
5.1	Composition of Main Aggregates of Gross Domestic Product	47
5.2	Percentage Change in Purchasing Power Parities for Gross Domestic Product and Individual Consumption Expenditure by Households—Reference Volume to New Hybrid	52

FIGURES

3.1	Economy Shares of Real and Nominal Gross Domestic Product, 2021	15
3.2	Real and Nominal Gross Domestic Product, 2021	16
3.3	Per Capita Real and Nominal Gross Domestic Product, 2021	17
3.4	Lorenz Curves for Per Capita Real and Nominal Gross Domestic Product, 2021	18
3.5	Price Level Indexes for Economies for Gross Domestic Product, 2021	20
3.6	Price Level Index versus Per Capita Real Gross Domestic Product, 2021	20
3.7	Lorenz Curves for Per Capita Real Gross Domestic Product and Per Capita Real Household Consumption Aggregates, 2021	24
3.8	Economy Shares of Real and Nominal Government Final Consumption Expenditure, 2021	27
3.9	Per Capita Real and Nominal Government Final Consumption Expenditure in Asia and the Pacific, 2021	28
3.10	Economy Shares of Real and Nominal Gross Fixed Capital Formation, 2021	30
3.11	Per Capita Real and Nominal Gross Fixed Capital Formation in Asia and the Pacific, 2021	31
4.1	Ratio of Revised to Original Purchasing Power Parities for Gross Domestic Product, 2017	36
4.2	Ratio of 2021 Purchasing Power Parities for Gross Domestic Product to Extrapolations from 2017 (Revised)	37
4.3	Real Gross Domestic Product, 2017 and 2021	39
5.1	International Comparison Program—Governance Structure	44
5.2	Workflow for the International Comparison Program	44
5.3	Pyramid Structure for Aggregates	46
5.4	The New Hybrid Approach for Comparisons of Prices and Real Expenditures for Housing	51

BOXES

2.1   Purchasing Power Parity Defined   6
3.1   Notes on Data and Results for the 2021 International Comparison Program in Asia and the Pacific   12

Foreword

The 2021 International Comparison Program (ICP) global cycle saw the participation of 176 economies with 21 economies from Asia and the Pacific. For the 2021 ICP cycle, the Asian Development Bank (ADB) served as the regional implementing agency (RIA) for the Asia and Pacific region for the fourth time, following the 2005, 2011, and 2017 cycles.

The ICP cycles had been set to transition from the previous 6-year gap to a 3-year interval after the 2017 ICP round, following recommendations of the United Nations Statistical Commission. The next cycle was due in 2020; however, the onset of the coronavirus disease (COVID-19) pandemic disrupted these plans, leading to a decision to shift the 2020 benchmark to 2021, a period when the regional and global economies were still recovering from the pandemic's aftermath. Providing continued leadership as the RIA during this challenging ICP cycle reflects ADB's commitment to fulfilling its role as a knowledge bank.

In the 2021 ICP cycle, 21 economies from the Asia and Pacific region participated—Bangladesh; Bhutan; Brunei Darussalam; Cambodia; the People's Republic of China; Fiji; Hong Kong, China; India; Indonesia; the Lao People's Democratic Republic; Malaysia; Maldives; Mongolia; Nepal; Pakistan; the Philippines; Singapore; Sri Lanka; Taipei,China; Thailand, and Viet Nam. Despite the challenges posed by COVID-19, the implementing agencies of the participating economies successfully conducted price surveys and employed innovative methods of price collection to overcome the mobility constraints imposed by lockdowns and completed the 2021 cycle. This achievement underscores the tireless efforts and unwavering commitment of the staff of participating statistical agencies, who overcame obstacles to adhere to established guidelines at both global and regional levels.

As the RIA, ADB developed innovative strategies to maintain data quality and integrity. Increased use of virtual meetings made it possible to provide continuous training and guidance to the implementing agencies throughout the cycle. Additionally, software tools were provided for the compilation, rigorous data validation, and management of price and other data required for the ICP exercise. In the 2021 ICP cycle, a breakthrough in methodology was achieved by ADB by developing a new hybrid approach for measuring comparison-resistant housing services. The hybrid approach combines the ICP's two recommended approaches for housing, namely, rental and volume approaches. After thorough review, this hybrid method was endorsed by the Regional Advisory Board and the ICP Technical Advisory Group, thus replacing the nonstandard reference volume approach used in the regional comparisons between 2005 and 2017.

This Report presents 2021 regional purchasing power parity (PPP) and PPP-based real gross domestic product (GDP) estimates and its major components for the 21 participating economies and the revised results for the 2017 ICP cycle. To explore more detailed results from the 2021 ICP cycle and the 2017 ICP revisions, users are encouraged to visit the results and data available online (https://icp.adb.org).

The global ICP results released by the World Bank in May 2024 incorporate these regional results, underscoring the pivotal role of Asia and the Pacific in the global economy. The 21 economies of the region represent over half of the world's population, and account for 27% of the world's GDP in exchange rate terms and 35% of global GDP in PPP terms in 2021.

I believe that the 2021 ICP regional results and the corresponding global ICP results will provide policy makers, practitioners, and general users with comprehensive information on price levels and PPP-based GDP expenditure values for comparative analysis and policy applications.

I wish to express my sincere appreciation to everyone who contributed to the success of this project, including the ICP Regional Advisory Board for Asia and the Pacific for their overall guidance, the ICP's group of experts for their technical and methodological advice, the World Bank ICP Global Office for their technical guidance to the regional program, and the dedicated ADB ICP team, under the guidance and overall supervision of Elaine S. Tan, Director, Data Division, Economic Research and Development Impact Department. Most importantly, I extend my appreciation and gratitude to the implementing agencies in the 21 participating economies whose resilience and commitment paved the way for the successful completion of this very challenging 2021 cycle.

Albert F. Park
Chief Economist and Director General
Economic Research and Development Impact Department
Asian Development Bank

Acknowledgments

The Data Division (formerly Statistics and Data Innovation Unit) of the Economic Research and Development Impact Department (ERDI) of the Asian Development Bank (ADB) implemented the 2021 International Comparison Program (ICP) for Asia and the Pacific. Kaushal Joshi, principal statistician, ERDI, served as the regional coordinator of the 2021 ICP cycle for the region and led the analysis of the results and preparation of this summary report with Prasada Rao.

Through the committed support and dedication of many governments, organizations, and individuals, the 2021 ICP for Asia and the Pacific was successfully completed. Our gratitude goes to the implementing agencies in the 21 participating economies, which rose to the challenge of COVID-19 by adopting innovative ways of collecting prices and estimating gross domestic product expenditure weights, which are the fundamental requirements for estimating the 2021 purchasing power parities for Asia and the Pacific. ADB is therefore deeply grateful to the heads of the following implementing agencies: Bangladesh Bureau of Statistics, Bangladesh; National Statistics Bureau, Bhutan; Department of Economic Planning and Statistics, Brunei Darussalam; National Institute of Statistics, Cambodia; National Bureau of Statistics of China, the People's Republic of China; Fiji Bureau of Statistics, Fiji; Census and Statistics Department, Hong Kong, China; Ministry of Statistics and Programme Implementation, India; Badan Pusat Statistik, Indonesia; Lao Statistics Bureau, the Lao People's Democratic Republic; Department of Statistics Malaysia, Malaysia; Maldives Bureau of Statistics, Maldives; National Statistics Office of Mongolia, Mongolia; National Statistics Office, Nepal; Pakistan Bureau of Statistics, Pakistan; Philippine Statistics Authority, the Philippines; Department of Statistics, Singapore; Department of Census and Statistics, Sri Lanka; Directorate-General of Budget, Accounting, and Statistics, Taipei,China; Trade Policy and Strategy Office, Thailand; and General Statistics Office, Viet Nam.

The successful conclusion of the 2021 ICP in Asia and the Pacific was made possible by the staunch support and commitment of the following coordinators and deputy coordinators of the ICP teams in 21 participating economies who led their teams in all facets of price data collection, validation, editing, submission, and coordination with ADB: Abdul Kadir Miah and Md. Nazmul Hoque, Bangladesh; Bikash Gurung and Karma Deki, Bhutan; Norsalina Mat Salleh and Siti Kamariyah Mohammad, Brunei Darussalam; Sim Ly and Keo Chettra, Cambodia; Yang Jialiang and Hu Xuemei, the People's Republic of China; Radhika Kumar and Bimlesh Krishna, Fiji; Lau Kwok Shun and Ma Wai Sze, Hong Kong, China; Narender Kumar Santoshi and Deepti Srivastava, India; Nurul Hasanudin and Windhiarso Ponco Adi Putranto, Indonesia; Salika Chanthalavong, Bannalath Khammerng, and Saykham Sisombath, the Lao People's Democratic Republic; Fuziah Md. Amin, Maslina Samsudin, and Nor Hashiah Othman, Malaysia; Aishath Hassan and Sajida Ahmed, Maldives; Erdenesan Eldev-Ochir and Oyunjargal Mangalsuren, Mongolia; Gyanendra Bajracharya and Arun Gautam, Nepal; Naseer Ahmad and Ahtasham Gul, Pakistan; Divina Gracia del Prado and Vivian Ilarina, the Philippines; Low Yan Hua Wendy and Ng Zhe Jing Sarah, Singapore; M. D. S. Senanayake, M. T. T. Thiloka, and

P. H. Walpita, Sri Lanka; Shwu-Chwen Chiou and Chih-Hung Tsao, Taipei,China; Wasinee Yaisawang, Nuntanut Chitsamphandhvej, and Wanviga Parktoop, Thailand; and Do Thi Ngoc and Nguyen Thu Oanh, Viet Nam.

The leadership and guidance provided by members of the 2021 ICP for Asia and the Pacific Regional Advisory Board through their meeting deliberations are gratefully acknowledged. These include the director general, National Institute of Statistics, Cambodia; director general, International Statistical Information Center, National Bureau of Statistics of China, the People's Republic of China; commissioner, Census and Statistics Department, Hong Kong, China; chief statistician of India and secretary, Ministry of Statistics and Programme Implementation; chief statistician, Department of Statistics Malaysia, Malaysia (co-chair); chief statistician, Maldives Bureau of Statistics, Maldives; and director general, Trade Policy and Strategy Office, Thailand. Thanks are also due to the institutional members of the Regional Advisory Board, namely, ADB through its chief economist and ERDI director general (co-chair) and Statistics Division, United Nations Economic and Social Commission for Asia and the Pacific through its director; as well as ex-officio members, including ICP global program manager, Development Data Group, World Bank. The regional coordinator of the ICP for Asia and the Pacific, ADB, and the member-secretary, ensured the smooth conduct of the Regional Advisory Board meetings.

The regional program significantly benefited from the technical advice of international experts Gholamreza Hajargasht; Aloke Kar; Arturo Pacificador, Jr.; Prasada Rao; Sergey Sergeev; Peter Tabor; and Aaron Wright at different stages of project implementation. Prasada Rao chaired the experts' group that provided technical guidance on methodology and reviewed the regional results. The ICP global office at the World Bank, led by Marko Olavi Rissanen, provided extensive technical advice through its global ICP team.

Albert Francis Park, chief economist and director general, ERDI, provided motivation and support to the project team at all stages. Criselda de Dios, economics and statistics analyst, provided technical and coordination support during the project's implementation. ADB's ICP project team included national consultants Paolo Kris Adriano, Rhea-Ann Bautista, Juan Miguel dela Cruz, Virginia Ganac, and Mario Ilagan II for the entire duration of the project, while Mel Lorenzo Accad, Kristine Faith Maningding, Gerson Pascua, and Eleanore Ramos supported at different stages. The team provided invaluable support in project implementation, extensive data validation to ensure high data quality, data analysis for calculation of regional results, and preparation of this report, in addition to technical and administrative support to the ICP teams of the participating economies. Ma. Roselia Babalo provided administrative support. Cherry Lynn Zafaralla edited the manuscript and Marjorie Celis proofread and performed page checking. Rhommell Rico created the cover design and Joseph Manglicmot prepared the layout. Guidance on production issues, overall compliance checks, and assistance in web dissemination were provided by the ADB Department of Communications and Knowledge Management.

Elaine S. Tan
Director, Data Division

Abbreviations

ADB	–	Asian Development Bank
AICH	–	actual individual consumption by households
COVID-19	–	coronavirus disease
CPD	–	country–product–dummy
Eurostat	–	Statistical Office of the European Union
GDP	–	gross domestic product
GFCE	–	government final consumption expenditure
GFCF	–	gross fixed capital formation
ICEH	–	individual consumption expenditure by households
ICP	–	International Comparison Program
LCU	–	local currency unit
NPISH	–	nonprofit institutions serving households
OECD	–	Organisation for Economic Co-operation and Development
PLI	–	price level index
PPP	–	purchasing power parity
RIA	–	regional implementing agency
SDG	–	Sustainable Development Goal
TAG	–	Technical Advisory Group
UNSC	–	United Nations Statistical Commission

CHAPTER 1

Introduction to the International Comparison Program in Asia and the Pacific

The International Comparison Program (ICP) is a global statistical initiative aimed at producing reliable estimates of purchasing power parities (PPPs) of currencies, price levels, and real expenditures, in accordance with international standards for statistical data set by the United Nations Statistical Commission (UNSC). In March 2016 during its 47th session, the UNSC instituted the ICP as a permanent element of the global statistical program to be implemented every three years from the 2017 cycle.

The ICP was established in 1968 as a joint research project of the United Nations Statistical Division and the International Comparisons Unit of the University of Pennsylvania with financial contributions from the Ford Foundation and the World Bank.[1] It started as a modest project covering 10 economies, but the ultimate goal was to set up a regular program of global PPP-based comparisons of gross domestic product (GDP). The ICP has since evolved into a comprehensive global statistical program. The last cycle of the ICP in 2017 encompassed 176 economies globally. The current cycle for 2021, which is the 10th in the series, covers 176 economies as well.

The ICP covers several regions, with a regional implementing agency (RIA) responsible for coordinating and implementing the program and producing regional PPPs and related results following uniform methods and standards. These RIAs are the Asian Development Bank (ADB) (for Asia and the Pacific), African Development Bank (for Africa), Interstate Statistical Committee of the Commonwealth of Independent States (for the Commonwealth of Independent States), Eurostat (for European countries), Organisation for Economic Co-operation and Development (OECD) (for non-European OECD countries), United Nations Economic Commission for Latin America and the Caribbean (for Latin America and the Caribbean), and United Nations Economic and Social Commission for Western Asia (for Western Asia). The ICP global office established at the World Bank as a permanent unit has been assigned the role of global implementing agency with the responsibility to coordinate with the RIAs and calculation of global PPPs and related results by linking the regional results following established methods.

In 2005, ADB assumed the role of RIA for the ICP in Asia and the Pacific, and continued in this capacity for the 2011, 2017, and 2021 cycles in the region. A hallmark of ADB's approach in implementing the ICP is its commitment to principles of transparency and maintaining the quality and integrity of data crucial for compiling PPPs and real expenditures. ADB has effectively cultivated cooperation and strong commitment among participating economies, fostering a sense of ownership for the regional program and its outcomes. All participating economies have diligently followed the guidelines established for the ICP at both global and regional levels.

The Asia and Pacific region, with ADB as RIA, leads an active research program aimed at enhancing the methodology used in the ICP. Significant contributions

---

1   World Bank. International Comparison Program—History. https://www.worldbank.org/en/programs/icp/history.

from the region to the ICP methodology development include the introduction in the 2005 and 2011 ICP cycles of a method for productivity adjustments for comparing government employees' compensation and the development of an innovative hybrid method in the 2021 ICP cycle that combines standard ICP approaches based on rental and volume data for comparing prices and real expenditures in the comparison-resistant housing services.

2021 International Comparison Program in Asia and the Pacific

The Asia and Pacific region, like the rest of the world, faced severe socioeconomic setbacks during the coronavirus disease (COVID-19) pandemic. The unprecedented health crisis affected all aspects of life and triggered the worst global economic crisis in a century. Governments worldwide implemented stringent measures to contain the virus, resulting in widespread disruptions to supply chains, a decline in international trade that profoundly impacted domestic demand, and a sharp contraction in economic activities. The pandemic triggered declining economic growth across global economies and a surge in unemployment, hitting sectors such as tourism, hospitality, and retail particularly hard. Lockdowns and social distancing measures caused businesses to shutter, leading to income losses for millions.

The crisis led to a surge in poverty, marking the first increase in decades (ADB 2021). Unprecedented levels of unemployment and income losses affected youth, women, self-employed, and casual workers with lower education levels. Governments responded with massive fiscal stimulus packages to mitigate the economic fallout, but the effects were varied, with some economies experiencing sharper contractions than others.

The lockdowns and mobility restrictions undertaken by the governments also had a severe impact on the statistical data collection activities of the national statistical agencies. The traditional methods like face-to-face data collection through surveys and censuses were either disrupted, lessened, or slowed down (ADB 2021). The ICP cycle originally scheduled for the reference year 2020 was affected from the very beginning leading to a decision to postpone the global program to the reference year 2021 (ECOSOC 2020).

Amidst these unprecedented challenges and even as most economies are still recovering from the effects of COVID-19, the 2021 ICP was undertaken globally including in the Asia and Pacific region. After more than 3 years of committed efforts by the participating economies and ADB in collection and validation of input data in the region, the 2021 ICP cycle has concluded and offers extensive statistical data on internationally comparable macroeconomic aggregates such as real GDP and several of its components for 2021. The 2021 ICP results, in conjunction with the 2017 ICP results, provide snapshots of economies in the region and offer a valuable opportunity for a comparative analysis of their conditions before and after the pandemic.

Participating Economies in Asia and the Pacific

ADB coordinated the regional program for the 2021 ICP in Asia and the Pacific with the following 21 ADB member economies participating: Bangladesh; Bhutan; Brunei Darussalam; Cambodia; the People's Republic of China; Fiji; Hong Kong, China; India; Indonesia; the Lao People's Democratic Republic; Malaysia; Maldives; Mongolia; Nepal; Pakistan; the Philippines; Singapore; Sri Lanka; Taipei,China; Thailand; and Viet Nam.[2]

---

2   Twenty-two economies participated in the 2017 ICP in Asia and the Pacific. These include the 21 economies that participated in the 2021 ICP with the then-participation of Myanmar. Effective 1 February 2021, ADB placed a temporary hold on sovereign project disbursements and new contracts in Myanmar. The bank continues to closely monitor the situation in the country and remains committed to supporting its people. ADB did not make any consultations with Myanmar for the data in this publication.

Under the ICP's global governance arrangements, ADB members that are also members of OECD, namely, Australia, Japan, the Republic of Korea, and New Zealand are participating in the PPP comparisons led by OECD; hence, are not part of the ICP in Asia and the Pacific. ADB regional developing member economies from Central Asia, namely, Armenia, Azerbaijan, Kazakhstan, the Kyrgyz Republic, Tajikistan, and Uzbekistan participated as per the existing arrangements with the Interstate Statistical Committee of the Commonwealth of Independent States as the RIA, while Georgia is included as a guest participant in the Eurostat–OECD comparison.

Despite comprising only 21 economies, Asia and the Pacific with its total population of 3.876 billion as of 2021 accounts for more than half of the global population. Economically, these 21 economies contribute significantly—approximately 27% of the world's nominal GDP and 35% of the world's real GDP in PPP terms, as per the global results of the 2021 ICP cycle recently released by the World Bank.[3] Hence, international comparisons facilitated by the ICP in Asia and the Pacific are pivotal for a comprehensive understanding of the global economy.

Structure of the Report

The main objective of this report is to provide economists, national policy makers, international organizations, and other stakeholders with an overview of the findings on PPPs of currencies and real expenditures of the 21 participating economies in the 2021 ICP in Asia and the Pacific. This report is, by design, concise, presenting highlights on the extensive data on PPPs, price levels, and real per capita expenditures available from the 2021 ICP cycle. It is hoped that users, after understanding the key results from the 2021 ICP in the region discussed in this report, will be encouraged to explore the detailed results available online (https://icp.adb.org) for further analyses.

Following this introduction, Chapter 2 explores key concepts that are vital for users of ICP results, such as PPPs, price level indexes, and nominal and real expenditure measures used for intereconomy comparisons of standards of living. The main findings from the 2021 ICP, including the relative sizes and contributions of the 21 participating economies, along with disparities in real per capita GDP, household expenditures, government expenditures, and investments made in the economy, are presented in Chapter 3. Chapter 4 assesses the PPPs estimated from the 2021 ICP in Asia and the Pacific in comparison to the 2021 PPPs extrapolated from the 2017 PPPs using suitable deflators. Chapter 5 is devoted to a brief description of the framework and methods used in compiling PPPs and real expenditures. It also describes methodological innovation introduced in the 2021 cycle for measuring price levels and real expenditures in housing services. Finally, Chapter 6 summarizes the 2021 ICP in Asia and the Pacific.

---

3   World Bank. DataBank: ICP 2021. https://databank.worldbank.org/source/icp-2021 (accessed 31 May 2024).

CHAPTER 2
Macroeconomic Measures and Intereconomy Comparisons

To make reliable intereconomy comparisons, monitor growth, and assist in evidence-based decision making, it is necessary to have reliable internationally comparable data on a range of macroeconomic aggregates. The primary objective of establishing the International Comparison Program (ICP) is to furnish internationally comparable metrics of economic activity across economies worldwide.

The national accounts compiled and published by national statistical offices provide the most comprehensive set of measures of economic activity. Gross domestic product (GDP), calculated as the gross value of output minus the value of goods and services utilized as intermediate outputs, along with taxes minus subsidies on products, serves as a gauge of economic activity from the production perspective. Per capita incomes are used for comparisons of standards of living. However, the ICP concentrates on an equivalent measure of GDP from the expenditure side, as it directly reflects the standard of living of residents within an economy. This measure encapsulates the market value of all final expenditures on goods and services within a given year in any economy. The ICP provides reliable and internationally comparable measures of the final expenditures on GDP based on purchasing power parities (PPPs) for the participating economies.

The ICP offers comparable measures of the following macroeconomic aggregates along with their more detailed components:

(i)   GDP;
(ii) individual consumption expenditure by households (ICEH), inclusive of expenditure by nonprofit institutions on behalf of households;

(iii) government final consumption expenditure, encompassing individual consumption and collective consumption expenditure by the government; and
(iv) gross capital formation, comprising gross fixed capital formation (GFCF), changes in inventories, and acquisitions minus disposals of valuables.

The ICP also provides other measures that are important from an analytical perspective. One such important measure is actual individual consumption by households, which is the sum of ICEH and individual consumption expenditure by the government and stands as a more comprehensive measure of welfare and standard of living, as it incorporates households' own consumption expenditure and expenditure made on their behalf by the government. Comparable measures of these major aggregates, as well as some subaggregates for the 21 participating economies of the region, are presented in Chapter 3. The Appendix tables provide measures of PPPs, price level indexes, total and per capita real expenditures for 35 economic indicators from the expenditure side of GDP.

International Comparisons: Exchange Rates or Purchasing Power Parities?

In Asia and the Pacific, what are the largest and smallest economies in 2021? Which are the richest and poorest economies? What are the relative costs of living? What are the cheapest tourist destinations? What is the level and per capita government expenditures on health or education in an economy vis-à-vis average per capita of the region?

Answering these questions is complex and challenging as economic aggregates are typically compiled by the national statistical agencies and expressed in local currency units (LCUs); therefore, they are not suitable for direct comparisons across economies. For example, the 2021 GDP of the People's Republic of China is CNY114.924 trillion and ₹227.243 trillion for India. Which economy is bigger? Similarly, per capita GDP in Hong Kong, China is HK$386,832 and S$106,943 for Singapore. Which of the two economies enjoys a higher per capita income?

These questions can be meaningfully answered only after converting these expenditures compiled in LCUs into a common currency. What currency conversion factors are appropriate for intereconomy comparisons?

Exchange Rates: Why Are They Inappropriate?

The use of exchange rates is a common method to convert economic data expressed in LCUs into a common currency, reference, or numeraire, such as the United States dollar.

The use of market exchange rate is justified as this is the rate at which currencies are exchanged in international currency markets, and international transactions take place at these rates. These rates are compiled in a very timely manner and are easily available for all economies. Exchange rates are used in the valuation of exports of an economy and determine its ability to purchase imports, as well as balance of payments and currency account balance; and for international official monetary transactions including foreign aid and other financial transactions.

However, the use of exchange rates is not appropriate for comparisons of real incomes and standards of living. Exchange rates are driven by several factors including the prices of traded goods, which are effectively set on world markets, whereas a large portion of goods and services consumed in most economies include, in large part, domestically produced goods and services that are not traded. Exchange rates are also influenced by currency speculation and short-term capital movements and are often subject to large, short-term swings of a speculative nature that can wrongly imply unexplainable shifts in relative living standards. For reliable comparisons, it is important to determine and compare the volumes or quantities of goods and services that incomes can buy in different economies. In this context, the use of exchange rates to convert GDP and per capita incomes can provide a misleading picture of standards of living as exchange rates do not reflect domestic price levels.

It has been shown in empirical studies that the use of exchange rates for comparing the size of economies systematically widens the gap between high-income and low-income economies. In assessing relative standards of living across economies, it is necessary to compare the relative volumes of goods and services purchased in different economies in a given period and which are determined by relative price levels in each of the economies under comparison.

Purchasing Power Parities of Currencies

Purchasing power parities, defined in Box 2.1, serve the dual purpose of converting macroeconomic aggregates expressed in LCUs into a common currency unit, while at the same time adjusting for spatial differences in prices prevailing in different economies.

Box 2.1: Purchasing Power Parity Defined

A working definition of a purchasing power parity is that it represents the number of currency units required to purchase the amounts of goods and services equivalent to what can be bought with one unit of the currency unit of the base or reference or numeraire economy.

Source: See Chapter 1, p. 19 of World Bank (2013).

Purchasing power parities are always expressed relative to a reference currency. In practice, any currency can be used as the reference currency. The Hong Kong dollar is the reference currency used in the ICP in Asia and the Pacific. This means that the results presented in Chapter 3 are either values expressed in Hong Kong dollars or as an index with Hong Kong, China = 100. It is important to note that the methodology used in the compilation of PPPs ensures that the relative price and volume comparisons across economies remain unchanged when the currency of a different economy is used as the reference currency. Hong Kong, China as the reference or base economy and Hong Kong dollar as the reference currency for regional comparisons implies that the exchange rate and the PPP for Hong Kong dollar would be equal to 1. Consequently, the nominal GDP, real GDP, and GDP in LCUs are all equal for the base economy.

The simplest and the most popular example of PPP is the Big Mac index published by *The Economist* magazine. The Big Mac index is a PPP that compares prices of a single commodity, the Big Mac sandwich. Table 2.1 shows Big Mac PPPs for the People's Republic of China; Hong Kong, China; Indonesia; and Thailand based on Big Mac prices observed in 2021.

Big Mac prices in LCUs for these economies can be expressed in PPPs using Hong Kong dollar as the reference currency by simply computing the ratios of Big Mac LCU prices in economies relative to the price in Hong Kong, China, which is calculated in column 4 of Table 2.1. This means that PPPs based on Big Mac prices for the People's Republic of China, Indonesia, and Thailand are, respectively, CNY1.07; Rp1619.05, and B6.10 per Hong Kong dollar. In comparison, exchange rates for these currencies in column 5 of Table 2.1 are CNY0.83, Rp1840.51, and B4.11 per Hong Kong dollar, respectively.

The Big Mac Index is a simple illustrative example of a PPP, and its main strength is that it is based on a single commodity that is easy to price, and the commodity is comparable in quality across all economies where it is available. However, it is of little use for making international comparisons of standards of living, as the Big Mac is not representative of the goods and services in household consumption and, more broadly, in GDP.

Table 2.1: Purchasing Power Parities, Exchange Rates, and Price Levels—An Illustrative Example, 2021

Economy	Local Currency Unit (LCU)	Price of Big Mac in LCU	PPP (HK$ = 1.00)	Exchange Rate (LCU per HK$)	Price Level Index (HKG = 100)
(1)	(2)	(3)	(4)	(5)	(6)
China, People's Republic of	yuan[a]	22.40	1.07	0.83	128.53
Hong Kong, China	Hong Kong dollar	21.00	1.00	1.00	100.00
Indonesia	rupiah	34,000.00	1,619.05	1,840.51	87.97
Thailand	baht	128.00	6.10	4.11	148.17

HK$ = Hong Kong dollar; HKG = Hong Kong, China; PPP = purchasing power parity.
Notes:
1. Exchange rates are expressed as the annual average rate for 2021 (period averages) based on data supplied by economies.
2. Big Mac prices in LCU as of July 2021 were obtained from The Economist. 2024. Burgernomics—The Big Mac Index. https://www.economist.com/big-mac-index (accessed 06 May 2024).
[a] The currency is the renminbi, while the currency unit is yuan.
Source: Asian Development Bank estimates.

To calculate PPPs for intereconomy comparisons, it is necessary to collect prices for a well-defined basket of goods and services purchased in the economies. Compilation of PPP for a representative basket of goods and services is a complex process. For the comparisons to be meaningful, the selected items for collection of prices should be comparable and be broadly representative of the goods and services purchased in the economies involved in the comparison (the methodology used in the compilation is briefly described in Chapter 5).

Purchasing Power Parities and Price Levels

Purchasing power parities are conversion factors that reflect differences in price levels of goods and services in different economies. However, PPPs by themselves are not measures of price levels. For example, what does a PPP of B6.10 per Hong Kong dollar in Table 2.1 mean for price levels? This question can be answered only by comparing the PPP with the exchange rate. Again, consider the data presented in Table 2.1. In the case of Thailand where HK$1.00 fetches B4.11 in 2021 from a currency exchange, one would need B6.10 to buy a Big Mac, indicating that the price level of the Big Mac is about 48% higher in Thailand compared to that in Hong Kong, China. However, in Indonesia, HK$1.00 could be exchanged for Rp1840.51 but only Rp1619.05 is needed to buy an equivalent of what HK$1.00 buys in Hong Kong, China. This means that the price level of the Big Mac in Indonesia is lower than that in Hong Kong, China.

In general, PPPs and exchange rates are used in defining a price level index (PLI), defined in equation (1) as:

$$\text{Price Level Index} = PLI_c = \frac{PPP_{HKG,c}}{XR_{HKG,c}} \times 100 \qquad (1)$$

Equation (2) exemplifies the case of Thailand,

$$PLI_{THA} = \frac{6.10}{4.11} \times 100 = 148.17 \qquad (2)$$

which means that price level of the Big Mac in Thailand is about 48% higher than that in Hong Kong, China.

Similarly, for Indonesia, using the data in Table 2.1, based on Big Mac prices, the PLI (equation [3]) is around 88, implying that the price of the Big Mac in Indonesia is cheaper by around 12% than that in Hong Kong, China.

$$PLI_{INO} = \frac{1619.05}{1840.51} \times 100 = 87.97 \qquad (3)$$

By definition, the PLI for the reference economy always equals 100. Price level indexes can also be expressed relative to price level in the whole region (equation [3]), i.e., with Asia and the Pacific = 100. Values of PLI relative to Hong Kong, China as well as with respect to Asia and the Pacific are both presented in the results tables in the Appendixes. Method of computing PLIs with Asia and the Pacific = 100 is explained in Appendix 5.

Nominal and Real Expenditures

For purposes of international comparisons of GDP and its components that are compiled in LCUs, both exchange rates and PPPs can be used. These serve different purposes. If the converted aggregates are to be used for comparing the volumes or real expenditures, i.e., standards of living, then PPPs need to be used for conversion.

The following nomenclature is used in international comparison literature and in this publication. The term *nominal expenditure* is used when exchange rate is used for conversion. As exchange rates simply convert aggregates into a common currency unit but do not necessarily reflect differences in prices across economies, exchange rate-converted aggregates are termed *"nominal"* aggregates. For example, nominal GDP of India, $NGDP_{HKG,IND}$, expressed in Hong Kong dollars is derived using exchange rate for conversion (equation [4]):

$$NGDP_{HKG,IND} = \frac{GDP_{IND}^{LCU}}{XR_{HKG,IND}} \qquad (4)$$

Real *expenditure* for a given aggregate, such as GDP or household consumption, is obtained by converting the aggregate expressed in LCUs using a PPP exchange rate that is appropriate for that aggregate. For example, real GDP of India, $RGDP_{HKG,IND}$, expressed in Hong Kong dollars, is Indian GDP in rupees converted to Hong Kong dollars using PPP for Indian rupee (equation [5]).

$$RGDP_{HKG,IND} = \frac{GDP_{IND}^{LCU}}{PPP_{HKG,IND}} \qquad (5)$$

The term *"real"* here reinforces the fact that using PPP for conversion adjusts for differences in prices for goods and services paid in Hong Kong, China and India.

Since PPP as well as exchange rate for the Hong Kong dollar, which is the reference currency, are equal to 1, real GDP and nominal GDP for Hong Kong, China are identical. Further, it is worth reinforcing the fact that exchange rates remain the same irrespective of which expenditure aggregate is being compared. In contrast, PPPs usually vary with the aggregate under consideration, as these are determined by the relative prices for goods and services relevant for the specific expenditure aggregate. This is illustrated in Table 2.2, which shows PPPs for GDP, ICEH, and GFCF for select economies for the 2021 ICP in the region. It may be seen that the PPPs for various aggregates for the five economies presented in columns 4, 5, and 6 are not the same except for Fiji, where the PPP for GDP and ICEH happen to be the same.

Table 2.3 summarizes the exchange rate- and PPP-based measures and/or indicators presented and discussed in this report. With the nominal and real expenditures for different economies expressed in the reference currency (Hong Kong dollar for the Asia and Pacific region), the nominal and real size of the whole region now can be measured, and the contribution of each economy to the region as a whole can now be assessed for each expenditure aggregate.

Table 2.2: Purchasing Power Parities for Gross Domestic Product, Individual Consumption Expenditure by Households, and Gross Fixed Capital Formation for Selected Economies, 2021

| | | | Purchasing Power Parity | | |
Economy	Local Currency Unit (LCU)	Exchange Rate (LCU per HK$)	Gross Domestic Product (HKG=1.00)	Individual Consumption Expenditure by Households (HKG=1.00)	Gross Fixed Capital Formation (HKG=1.00)
(1)	(2)	(3)	(4)	(5)	(6)
Cambodia	riel	527.23	243.01	246.92	245.34
China, People's Republic of	yuan[a]	0.83	0.68	0.63	0.71
Fiji	Fiji dollar	0.27	0.15	0.15	0.16
Hong Kong, China	Hong Kong dollar	1.00	1.00	1.00	1.00
India	Indian rupee	9.51	3.53	3.05	4.23

HK$ = Hong Kong dollar; HKG = Hong Kong, China.
[a] The currency is the renminbi, while the currency unit is yuan.
Source: Asian Development Bank estimates based on data supplied by the participating economies.

Having discussed some basic concepts and terminologies related to ICP and armed with the concepts and measures summarized in Table 2.3, it is now possible to answer the questions posed in the beginning of this chapter: What are the largest and smallest economies in 2021 in the region? Which are the richest and poorest economies? What are the relative costs of living? What are the cheapest tourist destinations? What is the level and per capita expenditures on health or education in an economy vis-à-vis average per capita of the region?

Uses and Applications of Purchasing Power Parities

Purchasing power parities serve as economically meaningful alternatives to exchange rates for compiling internationally comparable national accounts aggregates or real expenditures that fully account for differences in price levels across economies. Measures of total and per capita levels of PPP-converted GDP and other aggregates, such as ICEH, GFCF, and government final consumption expenditures allow meaningful intereconomy comparisons of standards of living and investments. With the increased number of participating economies since the program's inception in 1968, particularly since the 2005 ICP cycle, PPPs have been widely utilized.[4]

The PPPs produced from the ICP are used in various indicators identified for tracking progress across several Sustainable Development Goals (SDGs). Among these, the primary use of PPPs is in setting the international poverty line to track the critical global target of eliminating extreme poverty. Recently, the extreme poverty line, used in estimating global and regional poverty, was revised from \$1.90/day at 2011 PPPs to \$2.15/day (based on the PPPs from the 2017 ICP). Additionally, other SDGs also require the use of PPPs to monitor progress on income inequality, zero hunger, quality of education, healthy lives and well-being, affordable and clean energy, labor productivity, clean and environmentally sound technologies, and sustainable cities and communities.

Table 2.3: Exchange Rate-Based and Purchasing Power Parity-Based Indicators

Exchange Rate-Based Indicators	PPP-based Indicators
(Uniform for all commodities)	(Different for each commodity)
n.a.	Price Level Indexes = $\dfrac{PPP}{XR} \times 100$
Nominal Expenditure = $\dfrac{Expenditure\ in\ LCU}{XR}$	Real Expenditure = $\dfrac{Expenditure\ in\ LCU}{PPP}$
Per Capita Nominal Expenditure = $\dfrac{Nominal\ Expenditure}{Population}$	Per Capita Real Expenditure = $\dfrac{Real\ Expenditure}{Population}$
Nominal Expenditure Share (%) to Region = $\dfrac{Nominal\ Expenditure_j}{Nominal\ Expenditure_{AP}} \times 100$	Real Expenditure Share (%) to Region = $\dfrac{Real\ Expenditure_j}{Real\ Expenditure_{AP}} \times 100$
Per Capita Nominal Expenditure Index = $\dfrac{Per\ Capita\ Nominal\ Expenditure_j}{Per\ Capita\ Nominal\ Expenditure_{HKG}} \times 100$	Per Capita Real Expenditure Index = $\dfrac{Per\ Capita\ Real\ Expenditure_j}{Per\ Capita\ Real\ Expenditure_{HKG}} \times 100$

j = refers to any economy which participated in the 2021 ICP for Asia and the Pacific; AP = Asia and the Pacific; HKG = Hong Kong, China; ICP = International Comparison Program; LCU = local currency unit; n.a. = not applicable; PPP = purchasing power parity; XR = exchange rate.
Source: Asian Development Bank (Economic Research and Development Impact Department).

4 More uses of PPPs can be found in World Bank. 2021. *Purchasing Power Parities for Policy Making: A Visual Guide to Using Data from the International Comparison Program*. World Bank, Washington, DC. http://hdl.handle.net/10986/35736.

International organizations extensively employ PPPs in their policy applications. While the PPPs are used by the United Nations in assessing progress against SDGs, the United Nations Development Program uses PPPs for its Human Development Index and Gender Development Index. The International Monetary Fund uses PPPs in its World Economic Outlook and for determining quota subscriptions of member countries; the European Commission uses PPPs for allocating Structural Funds to its member states; and the World Bank uses PPPs for its World Development Indicators and various research and policy analyses. ADB's Corporate Results Framework, 2019–2024 (ADB 2019) integrates SDGs and some indicators related to development progress in Asia and the Pacific, and includes indicators whose measurement depends on purchasing power parities.

Additionally, PPPs from the ICP are used for productivity comparisons, assessing economic performance, catch-up and convergence, measuring global and regional inequality levels and trends, determining cost-of-living adjustments for expatriates, and studying competitiveness. More recently, price data used in compiling PPPs are being utilized for nutrition-based measures of poverty. It is also important for users to apply the relevant PPPs for converting expenditures in local currency units, as PPPs are specific to a select basket of goods and services.

Despite the numerous uses of PPPs, caution is advised in using exact rankings of economies based on PPP-converted aggregates when the differences in real expenditures are not significant, as PPPs are subject to sampling and other errors. Further, PPPs should not be used in making temporal comparisons of PPP-converted GDP or other economic measures, as the PPPs are meant for spatial comparisons for the given benchmark. PPPs should also not be used to make any judgment on the overvaluation or undervaluation of a currency, as PPPs from ICP cover both tradable and nontradable goods and services, whereas exchange rates are determined by the total demand for currencies, such as for financing external trade and capital transfers.

CHAPTER 3

Summary Results from the 2021 International Comparison Program in Asia and the Pacific

Comparative assessment of economic performance of economies of the Asia and Pacific region needs comparable macroeconomic data on total and per capita levels of gross domestic product (GDP), household consumption expenditures, government expenditures, and investments. As posed in Chapter 2, questions like which are the richest and poorest economies in Asia and the Pacific or what are the relative costs of living across economies of the region can be answered with the help of estimates of purchasing power parities (PPPs) of currencies from the just concluded 2021 International Comparison Program (ICP) in the region.

This chapter presents the key findings of the 2021 ICP in Asia and the Pacific. It covers PPPs, price level indexes (PLIs), total and per capita levels of real and nominal expenditures, and real and nominal shares for GDP and its major aggregates for the 21 participating economies. Real expenditure measures are derived by converting national accounts expenditure aggregates available in local currency units using PPPs with Hong Kong, China as the reference economy and Hong Kong dollar (HK\$) as the reference currency. (Chapter 5 provides a brief description of the approaches used to collect and validate data and estimate PPPs for its various GDP components.)

Findings for the following major aggregates are discussed in this chapter:

(i)   *GDP.* This is a measure of the size of the total economy. The expenditure side measure of GDP consists of individual consumption expenditure by households (ICEH),[5] government final consumption expenditure (GFCE), gross capital formation, and net exports.

(ii) *ICEH.* This includes household consumption expenditure and expenditures by nonprofit institutions serving households (NPISH) on behalf of households.

(iii) *Actual individual consumption by households (AICH).* This encompasses all goods and services consumed by households, including ICEH, NPISH expenditures, and individual consumption expenditure by government on behalf of households (ICEG). Actual individual consumption by households is a more accurate measure of material well-being than GDP as it covers all goods and services consumed by households.

(iv) *GFCE.* This includes ICEG comprising expenditures made by the government on behalf of households predominantly on education and health; and collective consumption expenditure by government (CCEG) made on collective services provided by the government to the community in general, e.g., general public services, defense, public order and safety, etc.

(v)   *Gross fixed capital formation (GFCF).* This represents the total value of acquisitions less disposals of all fixed assets, including expenditures on construction, machinery and equipment, and other products.

Tables showing the detailed results for GDP, ICEH, AICH, GFCE, GFCF, domestic absorption, total consumption, and several other disaggregated expenditure aggregates are given in the tables presented in Appendix 1.

Box 3.1 presents some special notes for the readers to keep in mind when looking at the results for the 2021 ICP in Asia and the Pacific.

Box 3.1: Notes on Data and Results for the 2021 International Comparison Program in Asia and the Pacific

The term "Asia and the Pacific" in this report refers to the 21 Asian Development Bank (ADB) members participating in the 2021 International Comparison Program (ICP) in Asia and the Pacific, with Fiji as the only Pacific economy.

The term "economies of the region," used interchangeably with "economies in Asia and the Pacific," refers to all 21 ADB members participating in the 2021 cycle for the Asia and Pacific region.

In the analysis, "real" refers to purchasing power parity-converted values of expenditure aggregates, while "nominal" refers to exchange rate-converted expenditure values converted to Hong Kong dollars.

Results presented in this report are produced by ADB as the ICP Asia and the Pacific regional implementing agency, based on data supplied by all the participating economies, in accordance with the methodology recommended by the ICP Technical Advisory Group and endorsed by the 2021 ICP Asia and the Pacific Regional Advisory Board. As such, these results are not produced by participating economies as part of the economies' official statistics. The results presented are based on the data finalized and submitted by the implementing agencies as of April 2024.

Bangladesh, India, Nepal, and Pakistan compile their gross domestic product (GDP) based on financial year, which is different from the calendar year. As the ICP requires calendar year GDP expenditures from the economies in local currency units, the financial year-based GDP estimates were converted to calendar year 2021 estimates using different approaches, depending on the availability of detailed expenditure estimates in each of these economies.

In some economies, household expenditure data includes the expenditures undertaken by the nonprofit institutions serving households (NPISH) due to challenges in segregating NPISH data, with the exception of the People's Republic of China, where NPISH data is included with government expenditures.

In accordance with ICP's requirements, GDP expenditures are to be disaggregated by 155 expenditure components (called basic headings) in the ICP classification. Accordingly, statistical discrepancy (if any) on the expenditure side is allocated to one or more basic headings by the economies based on their best judgment. Due to the adjustment of the statistical discrepancy in some basic headings, the expenditures in local currency units presented in the tables in this report for some expenditure aggregates may be different from the published expenditure estimates by the economies.

Following the data revision policy of ICP, the results from the 2017 ICP in Asia and the Pacific were also revised based on (i) revisions in the 2017 estimates of GDP, population, and exchange rates; (ii) implementation of a new, hybrid approach of estimating actual and imputed rentals for housing; (iii) updates to the productivity-adjusted PPPs for government; and (iv) uniform treatment of concepts across economies and over the two cycles. As with the 2021 findings, the 2017 revised results are produced by ADB as the ICP Asia and the Pacific regional implementing agency, based on data supplied by all the participating economies, and in accordance with the methodology recommended by the ICP Technical Advisory Group and endorsed by the 2021 ICP Asia and the Pacific Regional Advisory Board. As such, these results are not produced by participating economies as part of the economies' official statistics.

In Chapter 4 where discussion on the consistency between the 2017 and 2021 ICP benchmark years are analyzed, results for 2017 are calculated for the same set of 21 economies that participated in the 2021 ICP cycle for comparability.

Source: Asian Development Bank (Economic Research and Development Impact Department).

Gross Domestic Product: Size and Shares of Economies of the Asia and Pacific Region

Comparison of the levels and relative shares of GDP and its subaggregates across economies require compiling PPPs relevant to each expenditure aggregate for the participating economies with reference to a base economy. The GDP is a standard measure of economic activity and is compiled by the economies following international standards established in the system of national accounts, the latest being the System of National Accounts 2008 (United Nations 2009). The PPPs estimated from ICP are used to calculate real measures of the size of the participating economies and for the Asia and Pacific region, thus making it possible to examine size and shares of these economies in the whole region.

Table 3.1 provides the set of summary results for GDP from the 2021 ICP for the 21 participating economies of the region. The table presents estimates of PPPs of currencies at the GDP level, exchange rates, and real and nominal GDP, along with levels of per capita real and nominal GDP, PLIs, and shares in real and nominal GDP. Population and GDP in local currency units provided by the participating economies are in columns (13) and (14), respectively.

The total size of the regional economy measured in PPP or real terms (column 4) is HK$317.918 trillion, and HK$204.629 trillion in nominal terms (column 5). It may be noted that the nominal GDP of the regional economy, computed using exchange rates, is significantly lower than the size of real GDP of the region. The explanation for this difference lies in the PPPs and exchange rates in columns (2) and (3) where PPPs for all economies are systematically lower than the respective exchange rates. Therefore, real GDP exceeds nominal GDP for all the economies except for Hong Kong, China, which being the reference economy, has the same GDP in columns (2) and (3).

Table 3.1 (column 4) also shows that the People's Republic of China with a real GDP of HK$169.242 trillion is the largest economy. India with a real GDP of HK$64.376 trillion is second in size, and Indonesia with HK$20.732 trillion is third. Meanwhile, the smallest economies are Bhutan at HK$61.28 billion; Maldives at HK$57.77 billion; and Fiji, the smallest at HK$57.52 billion, very close to Maldives.

Shares in GDP of the 21 participating economies in the real and nominal GDP of the region are presented in Figure 3.1, which are based on Table 3.1.

The left side panel of Figure 3.1 shows the 11 largest economies of the region with shares of 1.0% or more in the region's real GDP. Their combined share is about 97.79%, while the remaining 10 smaller economies account for only about 2.21% share in the region's GDP. The right panel in Figure 3.1 shows the breakdown for these 10 smallest economies in the region with Hong Kong, China having the largest share of about 0.90% among them.

The three largest economies both in real and nominal GDP terms in the Asia and Pacific region, are the People's Republic of China with a share of 53.23%; India, 20.25%; and Indonesia, 6.52%. While the People's Republic of China accounts for more than half of the share of real GDP, the three largest economies together account for four-fifths of the region's GDP. These three economies are also the biggest in terms of population size, with shares of 36.44% (People's Republic of China), 35.28% (India), and 7.04% (Indonesia), for a combined share of 78.75% of the region's population. In PPP terms, the smallest economies are Bhutan, Maldives, and Fiji, each with a share of nearly 0.02%.

Another feature in Figure 3.1 that may be noted is in terms of shares of the economies. For most economies, real shares are larger than their nominal shares except for five economies namely, Hong Kong, China; Maldives; the People's Republic of China; Singapore; and Taipei,China. These are the economies that have

Table 3.1: Summary Results for Gross Domestic Product, 2021
(Hong Kong, China as Base)

Economy	PPPs (HK$ = 1.00)	Exchange Rates (HK$ = 1.00)	Expenditure (HK$ billion)		Expenditure per Capita (HK$)		Shares (Asia and the Pacific = 100.00)			Price Level Indexes		Reference Data	
							Expenditure		Population				
			Based on PPPs	Based on XRs	Based on PPPs	Based on XRs	Based on PPPs	Based on XRs	Population	Asia and the Pacific = 100	HKG=100	Population (million)	Expenditure in LCU (billion)
(1)	(2)	(3)	(4)	(5)	(6)	(7)	(8)	(9)	(10)	(11)	(12)	(13)	(14)
Bangladesh	4.82	10.95	7,784	3,427	45,717	20,125	2.45	1.67	4.39	68.4	44.0	170.26	37,510
Bhutan	3.34	9.51	61	22	81,049	28,458	0.02	0.01	0.02	54.6	35.1	0.76	205
Brunei Darussalam	0.09	0.17	208	109	470,955	247,106	0.07	0.05	0.01	81.5	52.5	0.44	19
Cambodia	243.01	527.23	455	210	27,407	12,632	0.14	0.10	0.43	71.6	46.1	16.59	110,506
China, People's Republic of	0.68	0.83	169,242	138,482	119,829	98,050	53.23	67.67	36.44	127.1	81.8	1,412.36	114,924
Fiji	0.15	0.27	58	33	64,376	37,458	0.02	0.02	0.02	90.4	58.2	0.89	9
Hong Kong, China	1.00	1.00	2,868	2,868	386,832	386,832	0.90	1.40	0.19	155.4	100.0	7.41	2,868
India	3.53	9.51	64,376	23,899	47,087	17,481	20.25	11.68	35.28	57.7	37.1	1,367.17	227,243
Indonesia	818.87	1,840.51	20,732	9,224	76,030	33,827	6.52	4.51	7.04	69.1	44.5	272.68	16,976,751
Lao People's Democratic Republic	516.29	1,247.48	358	148	48,828	20,208	0.11	0.07	0.19	64.3	41.4	7.34	184,982
Malaysia	0.26	0.53	6,004	2,906	184,316	89,211	1.89	1.42	0.84	75.2	48.4	32.58	1,549
Maldives	1.40	1.98	58	41	101,638	71,856	0.02	0.02	0.01	109.8	70.7	0.57	81
Mongolia	148.19	366.52	294	119	89,532	36,200	0.09	0.06	0.08	62.8	40.4	3.28	43,555
Nepal	5.53	15.20	821	299	28,263	10,288	0.26	0.15	0.75	56.6	36.4	29.06	4,543
Pakistan	7.40	20.92	8,277	2,927	36,821	13,021	2.60	1.43	5.80	54.9	35.4	224.78	61,230
Philippines	3.30	6.34	5,883	3,064	53,383	27,801	1.85	1.50	2.84	80.9	52.1	110.20	19,411
Singapore	0.14	0.17	4,223	3,373	774,311	618,583	1.33	1.65	0.14	124.1	79.9	5.45	583
Sri Lanka	9.46	25.58	1,861	688	84,007	31,051	0.59	0.34	0.57	57.4	37.0	22.16	17,600
Taipei,China	2.45	3.60	8,836	6,010	376,515	256,084	2.78	2.94	0.61	105.7	68.0	23.47	21,663
Thailand	1.90	4.11	8,527	3,935	122,360	56,469	2.68	1.92	1.80	71.7	46.1	69.69	16,189
Viet Nam	1,212.53	2,979.15	6,993	2,846	70,994	28,895	2.20	1.39	2.54	63.2	40.7	98.51	8,479,667
Asia and the Pacific	n.a.	n.a.	317,918	204,629	82,030	52,799	100.00	100.00	100.00	100.0	64.4	3,875.65	n.a.

ADB = Asian Development Bank; HK$ = Hong Kong dollar; HKG = Hong Kong, China; LCU = local currency unit; n.a. = not applicable; PPP = purchasing power parity; XR = exchange rate.
Notes:
1. Expenditures in local currency units, mid-year population estimates, and exchange rates were supplied by the participating economies for the International Comparison Program.
2. The PPPs used to calculate real expenditures are ADB estimates based on data supplied by the participating economies.
Source: Asian Development Bank estimates.

Figure 3.1: Economy Shares of Real and Nominal Gross Domestic Product, 2021

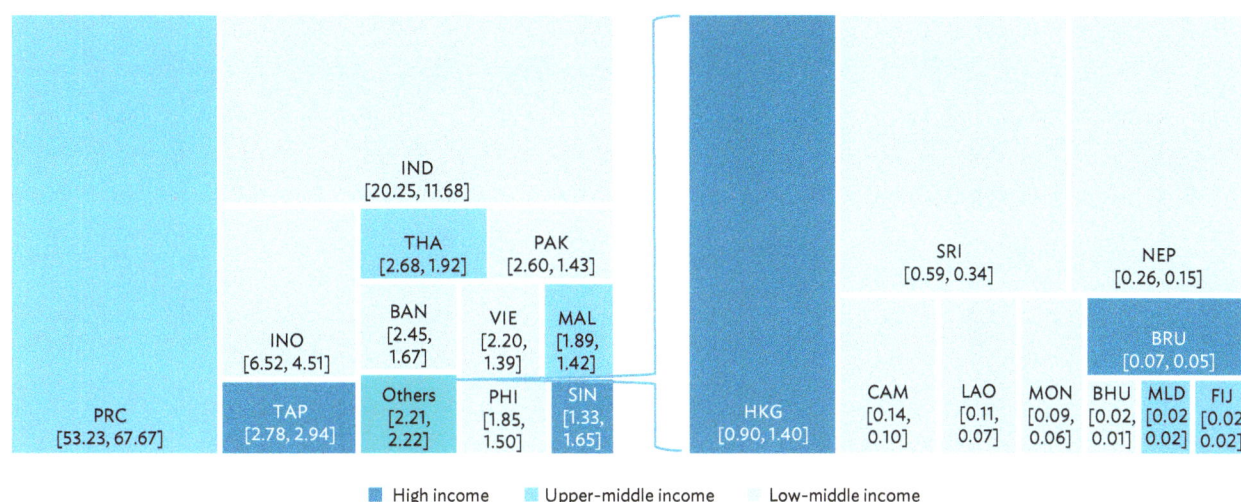

■ High income   ■ Upper-middle income   ■ Low-middle income

ADB = Asian Development Bank; BAN = Bangladesh; BHU = Bhutan; BRU = Brunei Darussalam; CAM = Cambodia; FIJ = Fiji; GDP = gross domestic product; HKG = Hong Kong, China; IND = India; INO = Indonesia; LAO = Lao People's Democratic Republic; MAL = Malaysia; MLD = Maldives; MON = Mongolia; NEP = Nepal; PAK = Pakistan; PHI = Philippines; PPP = purchasing power parity; PRC = People's Republic of China; SIN = Singapore; SRI = Sri Lanka; TAP = Taipei,China; THA = Thailand; VIE = Viet Nam.
Notes:
1. The sizes of the treemap segments are based on economy shares of real GDP to the Asia and Pacific region.
2. The first value shown in the label represents the share of real GDP, while the second value represents the share of nominal GDP.
3. The PPPs used to calculate real expenditures are ADB estimates based on data supplied by the participating economies.
Source: ADB estimates.

price levels above the regional average (Asia and the Pacific = 100), whereas the rest of the 16 economies have PLIs that are below 100 (see Table 3.1).

Levels of real and nominal GDP are shown in Figure 3.2 arranged by the size of GDP in real terms. As pointed out earlier, for all economies (except for Hong Kong, China, the reference economy) the real GDP is much higher than the nominal GDP, indicating that the PPPs for GDP are lower than the exchange rates.

It can be inferred from Figure 3.2, which is based on Table 3.1, that the top five economies maintain the same ranks under both measures. However, there are some shifts in ranks in the seven economies below the top five economies, namely: Bangladesh; Hong Kong, China; Malaysia; Pakistan; the Philippines; Singapore; and Viet Nam. The biggest upward shifts in the ranks from nominal to real are observed for Pakistan (from 9th to 6th) and Viet Nam (from 12th to 8th). The biggest downward shifts are for Singapore (7th to 11th) and the Philippines (8th to 10th). The shifts

in ranks between nominal and real GDP are driven by the relative differences in the PPPs vis-à-vis corresponding exchange rates.

Finally, a more meaningful measure of the relative contributions of various economies is the ratio of their share of real GDP in the economy relative to their population share (Table 3.1) as measured by the ratios of shares in real GDP shown in column (8), and shares in population of the region shown in column (10). A ratio of 1.00 or above implies an equal or a higher share in regional real GDP compared to the share in regional population, while a ratio below 1.0 implies a lower share in real GDP vis-à-vis share in population. Singapore is the best-performing economy with its share in GDP being 9.4 times the share in population of the region, followed by Brunei Darussalam (5.7 times); Hong Kong, China (4.7 times); and Taipei,China (4.6 times). These four economies accordingly enjoy high per capita real incomes among the 21 economies. Among the two largest economies, for the People's Republic of China,

Figure 3.2: Real and Nominal Gross Domestic Product, 2021
(HK$ billion)

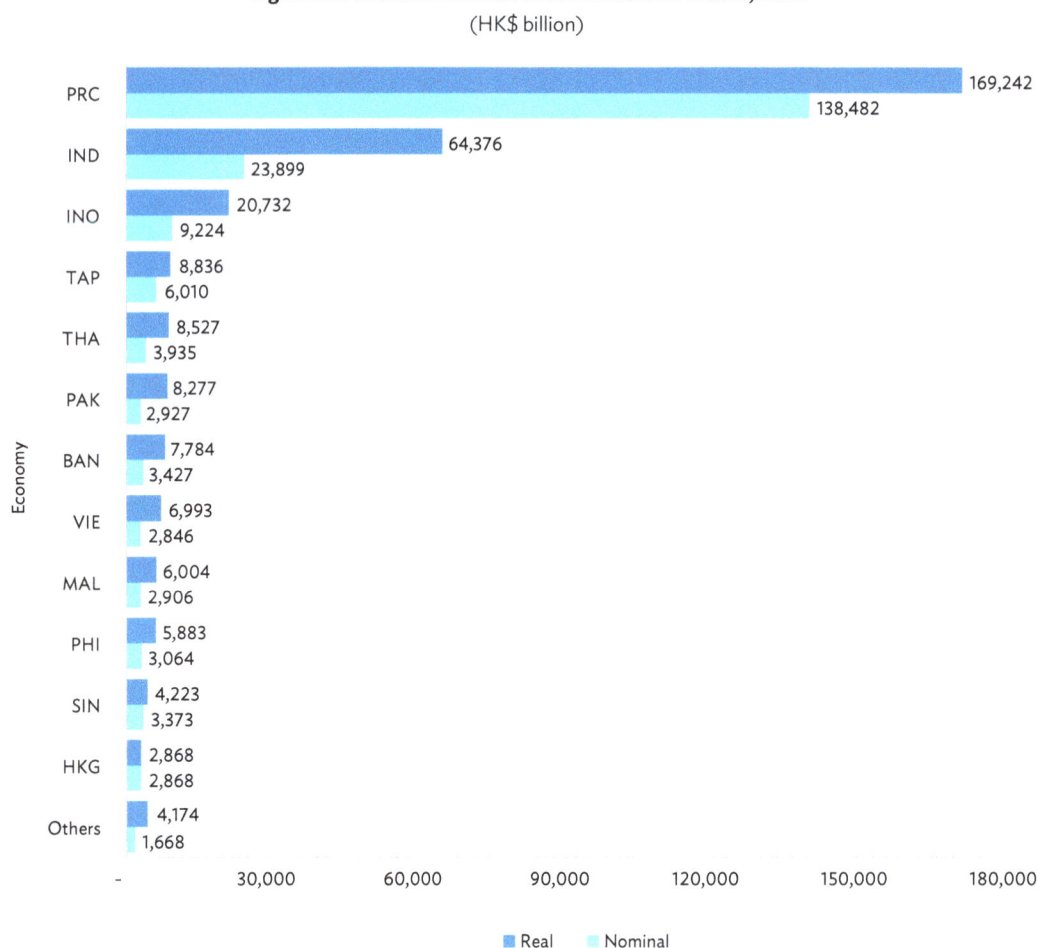

BAN = Bangladesh; HK$ = Hong Kong dollar; HKG = Hong Kong, China; IND = India; INO = Indonesia; MAL = Malaysia; PAK = Pakistan; PHI = Philippines; PRC = People's Republic of China; SIN = Singapore; TAP = Taipei,China; THA = Thailand; VIE = Viet Nam.
Source: Asian Development Bank estimates based on data supplied by the participating economies.

the ratio is 1.46, whereas for India it is 0.57. Cambodia and Nepal have the lowest ratios of 0.33 and 0.34, respectively, indicating that these economies also have the lowest per capita real incomes.

Per Capita Real Gross Domestic Product and Standards of Living

Per capita GDP or income is a commonly employed measure of standard of living. Stiglitz, Sen, and Fitoussi (2009) identified several shortcomings of real per capita income as a measure of welfare.

However, per capita income remains the single most important indicator of welfare as it correlates strongly with several indicators of economic and social well-being. Columns (6) and (7) of Table 3.1 show the real and nominal per capita incomes in the 21 participating economies, where the average per capita real GDP for the Asia and Pacific region is HK$82,030—much higher than the per capita nominal expenditure of HK$52,799. Graphically, the real and nominal per capita GDP values for the 21 economies are shown in Figure 3.3. Again, because the PPPs are lower than the exchange rates (except for Hong Kong, China), per capita real GDP values are much higher than per capita nominal values.

In identifying the richest and poorest economies, ranking economies by their per capita real income or GDP is used. The richest economy is Singapore with a per capita real income of HK$774,311, which is almost 64% higher than the next highest per capita GDP of HK$470,955 for Brunei Darussalam. Cambodia with per capita real income of HK$27,407 and Nepal marginally higher at HK$28,263 have the lowest per capita incomes. The largest economies of the region, the People's Republic of China with a per capita income of HK$119,829 ranked 7th, and India, the second-largest economy, ranked 17th with a per capita income of HK$47,087.

Per capita nominal GDP, based on exchange rates conversion, shows bigger gaps between the richest and the poorest economies. In Singapore, the richest economy, the per capita real income is around 28 times of Cambodia with the lowest per capita.

Figure 3.3: Per Capita Real and Nominal Gross Domestic Product, 2021

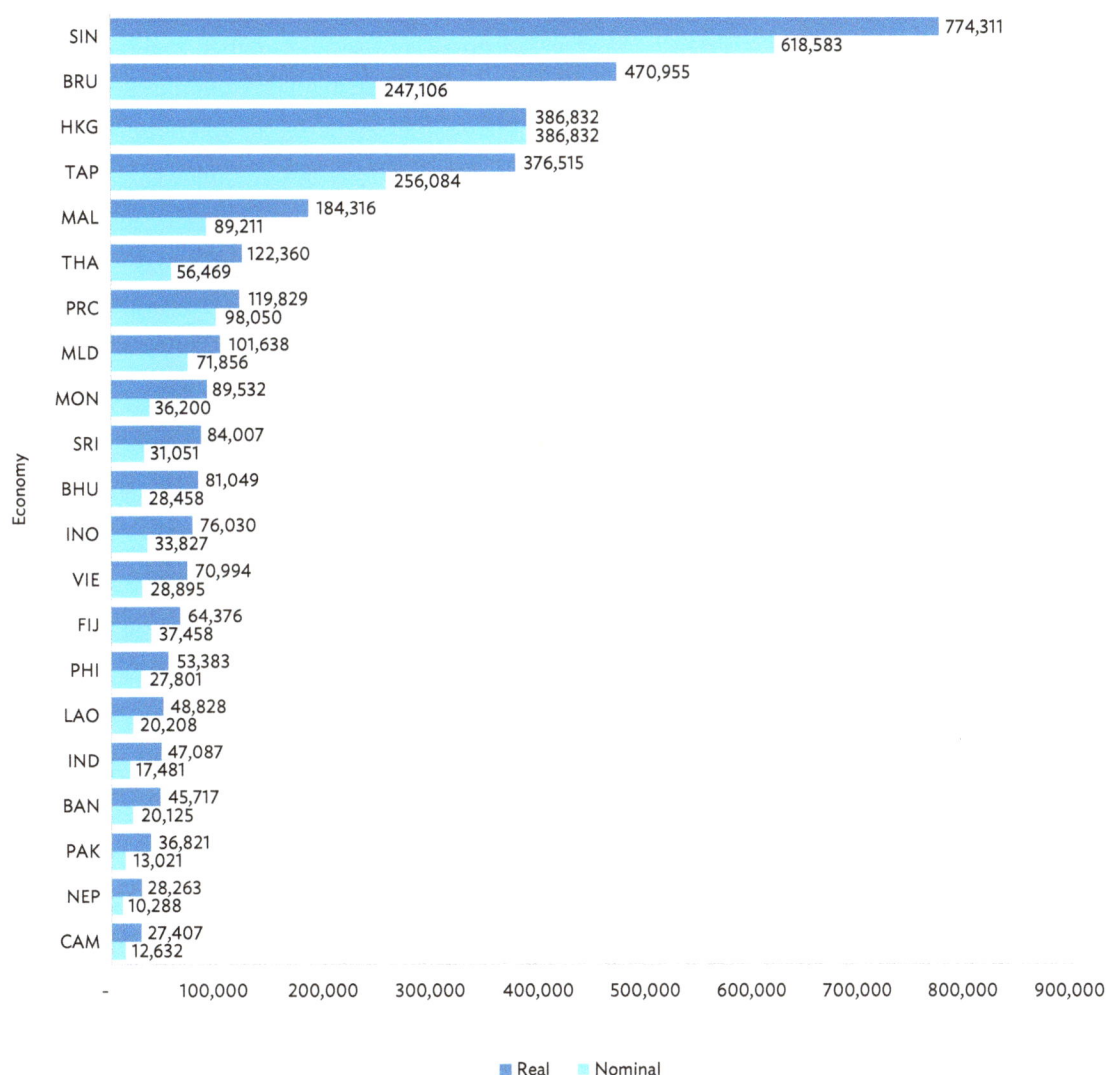

(HK$)

Economy	Real	Nominal
SIN	774,311	618,583
BRU	470,955	247,106
HKG	386,832	386,832
TAP	376,515	256,084
MAL	184,316	89,211
THA	122,360	56,469
PRC	119,829	98,050
MLD	101,638	71,856
MON	89,532	36,200
SRI	84,007	31,051
BHU	81,049	28,458
INO	76,030	33,827
VIE	70,994	28,895
FIJ	64,376	37,458
PHI	53,383	27,801
LAO	48,828	20,208
IND	47,087	17,481
BAN	45,717	20,125
PAK	36,821	13,021
NEP	28,263	10,288
CAM	27,407	12,632

■ Real ■ Nominal

BAN = Bangladesh; BHU = Bhutan; BRU = Brunei Darussalam; CAM = Cambodia; FIJ = Fiji; HK$ = Hong Kong dollar; HKG = Hong Kong, China; IND = India; INO = Indonesia; LAO = Lao People's Democratic Republic; MAL = Malaysia; MLD = Maldives; MON = Mongolia; NEP = Nepal; PAK = Pakistan; PHI = Philippines; PRC = People's Republic of China; SIN = Singapore; SRI = Sri Lanka; TAP = Taipei,China; THA = Thailand; VIE = Viet Nam.
Source: Asian Development Bank estimates based on data supplied by the participating economies.

However, this gap between the two increases to roughly 49 times when per capita nominal incomes are compared, indicating that comparisons based on exchange rate conversions grossly underestimate the size of poorer economies.

Inequality in the distribution of per capita real and nominal incomes for the 21 economies is shown in Figure 3.4 in the form of Lorenz curves, which shows the plot of cumulative percentage shares of expenditures against cumulative population starting with the poorest to the richest economy. The plot shows that when per capita real GDP is used, the income distribution is more equal than when using nominal GDP. The share of total expenditure that is associated with the poorest 40% in the region in real terms is about 22%, which is only about 13% in nominal terms. It may, however, be

noted that there are inequalities within economies. The Lorenz curve in Figure 3.4 only measures inequality in the distribution of income between the participating economies, without accounting for inequality within each economy.

Deviation of the Lorenz curve from the equal distribution or egalitarian line, represented by the diagonal, shows severity in inequality in the distribution of income. The Gini coefficient, a standard measure for inequality, equals twice the area between the Lorenz curve and the equal distribution line. Figure 3.4 shows that intereconomy inequality is much higher with a Gini coefficient of 0.414 when nominal per capita incomes are used than when real per capita incomes are used, which has a Gini coefficient of 0.270.

Figure 3.4: Lorenz Curves for Per Capita Real and Nominal Gross Domestic Product, 2021

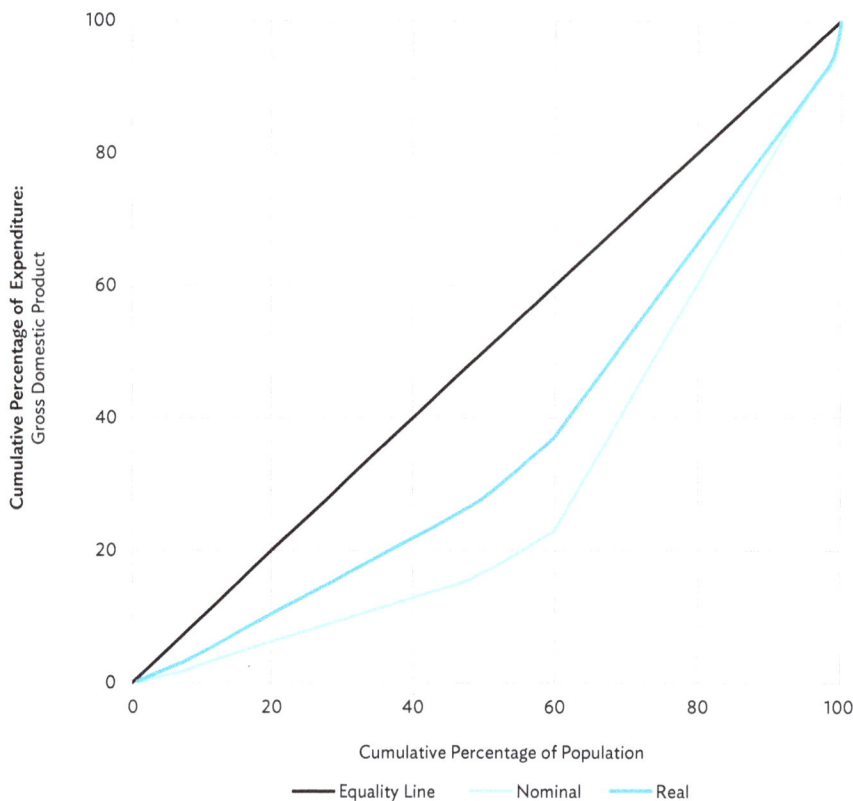

Note: Expenditure is represented by the economy-specific per capita gross domestic product.
Source: Asian Development Bank estimates based on data supplied by the participating economies.

Purchasing Power Parities and Price Levels of Economies for Gross Domestic Product in Asia and the Pacific

Turning to PPPs and price levels for GDP for 2021, shown in column (2) and column (12), respectively, of Table 3.1, PPP for Bangladesh is Tk4.82. This means that Tk4.82 has the same purchasing power as HK$1.00 in Hong Kong, China with respect to broadly defined goods and services that form GDP. In contrast, the market exchange rate for the same period is Tk10.95 per Hong Kong dollar (column 3). This means that, while HK$1.00 fetches Tk10.95, only Tk4.82 are needed in Bangladesh to buy what HK$1.00 buys in Hong Kong, China. This means that goods and services that constitute GDP are generally cheaper to buy in Bangladesh than in Hong Kong, China.

The PLI in column (12) with Hong Kong, China = 100 is the ratio of PPP (column 2) to exchange rate (column 3) times 100, which is a standardized index that represents price levels with reference to the base economy. The PLI for Bangladesh is 44.0, which is below 100, the PLI for the reference economy. This PLI of 44.0 for Bangladesh means that the general price level in Bangladesh's economy is roughly 44%, or less than half, that of Hong Kong, China. The cheapest among all economies is Bhutan with a PLI of 35.1 followed by Pakistan (35.4) and Nepal (36.4). The economy with the highest PLI after Hong Kong, China is the People's Republic of China where prices are roughly 82% of that in Hong Kong, China, followed by Singapore with a PLI at around 80.

One significant observation from the Table 3.1 is that, except for the reference economy Hong Kong, China, PPPs differ significantly from exchange rates for most economies. This implies that exchange rates are not suitable for the purpose of converting measures of economic activity, such as GDP, and that the PPPs that account for the price level differences across economies

provide more accurate measures for converting GDP and its main aggregates to a common currency.

The second observation is that all the economies in the region have price levels lower than that in Hong Kong, China, implying that the price levels in all economies relative to Hong Kong, China are lower. Price levels can be expressed relative to the regional average (Asia and the Pacific = 100) instead of using Hong Kong, China as the reference (see Appendix 5). These are presented in Figure 3.5 for the 21 economies, which shows that Hong Kong, China with a PLI of 155.4 is about 55% more expensive than the regional average of 100. This is followed by the People's Republic of China (127.1); Singapore (124.1); Maldives (109.8); and Taipei,China (105.7), which all have PLIs higher than the regional average. Five economies from South Asia namely, Bhutan (54.6), Pakistan (54.9), Nepal (56.6), Sri Lanka (57.4), and India (57.7) have the lowest PLIs among the 21 economies.

An important observation from Figure 3.5 is that price levels generally increase with income levels or, equivalently, price levels are lower in lower-middle-income economies. The general pattern of relationship between price levels and real per capita expenditure is shown in Figure 3.6.

Figure 3.6 shows a positive relationship between price levels and per capita real expenditure. This relationship is referred to as the Penn Effect and is largely attributed to the Balassa–Samuelson effect (Balassa 1964, Samuelson 1964), which implies that productivity differentials between developed and less developed economies in the traded goods' sectors affect wages and prices in the nontradable goods sectors that in turn are reflected in general price levels. An important implication of this is that the price levels in the economies would be generally higher for those aggregates that largely comprise highly traded goods, compared to nontraded goods for which price levels tend to be lower in low-income economies. In general, this is observed for the PPPs

Figure 3.5: Price Level Indexes for Economies for Gross Domestic Product, 2021

(Asia and the Pacific = 100)

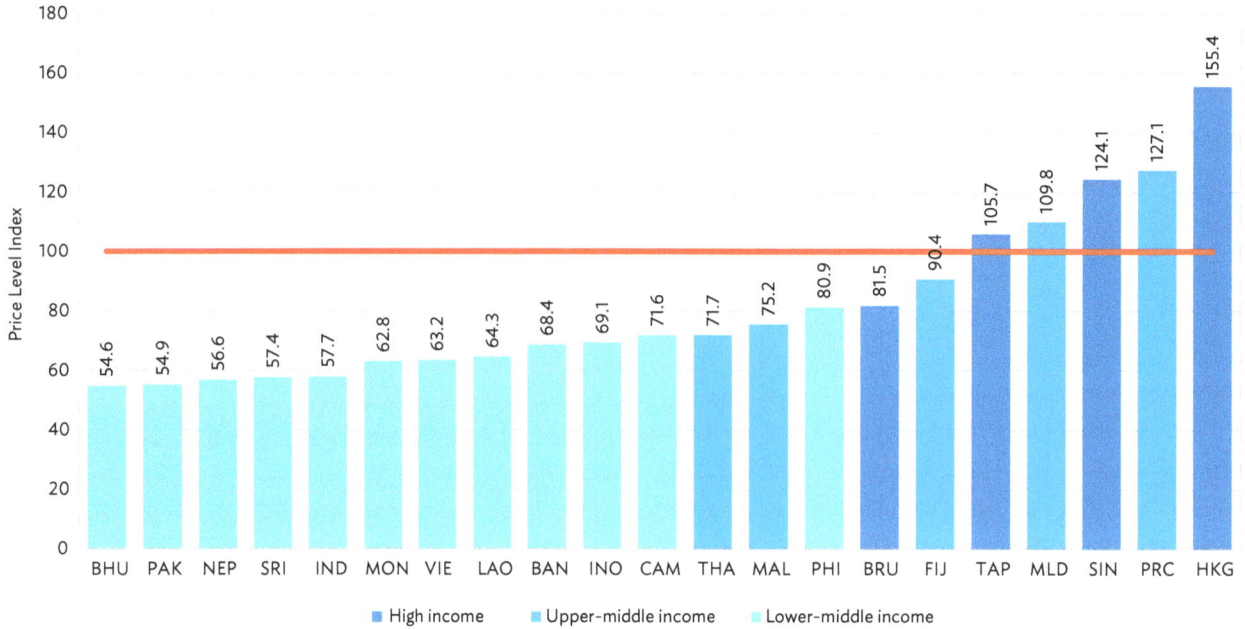

BAN = Bangladesh; BHU = Bhutan; BRU = Brunei Darussalam; CAM = Cambodia; FIJ = Fiji; HKG = Hong Kong, China; IND = India; INO = Indonesia; LAO = Lao People's Democratic Republic; MAL = Malaysia; MLD = Maldives; MON = Mongolia; NEP = Nepal; PAK = Pakistan; PHI = Philippines; PRC = People's Republic of China; SIN = Singapore; SRI = Sri Lanka; TAP = Taipei,China; THA = Thailand; VIE = Viet Nam.

Source: Asian Development Bank estimates based on data supplied by the participating economies.

Figure 3.6: Price Level Index versus Per Capita Real Gross Domestic Product, 2021

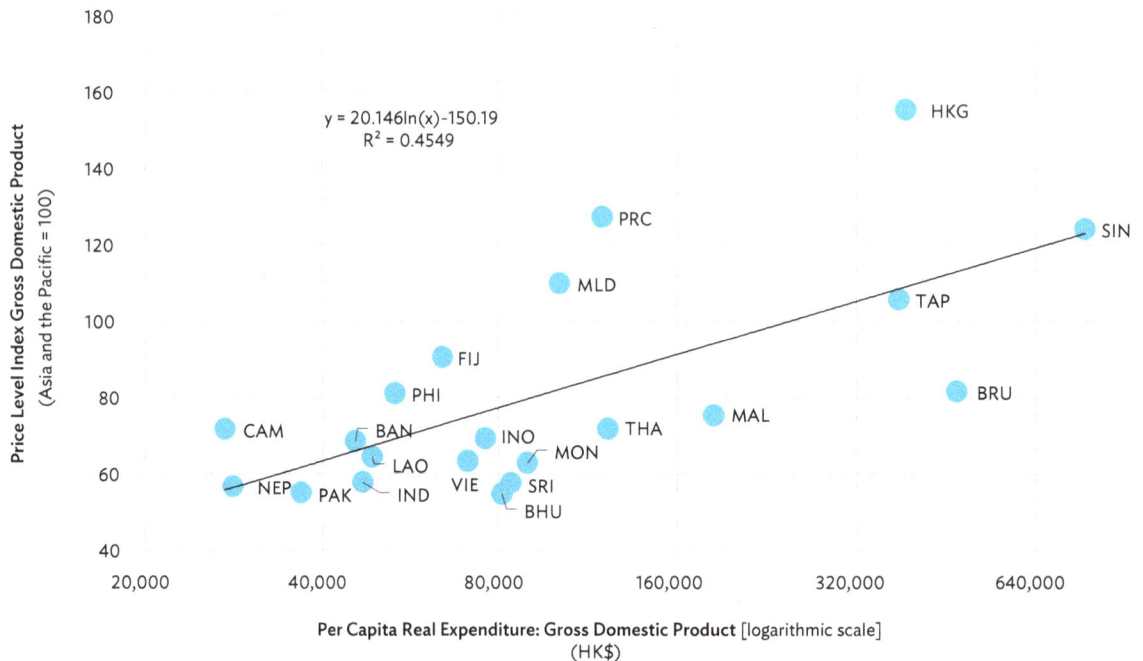

BAN = Bangladesh; BHU = Bhutan; BRU = Brunei Darussalam; CAM = Cambodia; FIJ = Fiji; HK$ = Hong Kong dollar; HKG = Hong Kong, China; IND = India; INO = Indonesia; LAO = Lao People's Democratic Republic; MAL = Malaysia; MLD = Maldives; MON = Mongolia; NEP = Nepal; PAK = Pakistan; PHI = Philippines; PRC = People's Republic of China; SIN = Singapore; SRI = Sri Lanka; TAP = Taipei,China; THA = Thailand; VIE = Viet Nam.

Source: Asian Development Bank estimates based on data supplied by the participating economies.

for machinery and equipment, which are largely imported by the regional economies, and where PPPs are closer to exchange rates than what is observed in the case of GDP or other aggregates in the region.

Household Final Consumption Expenditure

The household consumption expenditure is a major component of GDP and is an indicator of the total volumes of goods and services consumed by the households in each period. Table 3.2 provides a summary of the PPPs, PLIs, real and nominal expenditures, per capita real and nominal expenditures, and shares for the 21 participating economies for individual consumption expenditure by households (ICEH). The measure ICEH is inclusive of the expenditures undertaken by the nonprofit institutions serving households.

In Table 3.2 (column 4), the total real ICEH (in PPP terms) for the 21 participating economies is HK$166.523 trillion, compared to nominal ICEH of HK$91.718 trillion (column 5). Similar to the results for GDP, the People's Republic of China with HK$69.972 trillion (42.02%), India with HK$45.534 trillion (27.34%), and Indonesia with HK$11.269 trillion (6.77%) are the three largest economies, with a combined share of more than three-quarters (76.13%) of the ICEH for the region.

The PPPs for ICEH (column 2) are lower than the exchange rates (column 3), implying that the relative prices of goods and services consumed by the household were lower in all economies with reference to Hong Kong, China = 1.00.

With Asia and the Pacific = 100 as the reference (column 11), the PLI of Hong Kong, China for ICEH is highest at 181.6 followed by 174.1 for Singapore. Four other economies with PLIs higher than the regional average are Maldives (147.3); the People's Republic of China (137.4); Taipei,China (123.8); and Fiji (100.8). India and

Pakistan are least expensive and have the lowest PLIs at about 58. The remaining 16 economies have PLIs below the regional average of 100 with five economies of South Asia, namely, Pakistan (57.8), India (58.2), Nepal (63.3), Bhutan (63.8), and Sri Lanka (64.8) having the lowest PLIs for individual consumption expenditure by households.

Per Capita Income and Household Expenditure

Per capita income or per capita GDP is used as a measure of standard of living. However, given that GDP comprises household consumption, government spending, gross fixed capital formation (GFCF), changes in inventories, acquisitions less disposals of valuables, and net balance of exports, focusing on per capita household consumption expenditure can provide insights into material well-being of the households. This section presents the real per capita GDP, real per capita AICH, and real individual consumption expenditure by households. The ICEH is inclusive of the expenditure made by NPISH, whereas AICH also includes expenditures made by the government on behalf of households and therefore provides a more comprehensive measure of material well-being.

Table 3.3 has three measures reflecting the standards of living enjoyed by people in the 21 economies. The first is per capita real income or GDP, which is an all-encompassing measure of welfare used by various international organizations including the United Nations in its Human Development Index. As mentioned earlier, GDP includes government expenditure, gross capital formation, and net exports, and per capita GDP may not reflect the level of welfare enjoyed by the households. For example, an economy with a large volume of exports will have a lower per capita consumption expenditure relative to per capita GDP. This is the case with Singapore, which has the highest per capita real GDP of HK$774,311 but has a much lower per capita real AICH (HK$213,002) and

Table 3.2: Summary Results for Individual Consumption Expenditure by Households, 2021
(Hong Kong, China as Base)

| Economy | PPPs (HK\$ = 1.00) | Exchange Rates (HK\$ = 1.00) | Expenditure (HK\$ billion) | | Expenditure per Capita (HK\$) | | Shares (Asia and the Pacific = 100.00) | | | Price Level Indexes | | Reference Data | |
| | | | Based on PPPs | Based on XRs | Based on PPPs | Based on XRs | Expenditure Based on PPPs | Expenditure Based on XRs | Population | Asia and the Pacific = 100 | HKG=100 | Population (million) | Expenditure in LCU (billion) |
(1)	(2)	(3)	(4)	(5)	(6)	(7)	(8)	(9)	(10)	(11)	(12)	(13)	(14)
Bangladesh	4.57	10.95	5,654	2,362	33,209	13,873	3.40	2.58	4.39	75.8	41.8	170.26	25,857
Bhutan	3.34	9.51	32	11	42,194	14,834	0.02	0.01	0.02	63.8	35.2	0.76	107
Brunei Darussalam	0.09	0.17	49	27	111,819	61,410	0.03	0.03	0.01	99.7	54.9	0.44	5
Cambodia	246.92	527.23	295	138	17,767	8,321	0.18	0.15	0.43	85.0	46.8	16.59	72,790
China, People's Republic of	0.63	0.83	69,972	52,963	49,543	37,499	42.02	57.75	36.44	137.4	75.7	1,412.36	43,953
Fiji	0.15	0.27	49	27	55,233	30,671	0.03	0.03	0.02	100.8	55.5	0.89	7
Hong Kong, China	1.00	1.00	1,863	1,863	251,347	251,347	1.12	2.03	0.19	181.6	100.0	7.41	1,863
India	3.05	9.51	45,534	14,594	33,305	10,675	27.34	15.91	35.28	58.2	32.1	1,367.17	138,767
Indonesia	838.02	1,840.51	11,269	5,131	41,328	18,817	6.77	5.59	7.04	82.7	45.5	272.68	9,443,965
Lao People's Democratic Republic	510.34	1,247.48	170	70	23,218	9,499	0.10	0.08	0.19	74.3	40.9	7.34	86,947
Malaysia	0.24	0.53	3,688	1,684	113,199	51,697	2.21	1.84	0.84	82.9	45.7	32.58	898
Maldives	1.60	1.98	24	19	41,808	33,912	0.01	0.02	0.01	147.3	81.1	0.57	38
Mongolia	149.94	366.52	154	63	46,902	19,187	0.09	0.07	0.08	74.3	40.9	3.28	23,086
Nepal	5.30	15.20	714	249	24,560	8,559	0.43	0.27	0.75	63.3	34.9	29.06	3,780
Pakistan	6.66	20.92	7,791	2,479	34,658	11,029	4.68	2.70	5.80	57.8	31.8	224.78	51,862
Philippines	3.25	6.34	4,498	2,306	40,821	20,923	2.70	2.51	2.84	93.1	51.3	110.20	14,609
Singapore	0.17	0.17	1,022	980	187,411	179,685	0.61	1.07	0.14	174.1	95.9	5.45	169
Sri Lanka	9.13	25.58	1,180	421	53,273	19,002	0.71	0.46	0.57	64.8	35.7	22.16	10,771
Taipei,China	2.46	3.60	3,949	2,693	168,267	114,735	2.37	2.94	0.61	123.8	68.2	23.47	9,706
Thailand	1.83	4.11	4,656	2,075	66,819	29,778	2.80	2.26	1.80	80.9	44.6	69.69	8,537
Viet Nam	1,175.71	2,979.15	3,959	1,563	40,194	15,862	2.38	1.70	2.54	71.7	39.5	98.51	4,655,057
Asia and the Pacific	n.a.	n.a.	166,523	91,718	42,967	23,665	100.00	100.00	100.00	100.0	55.1	3,875.65	n.a.

ADB = Asian Development Bank; HK\$ = Hong Kong dollar; HKG = Hong Kong, China; LCU = local currency unit; n.a. = not applicable; PPP = purchasing power parity; XR = exchange rate.
Notes:
1. In this table, individual consumption expenditure by households includes expenditure by nonprofit institutions serving households.
2. Expenditures in local currency units, mid-year population estimates, and exchange rates were supplied by the participating economies for the International Comparison Program.
3. The PPPs used to calculate real expenditures are ADB estimates based on data supplied by the participating economies.
Source: Asian Development Bank estimates.

Table 3.3: Per Capita Real Gross Domestic Product, Actual Individual Consumption by Households, and Individual Consumption Expenditure by Households, 2021

Economy	Population (million)	Gross Domestic Product		Actual Individual Consumption by Households		Individual Consumption Expenditure by Households	
		Per Capita Real GDP (HK$)	Ranking Based on Per Capita Real GDP	Per Capita Real AICH[a] (HK$)	Ranking Based on Per Capita Real AICH	Per Capita Real ICEH[b] (HK$)	Ranking Based on Per Capita Real ICEH
(1)	(2)	(3)	(4)	(5)	(6)	(7)	(8)
Singapore	5.45	774,311	1	213,002	2	187,411	2
Brunei Darussalam	0.44	470,955	2	142,700	4	111,819	5
Hong Kong, China	7.41	386,832	3	270,778	1	251,347	1
Taipei,China	23.47	376,515	4	200,823	3	168,267	3
Malaysia	32.58	184,316	5	128,303	5	113,199	4
Thailand	69.69	122,360	6	81,569	6	66,819	6
China, People's Republic of	1,412.36	119,829	7	56,404	10	49,543	9
Maldives	0.57	101,638	8	54,102	11	41,808	12
Mongolia	3.28	89,532	9	57,434	9	46,902	10
Sri Lanka	22.16	84,007	10	61,629	8	53,273	8
Bhutan	0.76	81,049	11	53,772	12	42,194	11
Indonesia	272.68	76,030	12	46,418	13	41,328	13
Viet Nam	98.51	70,994	13	46,308	14	40,194	15
Fiji	0.89	64,376	14	62,029	7	55,233	7
Philippines	110.20	53,383	15	44,835	15	40,821	14
Lao People's Democratic Republic	7.34	48,828	16	26,096	20	23,218	20
India	1,367.17	47,087	17	34,898	17	33,305	17
Bangladesh	170.26	45,717	18	34,664	18	33,209	18
Pakistan	224.78	36,821	19	36,577	16	34,658	16
Nepal	29.06	28,263	20	26,353	19	24,560	19
Cambodia	16.59	27,407	21	19,946	21	17,767	21
Asia and the Pacific	3,875.65	82,030	n.a.	47,588	n.a.	42,967	n.a.

AICH = actual individual consumption by households, GDP = gross domestic product, ICEH = individual consumption expenditure by households, n.a. = not applicable.
[a] Includes individual consumption expenditure by households, nonprofit institutions serving households, and government.
[b] Includes expenditure by nonprofit institutions serving households.
Source: Asian Development Bank estimates based on data supplied by the participating economies.

per capita real ICEH of HK$187,411, the latter being roughly a quarter of per capita real GDP. Brunei Darussalam is another example where per capita real GDP is HK$470,955 and per capita real ICEH is HK$111,819, with household consumption nearly a quarter of per capita GDP. Hong Kong, China ranks 3rd in terms of per capita real GDP, but ranks 1st when per capita AICH and ICEH are considered. Out of 21 economies, the People's Republic of China, the top-ranked economy of the region in terms of size of its economy, is ranked 7th in terms of per capita GDP, 10th in terms of AICH, and 9th in terms of ICEH. India, the second-largest economy, consistently ranked 17th in terms of per capita GDP, ICEH, and AICH. Per capita measures in columns shown in Table 3.3 are drawn from more detailed tables in Appendix 1 for GDP, AICH, and ICEH.

Intereconomy disparities in per capita household expenditures are less striking compared to those in per capita GDP. Relative inequalities in the distribution of these three measures are shown in the form of Lorenz curves in Figure 3.7. The Lorenz curves plot the cumulative percentage shares of expenditures on GDP, ICEH, and AICH of the economies in Asia and the Pacific against the cumulative percentage shares of population, beginning with the economy with the lowest per capita expenditure to the highest. For example, the Lorenz curve for GDP plots the cumulative population shares of economies starting from the economy with the lowest per capita income to the highest. Inequality in per capita GDP is significantly higher than that seen for ICEH and AICH. For example, the poorest or bottom 20% of population receives about 10% of real GDP whereas the share of around 16% is higher for AICH and ICEH.

**Figure 3.7: Lorenz Curves for Per Capita Real Gross Domestic Product
and Per Capita Real Household Consumption Aggregates, 2021**

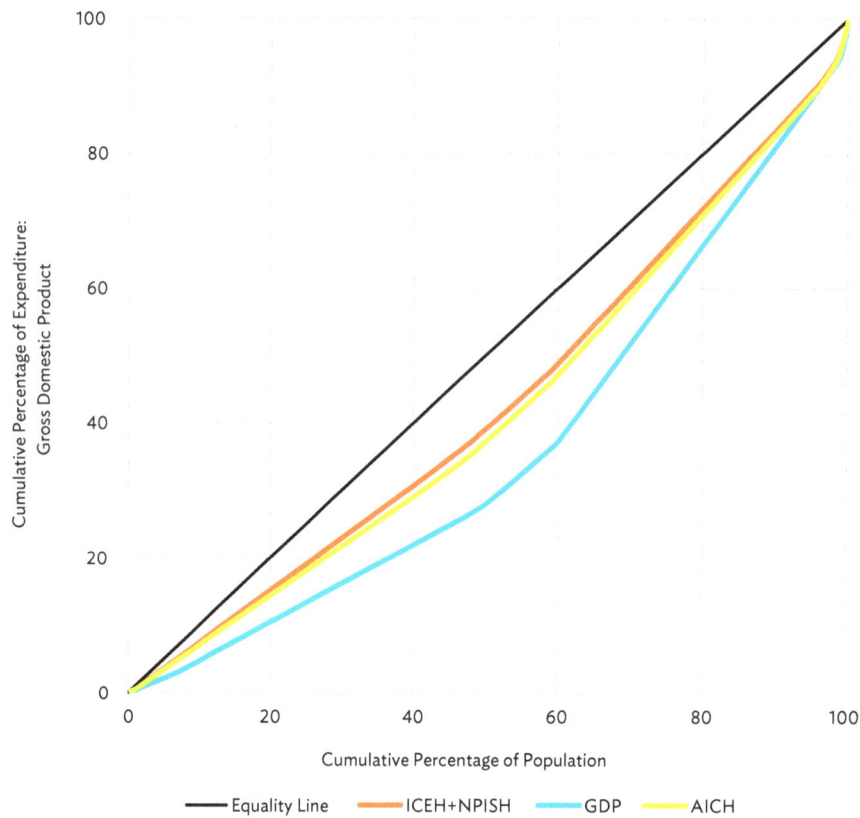

AICH = actual individual consumption by households, GDP = gross domestic product, ICEH = individual consumption expenditure by households, NPISH = nonprofit institutions serving households.
Note: Expenditure is represented by the economy-specific per capita real expenditure (GDP, ICEH, NPISH, and AICH.)
Source: Asian Development Bank estimates based on data supplied by the participating economies.

Per Capita Expenditures for Selected Aggregates

The ICP is a rich source of internationally comparable data on price levels and real expenditures at the aggregate level, such as GDP; consumption and investment; commodity groups; as well as categories such as food, clothing, transport, machinery, and equipment. Table 3.4 presents indexes of per capita real consumption expenditure levels for selected commodity groups, including AICH, for all 21 participating economies, expressed relative to the regional average (Asia and the Pacific = 100). Per capita real AICH for the whole region is HK$47,588.

For the AICH aggregate, Hong Kong, China is ranked at the top with per capita AICH 5.7 times that of the

regional average. In contrast, the lowest level, which is only 42% of the regional average, is observed for Cambodia. Per capita AICH shows a significant level of disparity with maximum per capita roughly 14 times that of the minimum. However, when it comes to "*food,*" the highest per capita is recorded for Malaysia with an index of 269 compared to 74 for Cambodia with a max–min ratio of only 3.6. This is the lowest recorded for any consumption aggregate. On the other hand, the level of intereconomy disparity observed is the highest for restaurants and hotels with a ratio of 130.3, with Singapore's index of 970 and Fiji's index being only 7, reflecting continued adverse impact of the pandemic in 2021 in Fiji. Several other interesting observations can be deduced by the readers about the relative per capita consumption expenditures of the economies for the

Table 3.4: Per Capita Real Expenditure Indexes for Actual Individual Consumption by Households and its Selected Components, 2021
(Asia and the Pacific = 100)

Economy	Actual Individual Consumption by Households[a]	Food	Bread and Cereals	Meat and Fish	Fruits and Vegetables	Services	Health[a]	Education[a]	Transportation and Communication	Recreation and Culture[a]	Restaurants and Hotels
(1)	(2)	(3)	(4)	(5)	(6)	(7)	(8)	(9)	(10)	(11)	(12)
Hong Kong, China	569.0	223.3	135.6	426.4	137.6	624.5	427.0	346.8	380.4	2,354.4	927.9
Singapore	447.6	175.4	158.8	207.8	142.1	578.0	392.2	420.1	325.7	1,898.3	970.4
Taipei,China	422.0	183.7	181.7	226.7	206.0	402.1	613.1	320.7	399.9	934.9	831.4
Brunei Darussalam	299.9	149.3	202.2	183.6	72.4	231.4	182.5	419.9	346.0	487.9	202.1
Malaysia	269.6	268.6	214.7	315.9	205.1	220.6	170.9	165.4	315.3	251.7	632.5
Thailand	171.4	147.2	136.8	147.3	209.0	157.0	225.3	230.5	128.2	238.2	291.0
Fiji	130.3	185.2	193.1	146.1	198.8	77.1	84.6	171.1	102.1	34.2	7.4
Sri Lanka	129.5	132.1	197.0	59.6	66.7	170.2	157.5	110.2	139.6	372.9	85.7
Mongolia	120.7	157.2	82.2	342.1	18.8	60.1	124.2	262.9	86.4	56.0	14.4
China, People's Republic of	118.5	88.3	54.4	145.8	92.8	119.9	143.6	112.5	126.9	137.1	137.3
Maldives	113.7	104.9	43.5	155.8	55.9	86.2	166.5	179.0	99.4	52.7	115.2
Bhutan	113.0	120.7	169.9	50.3	129.2	74.7	125.0	218.4	66.5	115.3	83.3
Asia and the Pacific	**100.0**	**100.0**	**100.0**	**100.0**	**100.0**	**100.0**	**100.0**	**100.0**	**100.0**	**100.0**	**100.0**
Indonesia	97.5	100.6	125.0	126.7	61.1	76.5	50.4	111.6	103.1	116.4	194.7
Viet Nam	97.3	83.9	113.8	124.1	48.1	101.3	115.7	147.8	115.8	140.5	120.8
Philippines	94.2	135.0	221.1	199.2	53.8	81.2	52.1	127.0	58.9	39.4	124.8
Pakistan	76.9	105.7	91.3	66.9	86.0	67.3	55.6	66.3	41.0	114.5	39.0
India	73.3	94.5	100.0	32.7	114.7	83.6	63.9	76.4	81.7	19.4	17.0
Bangladesh	72.8	140.9	277.9	93.3	108.7	46.4	35.5	57.0	21.1	37.0	39.7
Nepal	55.4	130.6	215.6	66.8	130.7	30.5	50.0	48.5	13.2	44.4	15.4
Lao People's Democratic Republic	54.8	75.4	102.7	125.3	40.4	40.5	29.8	87.0	24.7	39.4	53.6
Cambodia	41.9	74.4	113.0	86.0	44.2	23.3	60.6	50.7	16.4	32.1	37.6

AICH = actual individual consumption by households.
Note: Economies in the table are arranged in the descending order of their per capita expenditure index for AICH (column 2).
[a] Includes individual consumption expenditure by households, nonprofit institutions serving households, and government.
Source: Asian Development Bank estimates based on data supplied by the participating economies.

detailed expenditure aggregates presented in the Tables in Appendix 1.

General Government Final Consumption Expenditure

Government final consumption expenditure (GFCE) comprises individual consumption expenditure by government (ICEG) and collective consumption expenditure by government (CCEG). Spending on health, education, housing, recreation, culture, and social protection on behalf of households is mainly covered by ICEG. The items in CCEG involve services provided to the entire community such as general public services, defense, public order and safety, economic affairs, environmental protection, and housing and community amenities.

Comparing per capita real GFCE and its components offers valuable insights into the diverse roles played by governments in different economies. Table 3.5 presents summary results for the PPPs, PLIs, and total and per capita real and nominal government expenditures for Asia and the Pacific.

The total GFCE in Asia and the Pacific in real terms is estimated at HK$43.554 trillion compared to nominal expenditure of HK$29.519 trillion. The People's Republic of China has the largest real GFCE (HK$25.564 trillion), which is roughly four times compared to the next largest economy, India. Relative to the reference economy (Hong Kong, China = 1.00), the PPPs (column 2) for GFCE and exchange rates (column 3) show that PPPs for GFCE, which are largely driven by the relative prices for compensation paid to government

Table 3.5: Summary Results for Government Final Consumption Expenditure, 2021
(Hong Kong, China as Base)

Economy	PPPs (HK$ = 1.00)	Exchange Rates (HK$ = 1.00)	Expenditure (HK$ billion)		Expenditure per Capita (HK$)		Shares (Asia and the Pacific = 100.00)			Price Level Indexes		Reference Data	
			Based on PPPs	Based on XRs	Based on PPPs	Based on XRs	Expenditure		Population	Asia and the Pacific = 100	HKG=100	Population (million)	Expenditure in LCU (billion)
							Based on PPPs	Based on XRs					
(1)	(2)	(3)	(4)	(5)	(6)	(7)	(8)	(9)	(10)	(11)	(12)	(13)	(14)
Bangladesh	3.96	10.95	548	198	3,216	1,164	1.26	0.67	4.39	53.4	36.2	170.26	2,170
Bhutan	1.75	9.51	27	5	35,085	6,452	0.06	0.02	0.02	27.1	18.4	0.76	46
Brunei Darussalam	0.06	0.17	74	24	167,259	55,517	0.17	0.08	0.01	49.0	33.2	0.44	4
Cambodia	186.24	527.23	43	15	2,580	911	0.10	0.05	0.43	52.1	35.3	16.59	7,971
China, People's Republic of	0.71	0.83	25,564	21,967	18,100	15,553	58.69	74.42	36.44	126.8	85.9	1,412.36	18,230
Fiji	0.13	0.27	16	8	17,794	8,843	0.04	0.03	0.02	73.3	49.7	0.89	2
Hong Kong, China	1.00	1.00	364	364	49,041	49,041	0.83	1.23	0.19	147.5	100.0	7.41	364
India	4.22	9.51	5,893	2,617	4,310	1,914	13.53	8.86	35.28	65.5	44.4	1,367.17	24,882
Indonesia	579.82	1,840.51	2,707	853	9,929	3,128	6.22	2.89	7.04	46.5	31.5	272.68	1,569,830
Lao People's Democratic Republic	283.34	1,247.48	88	20	11,956	2,716	0.20	0.07	0.19	33.5	22.7	7.34	24,859
Malaysia	0.24	0.53	829	370	25,439	11,343	1.90	1.25	0.84	65.8	44.6	32.58	197
Maldives	0.94	1.98	16	8	28,346	13,420	0.04	0.03	0.01	69.9	47.3	0.57	15
Mongolia	73.79	366.52	88	18	26,815	5,398	0.20	0.06	0.08	29.7	20.1	3.28	6,495
Nepal	4.88	15.20	77	25	2,666	856	0.18	0.08	0.75	47.4	32.1	29.06	378
Pakistan	7.69	20.92	851	313	3,786	1,393	1.95	1.06	5.80	54.3	36.8	224.78	6,548
Philippines	2.84	6.34	1,066	477	9,674	4,331	2.45	1.62	2.84	66.1	44.8	110.20	3,024
Singapore	0.13	0.17	466	358	85,388	65,731	1.07	1.21	0.14	113.6	77.0	5.45	62
Sri Lanka	5.49	25.58	303	65	13,676	2,937	0.70	0.22	0.57	31.7	21.5	22.16	1,665
Taipei,China	2.01	3.60	1,463	817	62,320	34,813	3.36	2.77	0.61	82.4	55.9	23.47	2,945
Thailand	1.47	4.11	2,028	724	29,097	10,394	4.66	2.45	1.80	52.7	35.7	69.69	2,980
Viet Nam	779.40	2,979.15	1,046	274	10,616	2,777	2.40	0.93	2.54	38.6	26.2	98.51	815,016
Asia and the Pacific	n.a.	n.a.	43,554	29,519	11,238	7,617	100.00	100.00	100.00	100.0	67.8	3,875.65	n.a.

ADB = Asian Development Bank; HK$ = Hong Kong dollar; HKG = Hong Kong, China; LCU = local currency unit; n.a. = not applicable; PPP = purchasing power parity; XR = exchange rate.
Notes:
1. Expenditures in local currency units, mid–year population estimates, and exchange rates were supplied by the participating economies for the International Comparison Program.
2. The PPPs used to calculate real expenditures are ADB estimates based on data supplied by the participating economies.
Source: Asian Development Bank estimates.

employees, are lower than the exchange rates for all economies except for Hong Kong, China. With Asia and the Pacific = 100, Hong Kong, China has the highest PLI with 147.5 followed by 126.8 for the People's Republic of China, and 113.6 for Singapore. These are the three economies whose PLIs for GFCE are higher than the regional average. At the other end, Bhutan has the lowest PLI of 27 followed by 30 for Mongolia. Seven economies have PLIs below 50 (nearly one-third that of Hong Kong, China) indicating relatively very low prices for government services in these economies.

Figure 3.8 shows the relative sizes of the 21 participating economies based on total GFCE in real and nominal terms of the region's economies. The left panel has 11 economies, each with at least 1% share in the region's real GFCE, and the right panel has 10 economies with the smallest sizes and less than 1% share. The People's Republic of China accounts for nearly three-fifths (58.69%) of the region's real expenditures in GFCE. Along with India

(13.53%) and Indonesia (6.22%), these three most populous economies together accounted for 78.44% of the region's real government expenditures.

The regional average per capita real GFCE is HK$11,238 while the per capita nominal GFCE is only HK$7,617 (see Table 3.5, columns 6 and 7). Per capita real and nominal GFCE are shown in Figure 3.9. As discussed earlier, since the PPPs are lower than the exchange rates for all economies, the per capita real GFCE are higher than the nominal counterparts for all economies, except for the reference economy Hong Kong, China for which both values are equal. Brunei Darussalam has the highest per capita real GFCE of HK$167,259 followed by Singapore with HK$85,388, which is almost half of Brunei Darussalam's per capita. Per capita real GFCE of Brunei Darussalam is roughly 64 times that of Cambodia, which has the lowest per capita real GFCE at HK$2,580. The People's Republic of China with HK$18,100 ranked 10th whereas India is ranked 17th with HK$4,310.

Figure 3.8: Economy Shares of Real and Nominal Government Final Consumption Expenditure, 2021 (%)

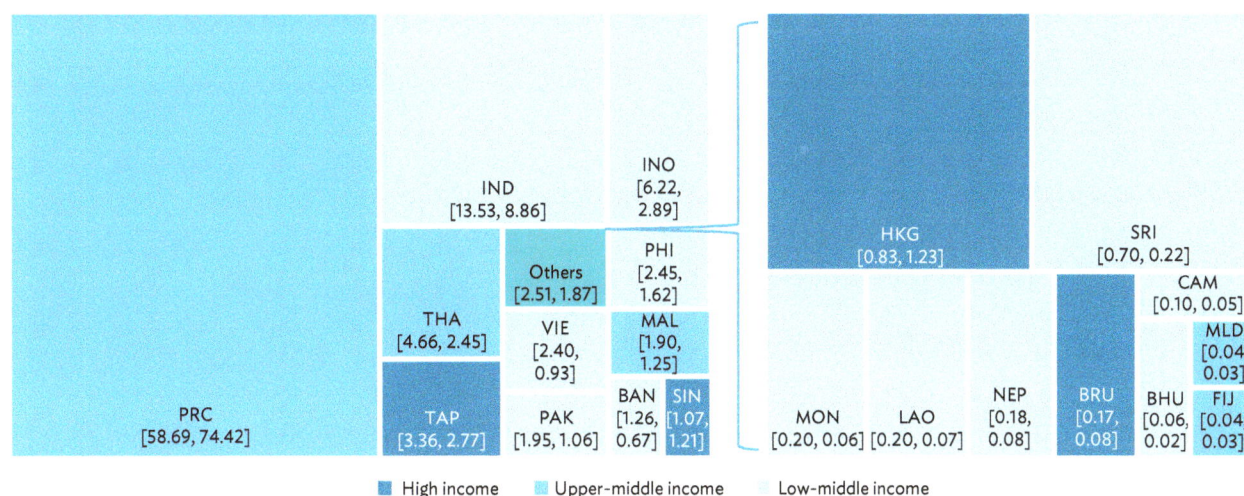

ADB = Asian Development Bank; BAN = Bangladesh; BHU = Bhutan; BRU = Brunei Darussalam; CAM = Cambodia; FIJ = Fiji; GFCE = government final consumption expenditure; HKG = Hong Kong, China; IND = India; INO = Indonesia; LAO = Lao People's Democratic Republic; MAL = Malaysia; MLD = Maldives; MON = Mongolia; NEP = Nepal; PAK = Pakistan; PHI = Philippines; PRC = People's Republic of China; SIN = Singapore; SRI = Sri Lanka; TAP = Taipei,China; THA = Thailand; VIE = Viet Nam.

Notes:

1. The sizes of the treemap segments are based on economy shares of real GFCE to the Asia and Pacific region.

2. The first value shown in the label represents the share of real GFCE, while the second value represents the share of nominal GFCE.

3. The PPPs used to calculate real expenditures are ADB estimates based on data supplied by the participating economies.

Source: ADB estimates.

Figure 3.9: Per Capita Real and Nominal Government Final Consumption Expenditure in Asia and the Pacific, 2021
(HK$)

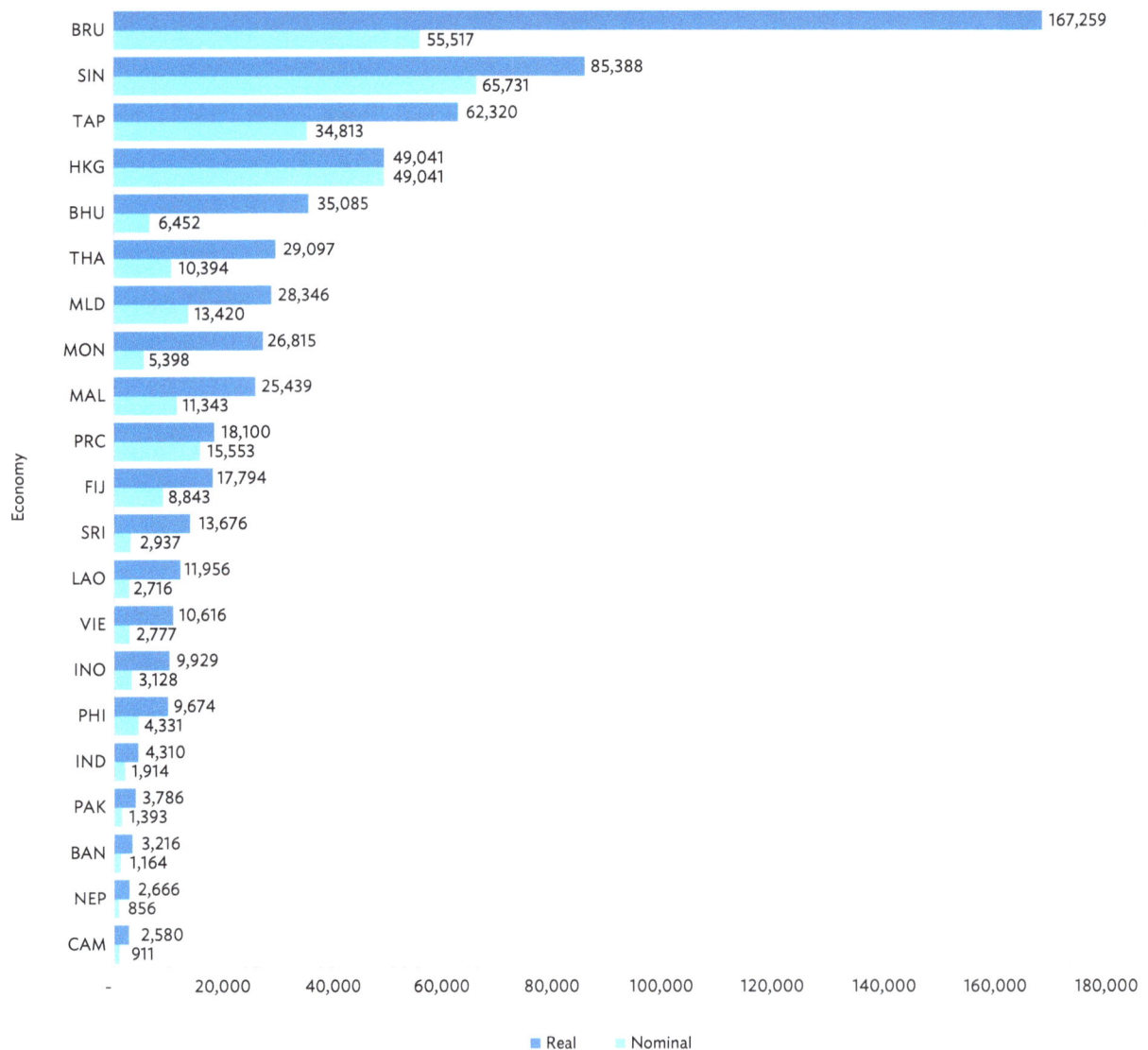

Economy	Real	Nominal
BRU	167,259	55,517
SIN	85,388	65,731
TAP	62,320	34,813
HKG	49,041	49,041
BHU	35,085	6,452
THA	29,097	10,394
MLD	28,346	13,420
MON	26,815	5,398
MAL	25,439	11,343
PRC	18,100	15,553
FIJ	17,794	8,843
SRI	13,676	2,937
LAO	11,956	2,716
VIE	10,616	2,777
INO	9,929	3,128
PHI	9,674	4,331
IND	4,310	1,914
PAK	3,786	1,393
BAN	3,216	1,164
NEP	2,666	856
CAM	2,580	911

■ Real ■ Nominal

BAN = Bangladesh; BHU = Bhutan; BRU = Brunei Darussalam; CAM = Cambodia; FIJ = Fiji; HK$ = Hong Kong dollar; HKG = Hong Kong, China; IND = India; INO = Indonesia; LAO = Lao People's Democratic Republic; MAL = Malaysia; MLD = Maldives; MON = Mongolia; NEP = Nepal; PAK = Pakistan; PHI = Philippines; PRC = People's Republic of China; SIN = Singapore; SRI = Sri Lanka; TAP = Taipei,China; THA = Thailand; VIE = Viet Nam.
Source: Asian Development Bank estimates based on data supplied by the participating economies.

Gross Fixed Capital Formation

An important component of GDP, GFCF comprises investments in machinery and equipment; construction of residential, nonresidential, and civil engineering structures; and other productive assets. While per capita individual or actual consumption expenditure by households reflect the relative standards of living enjoyed by populations in different economies, per capita GFCF is indicative of the future potential for growth, as investment in construction and machinery and equipment provide basic infrastructure and capital stock for production and GDP growth.

Table 3.6: Summary Results for Gross Fixed Capital Formation, 2021
(Hong Kong, China as Base)

Economy	PPPs (HK$ = 1.00)	Exchange Rates (HK$ = 1.00)	Expenditure (HK$ billion)		Expenditure per Capita (HK$)		Shares (Asia and the Pacific = 100.00) Expenditure			Price Level Indexes		Reference Data	
			Based on PPPs	Based on XRs	Based on PPPs	Based on XRs	Based on PPPs	Based on XRs	Population	Asia and the Pacific = 100	HKG=100	Population (million)	Expenditure in LCU (billion)
(1)	(2)	(3)	(4)	(5)	(6)	(7)	(8)	(9)	(10)	(11)	(12)	(13)	(14)
Bangladesh	5.74	10.95	2,063	1,081	12,116	6,352	2.00	1.43	4.39	71.3	52.4	170.26	11,838
Bhutan	5.07	9.51	18	9	23,479	12,519	0.02	0.01	0.02	72.6	53.3	0.76	90
Brunei Darussalam	0.10	0.17	60	34	136,314	76,811	0.06	0.04	0.01	76.7	56.3	0.44	6
Cambodia	245.34	527.23	103	48	6,210	2,890	0.10	0.06	0.43	63.3	46.5	16.59	25,281
China, People's Republic of	0.71	0.83	68,223	58,296	48,304	41,275	66.11	76.86	36.44	116.3	85.4	1,412.36	48,378
Fiji	0.16	0.27	11	6	11,966	7,268	0.01	0.01	0.02	82.7	60.7	0.89	2
Hong Kong, China	1.00	1.00	483	483	65,157	65,157	0.47	0.64	0.19	136.1	100.0	7.41	483
India	4.23	9.51	15,435	6,872	11,289	5,026	14.96	9.06	35.28	60.6	44.5	1,367.17	65,339
Indonesia	845.84	1,840.51	6,181	2,840	22,666	10,417	5.99	3.75	7.04	62.5	46.0	272.68	5,227,854
Lao People's Democratic Republic	656.39	1,247.48	128	67	17,469	9,192	0.12	0.09	0.19	71.6	52.6	7.34	84,137
Malaysia	0.28	0.53	1,080	560	33,145	17,189	1.05	0.74	0.84	70.6	51.9	32.58	298
Maldives	1.33	1.98	17	12	30,309	20,395	0.02	0.02	0.01	91.6	67.3	0.57	23
Mongolia	195.57	366.52	60	32	18,205	9,714	0.06	0.04	0.08	72.6	53.4	3.28	11,688
Nepal	7.35	15.20	183	89	6,295	3,046	0.18	0.12	0.75	65.8	48.4	29.06	1,345
Pakistan	10.02	20.92	823	394	3,662	1,754	0.80	0.52	5.80	65.2	47.9	224.78	8,247
Philippines	3.39	6.34	1,276	683	11,580	6,194	1.24	0.90	2.84	72.8	53.5	110.20	4,325
Singapore	0.14	0.17	951	752	174,296	137,889	0.92	0.99	0.14	107.6	79.1	5.45	130
Sri Lanka	12.47	25.58	371	181	16,757	8,167	0.36	0.24	0.57	66.3	48.7	22.16	4,629
Taipei,China	2.70	3.60	2,111	1,579	89,960	67,283	2.05	2.08	0.61	101.8	74.8	23.47	5,692
Thailand	2.13	4.11	1,802	933	25,858	13,394	1.75	1.23	1.80	70.5	51.8	69.69	3,840
Viet Nam	1,459.47	2,979.15	1,821	892	18,489	9,058	1.76	1.18	2.54	66.7	49.0	98.51	2,658,069
Asia and the Pacific	n.a.	n.a.	103,199	75,844	26,628	19,569	100.00	100.00	100.00	100.0	73.5	3,875.65	n.a.

ADB = Asian Development Bank; HK$ = Hong Kong dollar; HKG = Hong Kong, China; LCU = local currency unit; n.a. = not applicable; PPP = purchasing power parity; XR = exchange rate.
Notes:
1. Expenditures in local currency units, mid-year population estimates, and exchange rates were supplied by the participating economies for the International Comparison Program.
2. The PPPs used to calculate real expenditures are ADB estimates based on data supplied by the participating economies.
Source: Asian Development Bank estimates.

Summary results for GFCF are presented in Table 3.6 for the 21 economies. Total size of GFCF in the region in real terms is HK$103.199 trillion, and in nominal terms is HK$75.844 trillion. As seen for the other aggregates, the People's Republic of China's real GFCF at HK$68.223 trillion is the largest; India at HK$15.435 trillion is second-largest; and Indonesia at HK$6.181 trillion is third-largest. The real GFCF for all economies is higher than the nominal GFCF, which is again explained by the fact that the PPPs for GFCF (column 2) are lower than the exchange rates (column 3) for all economies. The PLIs shown in column (11) with Asia and the Pacific = 100 show that Hong Kong, China has the highest PLI of 136.1 followed by 116.3 for the People's Republic of China, while India has the lowest PLI of 60.6 followed by 62.5 for Indonesia and 63.3 for Cambodia.

Figure 3.10 shows that only 9 of the 21 economies had a share of more than 1% in the region's real GFCF with a combined share to real and nominal

GFCF of about 96.89% as seen on the left panel. The largest contributor to the region's GFCF, the People's Republic of China, accounted for 66.11% of real GFCF and 76.86% of the nominal share. India followed with 14.96% real GFCF and 9.06% nominal share. The remaining 12 economies each with a contribution below 1% have a combined share of about 3.11% (slightly larger than the 2.78% share in nominal GFCF). Among the high-income economies, the shares of Brunei Darussalam; Hong Kong, China; and Singapore to the real and nominal GFCF are below 1%. Singapore contributes roughly 0.92% in real and 0.99% in nominal terms. The shares of Hong Kong, China are 0.47% for real and 0.64% for nominal GFCF. Brunei Darussalam's share is 0.06% in real terms and 0.04% in nominal terms.

However, the economy rankings are very different when the per capita levels of GFCF are considered, as shown in Figure 3.11.

Figure 3.10: Economy Shares of Real and Nominal Gross Fixed Capital Formation, 2021 (%)

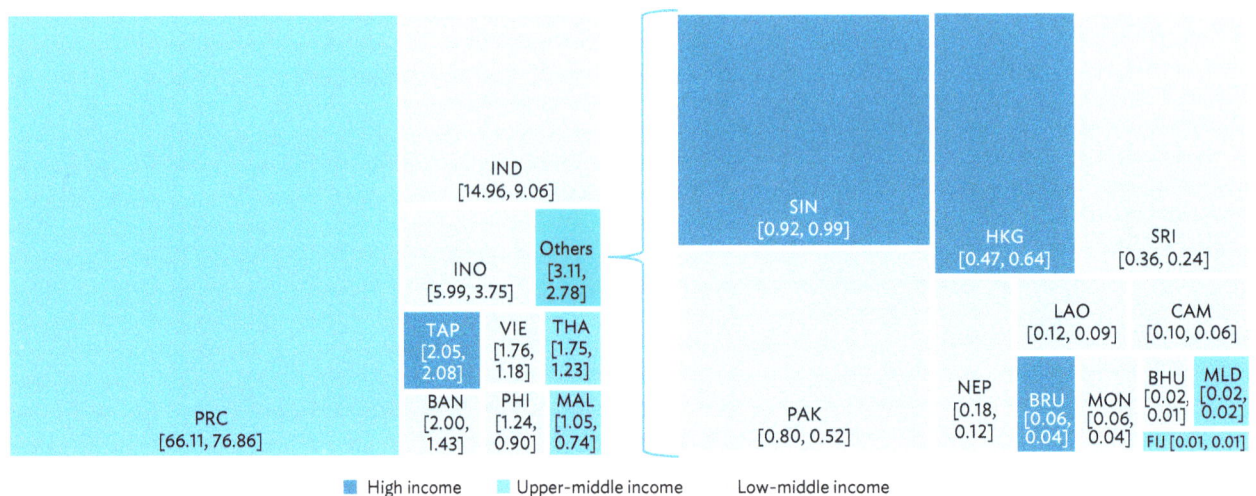

ADB = Asian Development Bank; BAN = Bangladesh; BHU = Bhutan; BRU = Brunei Darussalam; CAM = Cambodia; FIJ = Fiji; GFCF = gross fixed capital formation; HKG = Hong Kong, China; IND = India; INO = Indonesia; LAO = Lao People's Democratic Republic; MAL = Malaysia; MLD = Maldives; MON = Mongolia; NEP = Nepal; PAK = Pakistan; PHI = Philippines; PPPs = purchasing power parities; PRC = People's Republic of China; SIN = Singapore; SRI = Sri Lanka; TAP = Taipei,China; THA = Thailand; VIE = Viet Nam.

Notes:

1. The sizes of the treemap segments are based on economy shares of real GFCF to the Asia and Pacific region.

2. The first value shown in the label represents the share of real GFCF, while the second value represents the share of nominal GFCF.

3. The PPPs used to calculate real expenditures are ADB estimates based on data supplied by the participating economies.

Source: ADB estimates.

Figure 3.11: Per Capita Real and Nominal Gross Fixed Capital Formation in Asia and the Pacific, 2021

(HK$)

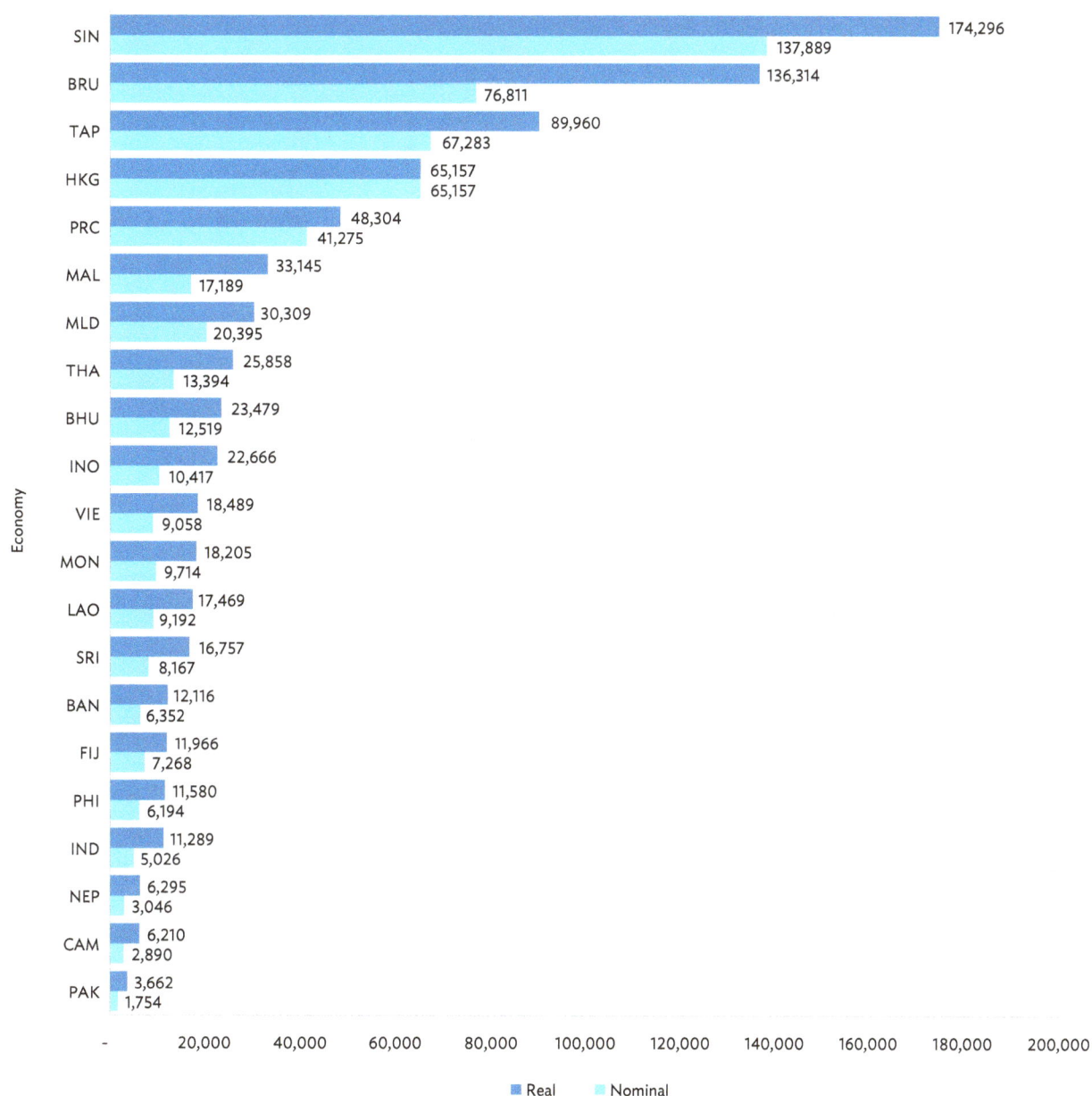

BAN = Bangladesh; BHU = Bhutan; BRU = Brunei Darussalam; CAM = Cambodia; FIJ = Fiji; HK$ = Hong Kong dollar; HKG = Hong Kong, China; IND = India; INO = Indonesia; LAO = Lao People's Democratic Republic; MAL = Malaysia; MLD = Maldives; MON = Mongolia; NEP = Nepal; PAK = Pakistan; PHI = Philippines; PRC = People's Republic of China; SIN = Singapore; SRI = Sri Lanka; TAP = Taipei,China; THA = Thailand; VIE = Viet Nam.

Source: Asian Development Bank estimates based on data supplied by the participating economies.

The average per capita real GFCF for Asia and the Pacific for 2021 is estimated at HK$26,628 in comparison to HK$19,569 per capita in nominal terms. Among the 21 participating economies, Singapore is ranked first with per capita real GFCF of HK$174,296 followed by Brunei Darussalam (HK$136,314); Taipei,China (HK$89,960); and Hong Kong, China (HK$65,157). The People's Republic of China with per capita real GFCF at HK$48,304 is ranked 5th while India with HK$11,289 is ranked 18th. Per capita GFCF in Singapore is roughly 48 times that in Pakistan, which has the lowest per capita real GFCF of HK$3,662.

Price Level Indexes for Gross Domestic Products and Its Major Components

Price level index is the ratio of an economy's PPP for the aggregate under consideration and the market exchange rate of its currency with the reference economy multiplied by 100. Hong Kong, China being the reference economy for Asia and the Pacific has a PPP (and exchange rate) equal to 1.00 and hence its PLI is also equal to 100. At the GDP level, the PLIs have shown a distinct pattern (Figure 3.4), described as the Penn effect, with low PLIs (resulting from low PPPs, which in turn reflect lower level of prices paid for goods and services) for low-income economies.

Price levels tend to be quite low in low-income economies. It is useful to examine whether similar patterns can be expected for other aggregates, especially for machinery and equipment where goods are freely traded across economies. In fact, many low-income economies tend to import equipment for major projects. At the other end of the spectrum, price levels for government expenditure tend to be low in low-income economies due to relatively low salaries and benefits enjoyed by public servants. The ICP makes an adjustment to salaries to account for differences in productivity of government employees. The PLIs of economies can also be expressed with respect to Asia and the Pacific = 100. The method to convert PLIs with Hong Kong, China as the reference economy with a PLI of 100, to corresponding PLIs with Asia and the Pacific = 100 as the reference is explained in Appendix 5. Table 3.7 presents PLIs for major components of GDP with Asia and the Pacific =100.

The first column shows PLIs for GDP, with Hong Kong, China registering the highest PLI of 155.4, i.e., about 55% higher than the regional average, while the lowest PLI of around 54.6 is observed for Bhutan, which is about 45% lower than the regional average. The ratio between the highest

and the lowest PLI is 2.8 implying that the price levels in Bhutan are roughly one-third of the prices in Hong Kong, China.

The relative price levels across economies are similar for individual and actual consumption expenditure by households (ICEH and AICH) though PLIs for AICH tend to be a little lower than those for ICEH. This is due to the inclusion in AICH of the expenditures incurred by the government on behalf of households.

Price level indexes for GFCE tended to be much lower in low-income economies than the PLIs for other aggregates. For example, Bhutan, the Lao People's Democratic Republic, Mongolia, and Viet Nam register PLIs below one-third of the regional average. The PLI for Singapore, 113.6, is lower than the PLI for the People's Republic of China (126.8) and Hong Kong, China (147.5). The ratio of the highest PLI to the lowest PLI for GFCE is 5.4, which is also the highest ratio in comparison to the similar ratios for GDP, AICH, ICEH, and GFCF, indicating wide disparities in the relative prices of government services, largely driven by relatively low wages of government employees in low-income economies. Among these aggregates, the ratio of the PLIs for GFCF between the highest PLI of 136.1 for Hong Kong, China to the lowest PLI of 60.6 for India is 2.2.

The PLIs for GFCF, machinery and equipment, and construction in low-income economies are quite different from PLIs for GDP and other aggregates. These indexes are even closer to 100 when it comes to machinery and equipment where the indexes are in the narrow range of 79.5 to 107.4, compared to the range of 55.4 to 155.4 for GDP, 57.8 to 181.6 for ICEH, and 27.1 to 147.5 for GFCE. That PLIs are closer to the regional average of 100 implies that the PPPs are closer to the exchange rates, which is expected for machinery and equipment that are highly tradeable items. In comparison, for construction, PLIs have a much wider range of 192.3 for Hong Kong, China to

Table 3.7: Price Level Indexes for Gross Domestic Product and its Major Components, 2021
(Asia and the Pacific = 100)

Economy	Gross Domestic Product	Actual Individual Consumption by Households[a]	Individual Consumption Expenditure by Households[b]	Government Final Consumption Expenditure	Gross Fixed Capital Formation		
					Total	Machinery and Equipment	Construction
(1)	(2)	(3)	(4)	(5)	(6)	(7)	(8)
Hong Kong, China	155.4	178.3	181.6	147.5	136.1	87.9	192.3
Singapore	124.1	169.7	174.1	113.6	107.6	98.2	132.4
China, People's Republic of	127.1	137.8	137.4	126.8	116.3	107.4	125.1
Maldives	109.8	133.2	147.3	69.9	91.6	93.1	96.2
Taipei,China	105.7	118.6	123.8	82.4	101.8	99.2	116.0
Asia and the Pacific	100.0	100.0	100.0	100.0	100.0	100.0	100.0
Brunei Darussalam	81.5	93.2	99.7	49.0	76.7	88.3	70.9
Fiji	90.4	97.2	100.8	73.3	82.7	91.0	78.5
Malaysia	75.2	80.6	82.9	65.8	70.6	88.1	60.4
Philippines	80.9	89.1	93.1	66.1	72.8	83.5	66.8
Thailand	71.7	77.1	80.9	52.7	70.5	90.0	56.5
Bangladesh	68.4	72.0	75.8	53.4	71.3	95.1	61.0
Cambodia	71.6	79.7	85.0	52.1	63.3	83.1	51.8
Indonesia	69.1	77.4	82.7	46.5	62.5	88.9	50.6
Lao People's Democratic Republic	64.3	67.8	74.3	33.5	71.6	87.8	62.3
Viet Nam	63.2	66.5	71.7	38.6	66.7	83.8	58.0
Mongolia	62.8	66.0	74.3	29.7	72.6	85.4	65.6
Sri Lanka	57.4	59.5	64.8	31.7	66.3	90.0	54.5
Pakistan	54.9	56.2	57.8	54.3	65.2	82.4	54.2
India	57.7	58.0	58.2	65.5	60.6	79.5	51.1
Nepal	56.6	60.1	63.3	47.4	65.8	82.1	56.7
Bhutan	54.6	57.4	63.8	27.1	72.6	94.2	59.7

[a] Includes individual consumption expenditure by households, nonprofit institutions serving households, and government.
[b] Includes expenditure by nonprofit institutions serving households.
Source: Asian Development Bank estimates based on data supplied by the participating economies.

50.6 for Indonesia, with a ratio between the highest and the lowest at 3.8, as construction uses substantial nontradeable resources of labor inputs and locally produced construction materials, which have lower relative prices in low-income economies.

The variability in the PLIs for GDP and some of its major components presented here serve as reminder to the users that PPPs are likely to differ significantly across different aggregates and commodity groups. Detailed results with PPPs, PLIs, and real expenditures are available online (https://icp.adb.org) for 45 expenditure categories. While using the PPPs for the purpose of converting expenditure aggregates in local currency units into comparable real expenditures, users are reminded that it is important to choose and use PPPs that closely align with the expenditure aggregates being considered.

CHAPTER 4

Comparative Analysis of Results from the 2017 and 2021 International Comparison Program in Asia and the Pacific

The 2021 International Comparison Program (ICP) cycle coincided with the year after devastating effects of the coronavirus disease (COVID-19) pandemic reverberated in 2020 throughout Asia and the Pacific. Due to variable responses from governments, the differential impacts of the pandemic on various sectors, and progress of national vaccination programs, the region's economies have exhibited significantly different patterns of growth, which is likely to alter the relative sizes and levels of well-being of their respective populations. The purchasing power parities (PPP) and real expenditure comparisons from the 2021 ICP in the region offer valuable insights into the relative performance of the 21 participating economies for the year 2021, when some economies were already on a strong recovery path while some others were still struggling with low or negative growth.

The size and distribution of the economies from the 2021 ICP were earlier presented in Chapter 3. This chapter offers a comparative assessment of the region's economies for the 2017 ICP benchmark with the 2021 ICP cycle in the region, when many economies were still recovering from the pandemic. The revised 2017 ICP results presented in the tables in Appendix 2 provide results for the full set of 22 economies that participated in the 2017 ICP cycle. In this chapter, comparisons presented between 2017 (revised) and 2021 results are made only for the 21 economies that are common to both 2017 and 2021 ICP cycles.

It has been a standard practice in the ICP to revise and/or update the PPPs and real expenditures results from the previous cycle by mainly incorporating revisions in national accounts and population data from participating economies, while keeping price data collected unchanged for

PPP and real expenditure computations. The 2017 ICP cycle concluded in early 2020 with a detailed report on the methodology used for international price comparisons in the region and an extensive analysis of the results published in October 2020 (ADB 2020).

Revisions to the 2017 International Comparison Program in Asia and the Pacific

There are four main sources that contributed revisions to the results from the 2017 ICP in the Asia and Pacific region:

(i) *Population data.* Except for upward revisions of about 4% for Pakistan and 2% for Thailand, and downward revisions of 3% for Nepal and about 2% for Mongolia, population data remained largely stable. The biggest revisions observed for Pakistan and Nepal are due to new data emerging from population censuses in 2017 and 2021, respectively.

(ii) *Gross domestic product (GDP).* There were significant upward revisions in GDP in many economies, primarily due to GDP revisions resulting from new surveys and/or base year revisions, with increases of 26% for Viet Nam, 25% for Nepal, 17% for Bangladesh, and 12% for Pakistan. Revisions to GDP also affect data for the main aggregates, individual consumption expenditure by households, government final consumption expenditure and gross capital formation, and their sub-aggregates leading to changes in the weights used in the aggregation of PPPs. While results presented here refer to GDP and its main components, users must be aware of similar changes for other aggregates.

(iii) *Productivity adjustment and changes in PPPs for government*. Changes in estimates of productivity adjustment factors used for adjusting productivity differentials in government services resulted in significant changes in these factors for some economies; however, the productivity adjustment methodology remained unchanged (Inklaar 2019). Most economies experienced changes in productivity adjustment factors, with notable increases of 38% for Maldives, 20% for Brunei Darussalam, and 14% for Cambodia. On the other hand, there were decreases of 25% for Sri Lanka and 7% for Pakistan. Conceptual consistency was ensured between 2017 and 2021 in estimating PPPs.

(iv) *Housing comparisons methodology*. The change in the methodology used for housing comparisons was introduced in the 2021 ICP cycle. Prior to the 2021 cycle, housing comparisons in Asia and the Pacific were based on the reference volume approach, which did not involve any rental or housing volume data collected during those cycles.[6] In the 2021 cycle, a new "hybrid" method incorporating quality-adjusted rental and quantity PPPs was introduced. To ensure comparability of 2021 results with the 2017 results, the 2017 ICP cycle results were recomputed using the new housing comparisons approach. A description of the new housing methodology introduced during the 2021 ICP in the region is provided in Chapter 5 on the framework and methodology for ICP in the region.

Figure 4.1 shows the ratio of revised PPPs for GDP for the 2017 benchmark year to the original PPPs published for 22 participating economies at the completion of the 2017 ICP cycle (ADB 2020).

By definition, PPP for Hong Kong, China equals 1.00. Out of the remaining economies, only Cambodia recorded around 1.6% increase, while Indonesia, Mongolia, and the Philippines recorded a small increase in PPPs. The remaining economies recorded a reduction of up to a maximum of about 4.5% for Thailand and about 4.4% for the People's Republic of China. Brunei Darussalam, Malaysia, Nepal, and Viet Nam recorded reductions between 3% to 4% in PPPs. For others, the reductions were below 3%. These revisions in PPPs are likely due to the adoption of the new hybrid methodology for housing and the result of revised productivity adjustment factors. Lower PPPs for all the economies except for Hong Kong, China (reference economy); Cambodia; Indonesia, Mongolia; and the Philippines would mean corresponding higher real GDP for the remaining economies compared to previously published results in the 2017 ICP (ADB 2020).

Consistency between the 2017 and 2021 Results

As mentioned, at the completion of each ICP cycle, it has been a standard practice to assess the latest cycle's results against those of the preceding benchmark. This consistency is evaluated by comparing PPPs from the current cycle with extrapolations of PPPs from the previous benchmark. The PPPs for each period reflect the relative prices for the given year. The new PPPs are a function of the PPPs from the previous period adjusted for the differences in price movements across economies during the period.

---

6   The reference volume approach was used in the past ICP cycles in Asia and the Pacific. This approach was not a standard approach recommended for ICP but was adopted due to the inability to get meaningful comparisons in the region following standard approaches, namely, rental approach and quantity approach. The reference volume method assumes that relative volumes of housing services between economies are equal to the relative volume of household expenditures, excluding housing. As such, the PPPs and real expenditures estimated from this approach are not based on actual housing data.

Figure 4.1: Ratio of Revised to Original Purchasing Power Parities for Gross Domestic Product, 2017

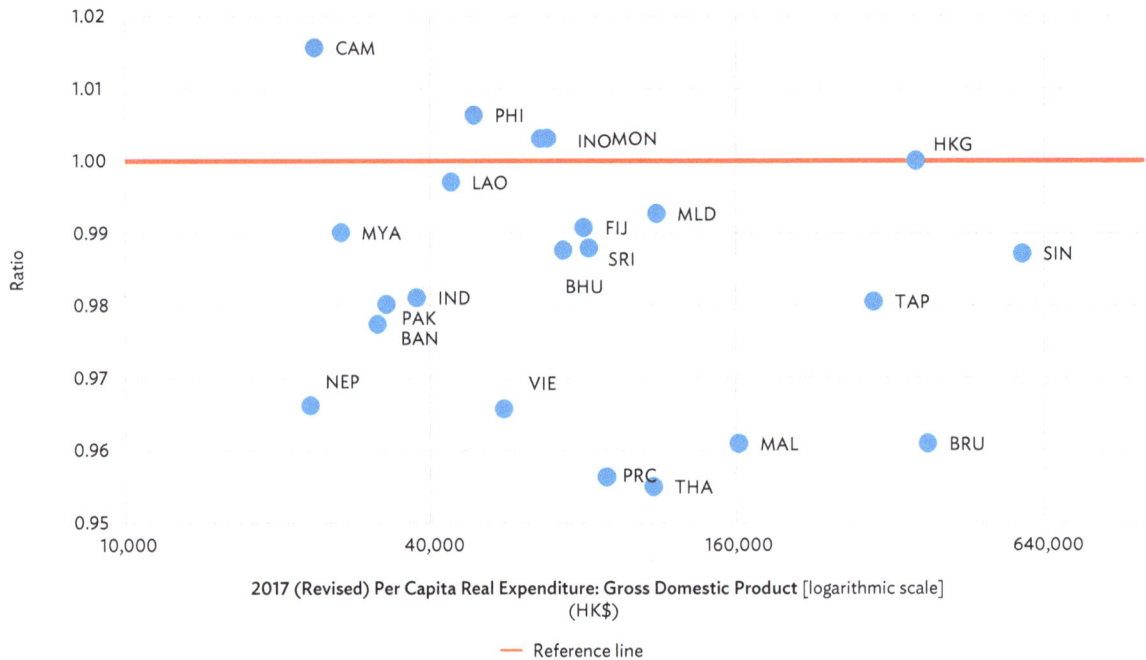

2017 (Revised) Per Capita Real Expenditure: Gross Domestic Product [logarithmic scale]
(HK$)

— Reference line

BAN = Bangladesh; BHU = Bhutan; BRU = Brunei Darussalam; CAM = Cambodia; FIJ = Fiji; HK$ = Hong Kong dollar; HKG = Hong Kong, China; ICP = International Comparison Program; IND = India; INO = Indonesia; LAO = Lao People's Democratic Republic; MAL = Malaysia; MLD = Maldives; MON = Mongolia, MYA = Myanmar; NEP = Nepal; PAK = Pakistan; PHI = Philippines; PRC = People's Republic of China; SIN = Singapore; SRI = Sri Lanka; TAP = Taipei,China; THA = Thailand; VIE = Viet Nam.

Notes:

1. The results in the graph pertain to 22 economies covered in the 2017 ICP cycle.

2. For Myanmar, total gross domestic product in local currency units, population (as of 1 October) were obtained from publicly available sources: (i) Central Statistical Organization. https://www.csostat.gov.mm (accessed 20 February 2024); and exchange rates from (ii) International Monetary Fund. International Financial Statistics. http://data.imf.org/ (accessed 26 January 2024).

Source: Asian Development Bank estimates based on data supplied by the participating economies.

However, there are both theoretical and practical arguments as to why PPPs from a benchmark year differ from its extrapolations from the past ICP cycle (ADB 2020, McCarthy 2013). Following the completion of the 2005 ICP and 2011 ICP rounds, a significant divergence between the 2011 benchmark results and extrapolations from the 2005 benchmark was observed, which is mainly attributed to significant shifts in ICP methodology Inklaar and Rao (2017). Since then, in line with the recommendations of the United Nations Statistical Commission, the ICP methodology has remained unchanged since the 2011 ICP round.

The broad consistency in results from the 2021 ICP cycle with those from the 2017 ICP benchmark is particularly relevant for two reasons. First, a new hybrid methodology for comparing price levels and real expenditures for housing has been introduced in 2021 ICP cycle. While new to Asia and the Pacific, the hybrid methodology for housing innovatively combines the rental and quantity approaches, which are the two standard methods recommended by the ICP Technical Advisory Group for housing comparisons and used in other ICP regions. Second, the COVID-19 pandemic had a severe impact on the schedule and implementation of the 2021 ICP cycle in the region. Mobility restrictions and lockdowns to contain the virus led to disruptions in the price surveys. As a result, price surveys were extended to 2022 in many economies requiring backcasting of prices collected outside the reference period to the corresponding period in 2021. With respect to expenditures, two important effects of the pandemic became evident: firstly, severe impacts on GDP growth rates, which led to most economies experiencing severe economic slowdown and/or negative growths over 2020 and 2021; secondly, changes in the composition and structure of GDP, reflected in changes in expenditure shares from 2019 to 2020 and then on to 2021. To ensure that the prices and GDP expenditures used in the calculation of the PPPs are of high quality, ADB undertook several

measures for data quality assurance. It undertook rigorous validation of prices and GDP data, conducted a series of data validation workshops, and developed standardized method and a tool for backcasting of price data.

Figure 4.2 compares PPPs for GDP from the 2021 ICP cycle with extrapolations from 2017. Extrapolations from 2017 PPPs are made using relative changes in GDP deflators between each economy and Hong Kong, China, the reference economy.

These ratios of actual to extrapolated PPPs for GDP for the participating economies indicate that for 9 of the 21 economies, the extrapolated PPPs closely

Figure 4.2: Ratio of 2021 Purchasing Power Parities for Gross Domestic Product to Extrapolations from 2017 (Revised)

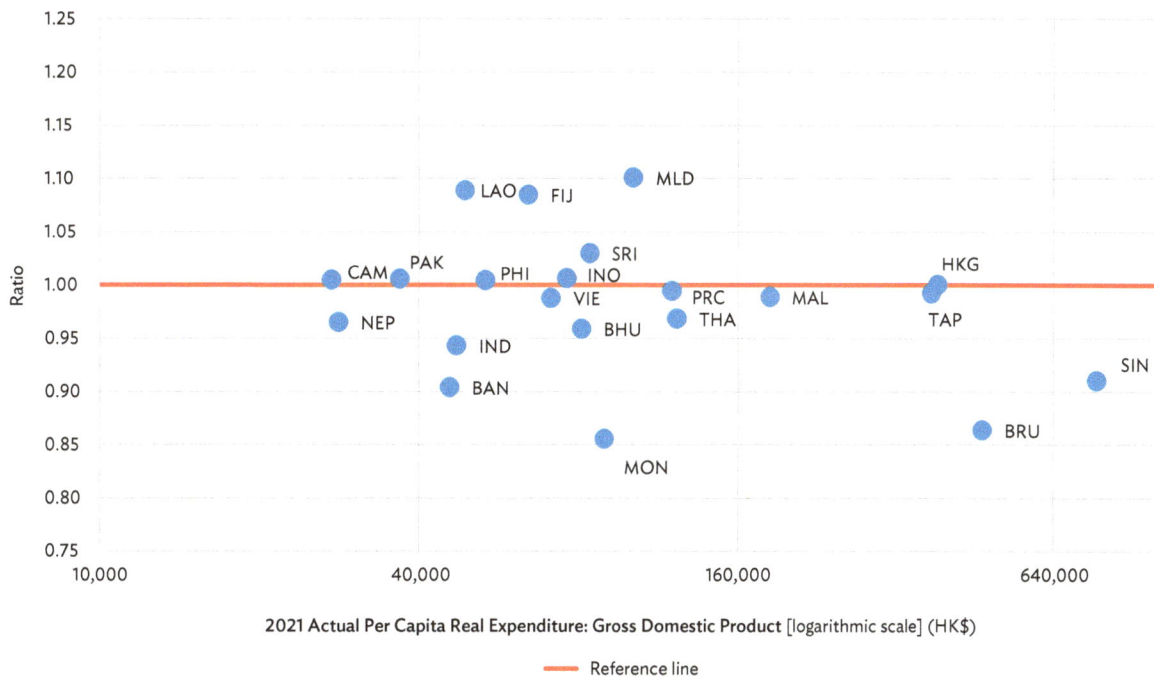

2021 Actual Per Capita Real Expenditure: Gross Domestic Product [logarithmic scale] (HK$)

— Reference line

ADB = Asian Development Bank; BAN = Bangladesh; BHU = Bhutan; BRU = Brunei Darussalam; CAM = Cambodia; FIJ = Fiji; GDP = gross domestic product; HK$ = Hong Kong dollar; HKG = Hong Kong, China; ICP = International Comparison Program; IND = India; INO = Indonesia; LAO = Lao People's Democratic Republic; MAL = Malaysia; MLD = Maldives; MON = Mongolia; NEP = Nepal; PAK = Pakistan; PHI = Philippines; PRC = People's Republic of China; SIN = Singapore; SRI = Sri Lanka; TAP = Taipei,China; THA = Thailand; VIE = Viet Nam.
Notes:
1. The 2017 results are calculated for the same set of 21 economies that participated in the 2021 ICP cycle for comparability.
2. GDP expenditures in local currency units were supplied by the participating economies.
3. Purchasing power parities used to calculate real GDP are based on data supplied by the economies.
4. The GDP deflators for Cambodia, Fiji, and the Lao People's Democratic Republic were sourced from ADB. 2023. *Key Indicators for Asia and the Pacific 2023.* For Thailand, GDP deflator based on data sourced from ADB. 2023. *Key Indicators for Asia and the Pacific 2023.* For Bangladesh, GDP deflator is based on data sourced from the Bangladesh Bureau of Statistics, Ministry of Planning, Statistics, and Informatics Division, Government of Bangladesh.
Source: ADB estimates based on data supplied by the participating economies.

match the actual PPPs. The median value for the ratio is 0.992. Fiji, the Lao People's Democratic Republic, and Maldives have actual PPPs at least 8% higher than extrapolated PPPs, while Bangladesh, Brunei Darussalam, Mongolia, and Singapore have lower PPPs in 2021 compared to extrapolations from 2017 (at least 9%). Overall, the values of the ratio ranged from 0.86 to 1.10, indicating an overall range of about 0.25. The ratios are seen randomly scattered above and below the line depicting a ratio equal to 1 (which implies no difference), and no systematic pattern is observed in the distribution of the ratios. A similar exercise in the 2017 ICP, comparing actual PPPs to extrapolations from 2011, showed a much broader range of 0.80 to 1.24, indicating a difference of 0.44. This suggests that differences in 2021 are much lower compared to those observed in 2017, and overall, no systematic pattern is noticed in these differences, thus exhibiting a greater level of consistency between extrapolated and actual PPPs for the 2021 ICP than those observed for the 2017 ICP.

Size and Relative Shares of Economies, 2017 and 2021

During the pandemic (2020–2021), several important questions arose. Which are the biggest and the smallest economies in the region? Have they changed over the pandemic years? Which are the richest and the poorest in the region in terms of real per capita income? Have the relative disparities increased during the pandemic? Answers to these and many more can be found in the detailed tables for the 2021 and 2017 benchmark comparisons in the Appendix Tables 1 and 2.

The size of the Asia and Pacific economy in PPP terms is shown to be HK\$317.92 trillion in 2021 and HK\$243.28[7] trillion in 2017. As these figures

are in price levels of the respective benchmark years, one should be careful in interpreting this change. A part of this change is due to growth in economies of the region; part of it is due to domestic inflation observed; and finally, part of this change is attributed to the differences in the PPPs of 2021 and 2017 used for conversion purposes. Measurement of contribution of these factors to the overall change in real GDP is discussed in the next section.

Figure 4.3 presents the real GDP levels of 21 economies in the Asia and Pacific region that are common to the 2017 and 2021 ICP cycles, arranged based on their 2021 real GDP levels. The economic growth in all economies was adversely affected by the COVID-19 pandemic resulting to a decline and/or slowdown in economic growth in 2020 and 2021. As a result, the growth in GDP in PPP terms between the two benchmark years 2017 and 2021 was also affected. Despite this, the People's Republic of China, India, and Indonesia maintained their positions as the top three economies in the region for both years. In contrast, Fiji and Maldives, both tourism-dependent economies, were the smallest economies in 2021, whereas Bhutan and Maldives were the smallest in 2017. Fiji slipped to become the smallest economy after the pandemic, with substantial declines in economic activity in 2020 and 2021, resulting from severe loss of tourism income to GDP. While Maldives also saw a severe decline in GDP in 2020, it recovered strongly in 2021. A closer look at the levels of real GDP of the three smallest economies reveals that the differences are small, suggesting that even small differences in the levels can lead to shifts in ranks. Some minor shifts in ranks were also observed in the upper-middle-income economies. While shifts in ranks at the GDP level are relatively small, it is quite possible that there could be bigger differences and major shifts in ranks when other aggregates are considered.

7   The results for 2017 are calculated for the same set of 21 economies that participated in the 2021 ICP cycle for comparability.

Figure 4.3: Real Gross Domestic Product, 2017 and 2021 (HK$ billion)

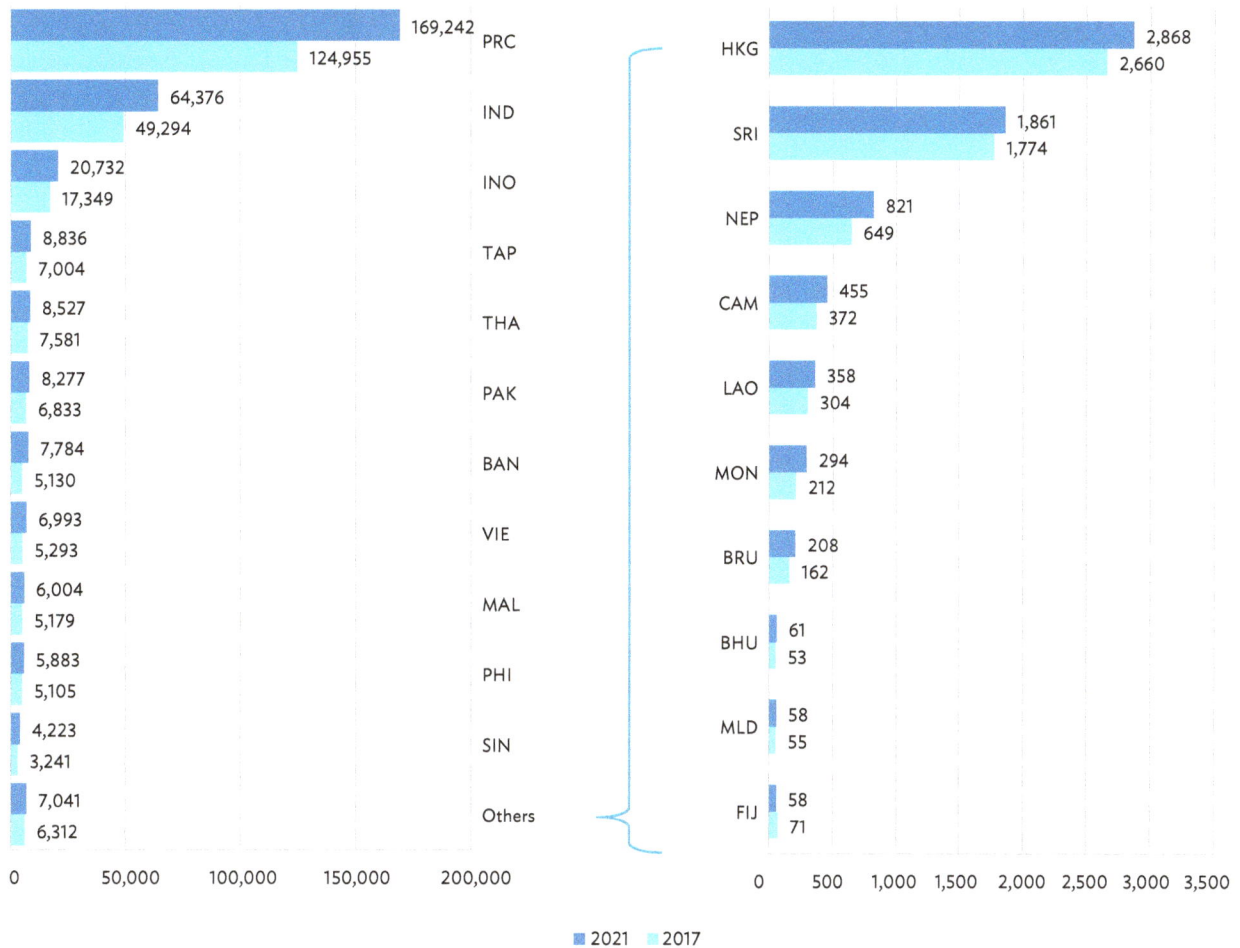

BAN = Bangladesh; BHU = Bhutan; BRU = Brunei Darussalam; CAM = Cambodia; FIJ = Fiji; HKG = Hong Kong, China; HK$ = Hong Kong dollar; IND = India; INO = Indonesia; LAO = Lao People's Democratic Republic; MAL = Malaysia; MLD = Maldives; MON = Mongolia; NEP = Nepal; PAK = Pakistan; PHI = Philippines; PRC = People's Republic of China; SIN = Singapore; SRI = Sri Lanka; TAP = Taipei,China; THA = Thailand; VIE = Viet Nam.
Note: The 2017 results are calculated for the same set of 21 economies that participated in the 2021 ICP cycle for comparability.
Source: Asian Development Bank estimates based on data supplied by the participating economies.

Interpreting and Decomposing Changes in the Size (Real) of Economies in Asia and the Pacific

From Table 4.1, it can be seen that the regional economy in PPP terms is HK$317.92 trillion in 2021 compared to HK$243.28 trillion[8] in 2017. Converted using exchange rate, GDP of the region changed from HK$151.34 trillion (footnote 8) in 2017 to HK$204.63 trillion in 2021. Therefore, both in PPP and exchange rate terms, the region's GDP has increased. However, as GDP in these years are valued at the prices of respective years, it is not possible to compare them directly, just as the economy-level GDP at current prices in 2021 cannot be compared with GDP in 2017 at current prices.

---

8   The results for 2017 are calculated for the same set of 21 economies that participated in the 2021 ICP cycle for comparability.

Table 4.1 provides a decomposition of change in GDP into growth and price change components for all the economies as well as the region. As PPPs used in conversion to real terms are themselves affected by prices, price change effect consists of the inflation observed in different economies and the differential effects of price changes on PPPs used in conversion.

Columns (6) and (7) of Table 4.1 show the real GDPs of economies for the years 2017 and 2021 respectively, converted into Hong Kong dollars using respective-year PPPs. For example, real GDP of Viet Nam was HK$5,293 billion in 2017 and HK$6,993 billion in 2021, showing a growth of 32.1%. As the PPPs used in conversion are based on relative prices prevailing in these years, these are not directly comparable.

With Viet Nam as illustration, what can be said about the observed 32.1% increase in real GDP over these two ICP cycles? Based on a methodology developed by Balk, Rambaldi, and Rao (2020) employed in the analysis of results for the 2017 ICP cycle (see Chapter 4 in ADB 2020), this change can be decomposed and contributions of three factors can be identified:

(i)   *GDP growth in the economy.* This is the growth in GDP and is measured as the ratio of GDP in local currency units expressed in constant prices in the two periods. During the 2017–2021 period, GDP at constant prices increased by 21.7% percent in Viet Nam (Column 9). Applied to real GDP of Viet Nam in 2017, this growth gives an estimate of real GDP of Viet Nam expressed in 2017 PPPs, which is HK$6,443 billion. Fiji is the only economy that posted a negative growth of 1.1% over the same period.

(ii) *Domestic inflation.* In Viet Nam, domestic inflation is observed at 10.7% (Column 8). Price increases between 2017 and 2021 will increase GDP in local currency units in 2021, which also increases real GDP in 2021 by 10.7%. This is the domestic inflation effect.

(iii) *PPP change effect.* Since GDP of Viet Nam in local currency units in 2017 and 2021 is converted to real GDP using PPPs for the respective year, change in real GDP from 2017 to 2021 is partly driven by changes in PPPs used in conversion. If ICP price increases in Viet Nam (relative to Hong Kong, China) are higher between 2017 and 2021, then PPP for Viet Nam currency will increase in 2021. Thus, the ratio of PPP in 2017 to PPP in 2021 is a measure of the PPP change effect (Column 10). In the case of Viet Nam, this ratio is 0.981 as the 2017 PPP for GDP is lower than the PPP for GDP in 2021.

The above three factors together explain the 32.1% increase in real GDP of Viet Nam from HK$5,293 billion in 2017 to HK$6,993 billion in 2021.

From Table 4.1, since inflation and PPP effects are driven by price changes, their product represents a measure of overall effect of price change shown in column (12). For Viet Nam, the overall price effect between 2017 and 2021 is 1.085. With Hong Kong, China as the reference economy, the PPPs for 14 economies increased in 2021 in comparison with the 2017 benchmark as seen from the ratios below 1.00 in column (10). Column (10) indicates that Pakistan's real GDP is driven downward by 26% due to increase in PPP from 2017 to 2021, followed by Sri Lanka with 14% increase in the PPP whereas real GDP of Brunei Darussalam and Thailand increased by about 14% and 8%, respectively, driven by lower PPPs in 2021.

Despite the profound impact of COVID-19, whose effects were most severe during 2020 and continued in many economies of the region in 2021, the economies of the region have shown a great resilience and growth. Many economies had bounced back by 2021, to a certain extent compensating for the recession in 2020 caused by the pandemic.

Table 4.1: Economy-Level Decomposition of Change in Real Gross Domestic Product, 2017–2021

Economy	GDP at Current Prices (LCU billion)		PPPs (HK$ = 1.00)		Real GDP in PPP at Current Prices (HK$ billion)		Domestic Inflation Effect 2021 / 2017	Domestic Growth Effect 2021 / 2017 [(3)/(2)]/(8)	PPP Change Effect 2017 / 2021 (4)/(5)	PPP Change 2021 / 2017 (5)/(4)	Price Effect 2021 / 2017 (8)*(10) = (8)/(11)	Growth in Real GDP in PPP at Current Prices (HK$) 2021 / 2017 (7)/(6) = (8)*(9)*(10)
	2017	2021	2017	2021	2017 (2)/(4)	2021 (3)/(5)						
(1)	(2)	(3)	(4)	(5)	(6)	(7)	(8)	(9)	(10)	(11)	(12)	(13)
Bangladesh	24,818	37,510	4.84	4.82	5,130	7,784	1.181	1.279	1.004	0.996	1.186	1.517
Bhutan	169	205	3.16	3.34	53	61	1.182	1.026	0.946	1.057	1.118	1.147
Brunei Darussalam	17	19	0.10	0.09	162	208	1.087	1.034	1.142	0.875	1.241	1.284
Cambodia	89,831	110,506	241.72	243.01	372	455	1.073	1.147	0.995	1.005	1.067	1.224
China, People's Republic of	83,204	114,924	0.67	0.68	124,955	169,242	1.100	1.256	0.981	1.020	1.078	1.354
Fiji	11	9	0.15	0.15	71	58	0.989	0.815	0.999	1.001	0.988	0.805
Hong Kong, China	2,660	2,868	1.00	1.00	2,660	2,868	1.072	1.006	1.000	1.000	1.072	1.078
India	166,281	227,243	3.37	3.53	49,294	64,376	1.190	1.149	0.956	1.046	1.137	1.306
Indonesia	13,589,826	16,976,751	783.31	818.87	17,349	20,732	1.114	1.122	0.957	1.045	1.065	1.195
Lao People's Democratic Republic	140,698	184,982	463.12	516.29	304	358	1.098	1.198	0.897	1.115	0.985	1.179
Malaysia	1,372	1,549	0.26	0.26	5,179	6,004	1.056	1.069	1.027	0.973	1.084	1.159
Maldives	74	81	1.35	1.40	55	58	1.012	1.077	0.962	1.039	0.974	1.049
Mongolia	28,011	43,555	131.84	148.19	212	294	1.409	1.104	0.890	1.124	1.253	1.383
Nepal	3,253	4,543	5.01	5.53	649	821	1.225	1.140	0.907	1.103	1.111	1.266
Pakistan	37,371	61,230	5.47	7.40	6,833	8,277	1.442	1.136	0.739	1.353	1.066	1.211
Philippines	16,557	19,411	3.24	3.30	5,105	5,883	1.086	1.079	0.983	1.017	1.068	1.152
Singapore	474	583	0.15	0.14	3,241	4,223	1.112	1.106	1.059	0.944	1.178	1.303
Sri Lanka	14,387	17,600	8.11	9.46	1,774	1,861	1.214	1.008	0.857	1.166	1.041	1.049
Taipei,China	17,983	21,663	2.57	2.45	7,004	8,836	1.032	1.168	1.047	0.955	1.080	1.262
Thailand	15,489	16,189	2.04	1.90	7,581	8,527	1.029	1.016	1.076	0.929	1.107	1.125
Viet Nam	6,293,905	8,479,667	1,189.01	1,212.53	5,293	6,993	1.107	1.217	0.981	1.020	1.085	1.321
Asia and the Pacific	n.a.	n.a.	n.a.	n.a.	243,276	317,918	1.124	1.196	0.972	1.028	1.093	1.307

ADB = Asian Development Bank, GDP = gross domestic product, HK$ = Hong Kong dollar, ICP = International Comparison Program, LCU = local currency unit, n.a. = not applicable, PPP = purchasing power parity.

Notes:

1. The 2017 revised results are calculated for the same set of 21 economies that participated in the 2021 ICP cycle for comparability.

2. Ratios may not be precisely replicated using the presented figures in this table due to rounding.

3. GDP expenditures in LCUs were supplied by the participating economies.

4. The PPPs used to calculate real GDP and data in columns 6 to 13 are ADB estimates based on data supplied by the economies.

5. The GDP deflators for Cambodia, Fiji, and the Lao People's Democratic Republic were sourced from ADB. 2023. *Key Indicators for Asia and the Pacific 2023*. For Thailand, GDP deflator based on data sourced from ADB. 2023. *Key Indicators for Asia and the Pacific 2023*. For Bangladesh, GDP deflator is based on data sourced from the Bangladesh Bureau of Statistics, Ministry of Planning, Statistics, and Informatics Division, Government of Bangladesh.

Source: ADB estimates based on data supplied by the participating economies.

In conclusion, comparing the 2017 and 2021 ICP cycles as a snapshot of the region recovering from COVID-19 reveals overall consistency in the results, indicating no systematic bias between extrapolations from 2017 and actual comparisons in 2021. This chapter has also demonstrated how data from these two ICP cycles can be utilized to evaluate the growth performance of the region and its participating economies. Because the ICP focuses on the expenditure side of the national accounts, if reliable deflators and growth rates in constant prices between 2017 and 2021 at the more detailed levels of expenditures are available, it would be possible to decompose the changes in real expenditures between 2017 and 2021 into the components of growth rate, inflation, and PPP effect to assess how growth and changes in the prices impact the changes in real expenditures between the two ICP benchmarks.

CHAPTER 5
Governance and Methodology

This chapter is designed to provide the user with an overview of the architecture of the International Comparison Program (ICP) and an introduction to the approach and methodology used in the compilation of purchasing power parities (PPPs) and real expenditures presented in Chapters 3 and 4. Further details with illustrative examples of the methodology described in this chapter can be found in Chapter 6 of the 2017 ICP in Asia and the Pacific Final Report produced by the Asian Development Bank (ADB 2020).

Governance and Structure

The ICP is a global statistical effort with the overarching aim of compiling PPPs and internationally comparable national accounts aggregates, including gross domestic product (GDP) and its components. The governance structure for the ICP is designed to engage all relevant stakeholders at the national, regional, and global levels and provides an efficient and effective mechanism to produce reliable and timely estimates of PPPs and real expenditures for all the participating economies. In its initial phases, the ICP was a global program; however, recognizing the challenges involved in implementing such a complex global program, it moved to a regional approach in 2005 with comparisons first organized by regions and then regional comparisons are linked together to obtain global comparisons.[9]

Figure 5.1 shows the current governance structure for the ICP that was put in place by the United Nations Statistical Commission during its 47th session in 2016 (ECOSOC 2016).

The ICP is conducted under the auspices of the United Nations Statistical Commission and coordinated globally by the World Bank, which is the global implementing agency under this structure. The ICP Governing Board is the strategic body that sets policies and timelines that govern the compilation of PPPs and release of results. The Technical Advisory Group (TAG) establishes and recommends methodology for ICP on an ongoing basis. The regional implementing agencies (RIAs) work within regions, collaborating directly with implementing agencies from economies participating in the regional comparisons. These regional agencies are responsible for the compilation and publication of results for their regions and provide necessary data to the global implementing agency, which is responsible for linking regional results to compile PPPs at the global level. The implementing agencies in the participating economies play a critical role in the ICP. They are responsible for conducting price surveys, collecting, validating, and submitting necessary data and metadata to the RIA for compiling PPPs and real expenditures.

ADB assumed responsibility as the RIA for the 2005 ICP and continued in this role for the 2011, 2017, and the current 2021 cycles of the ICP in the region.

Figure 5.2 demonstrates a simplified workflow of ICP data collection by implementing agencies in participating economies in each ICP region and computation of regional and global results by the RIAs and the World Bank, respectively, within the current ICP structure. Under the regional approach adopted for ICP since 2005, a two-stage approach has been implemented for global comparisons. In the first stage,

---

Figure 5.1: International Comparison Program—Governance Structure

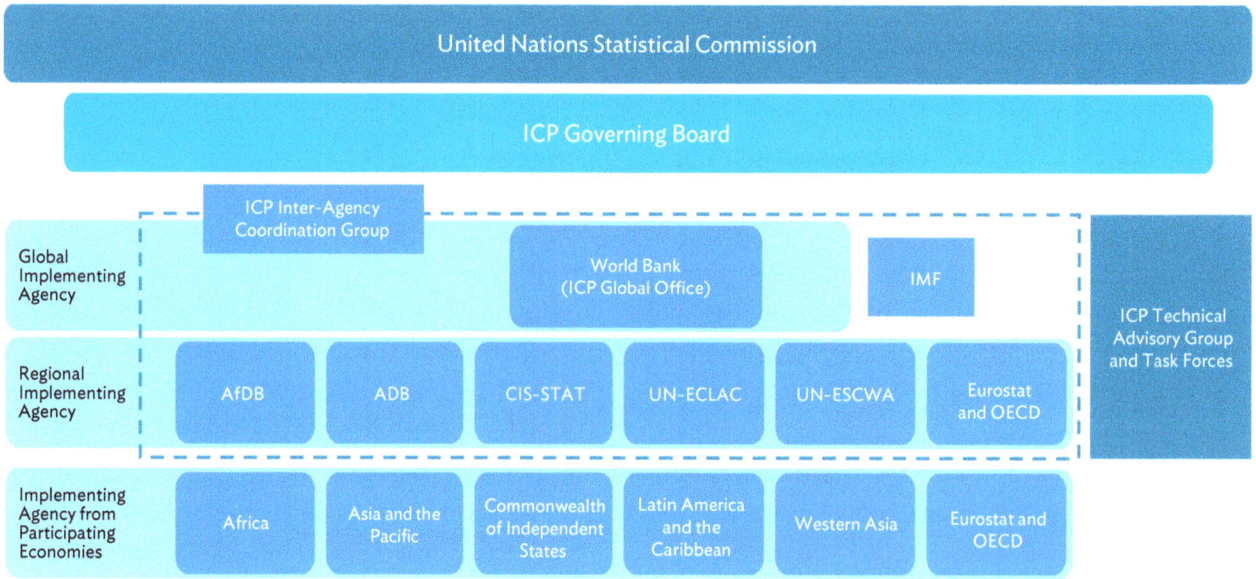

ADB = Asian Development Bank, AfDB = African Development Bank, CIS-STAT = Interstate Statistical Committee of the Commonwealth of Independent States, Eurostat = Statistical Office of the European Union, ICP = International Comparison Program, IMF = International Monetary Fund, OECD = Organisation for Economic Co-operation and Development, UN-ECLAC = United Nations Economic Commission for Latin America and the Caribbean, UN-ESCWA = United Nations Economic and Social Commission for Western Asia.
Source: World Bank. 2020. *Purchasing Power Parities and the Size of the World Economies: Results from the 2017 International Comparison Program*. https://openknowledge.worldbank.org/handle/10986/33623.

Figure 5.2: Workflow for the International Comparison Program

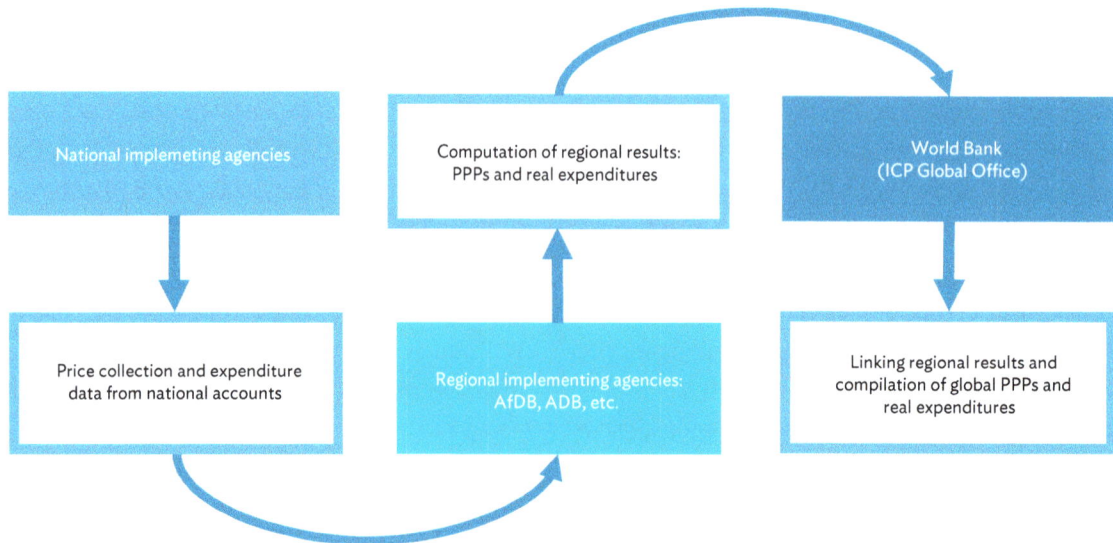

ADB = Asian Development Bank, AfDB = African Development Bank, ICP = International Comparison Program, PPPs = purchasing power parities.
Source: Asian Development Bank (Economic Research and Development Impact Department).

PPPs are computed, and real income comparisons are made at the regional level by applying standard methods using prices collected for a basket of goods and services for regional comparison purposes. The regions comprise relatively homogeneous groups of economies accounting for differences in the availability of types of goods and services comprising final expenditures in the GDP of the economies. In the second stage, a set of global comparisons is compiled by the World Bank with the application of specially designed linking procedures using regional comparisons and prices collected by all participating economies for a common basket of goods and services across the world.

In the remaining sections of this chapter, the methodology used in the compilation of PPPs in the Asia and Pacific region is presented in a nutshell.

Methodology for the International Comparison Program in Asia and the Pacific

The main objective of the ICP is to compile national accounts aggregates that are comparable across participating economies. Macroeconomic measures such as GDP, household consumption, and gross fixed capital formation are all expressed in local currency units. The ICP methodology implements the notion of PPP exchange rates, which serve both as currency conversion factors and adjustment for price level differences resulting in real expenditures that are comparable across economies. It may be noted that the methodology for regional comparisons in the 2017 and 2021 ICP cycles remained the same except for the new approach adopted for housing comparisons that combines the recommended ICP approaches—rental and quantity approaches, instead of the previously used reference volume approach. This new approach is presented subsequently in this chapter.

Index Number Decomposition of Gross Domestic Product and Other Aggregates

Consider the GDP of two economies A and B, denoted by GDP_A and GDP_B expressed in local currency units. The aim of the ICP is to decompose this GDP into components of volume and price level, denoted by Q_A and P_A, respectively, such that $GDP_A = Q_A \cdot P_A$. The relative volumes of GDP in these economies is given in equation (1):

$$\frac{Q_A}{Q_B} = \frac{\frac{GDP_A}{P_A}}{\frac{GDP_B}{P_B}} = \frac{GDP_A}{GDP_B} \cdot \frac{P_B}{P_A} \qquad (1)$$

Since these comparisons would be the same if the price levels are multiplied by a constant, it is necessary to express them relative to the price level of a reference economy, say Hong Kong, China.

Noting that purchasing power is the reciprocal of price level, quantity comparisons with Hong Kong, China as reference economy can be derived as shown in equation (2):

$$\frac{Q_{HKG,A}}{Q_{HKG,B}} = \frac{\frac{GDP_A}{P_{HKG,A}}}{\frac{GDP_B}{P_{HKG,B}}} = \frac{GDP_A \cdot PPP^*_{HKG,A}}{GDP_B \cdot PPP^*_{HKG,B}} \quad \text{where}$$

$$PPP^*_{HKG,A} = \frac{1}{P_{HKG,A}} \quad \text{and} \quad PPP^*_{HKG,B} = \frac{1}{P_{HKG,B}} \qquad (2)$$

Here, $PPP^*_{HKG,A}$ shows the number of Hong Kong dollars that have the same purchasing power as one unit of currency of economy—this is the reciprocal of *PPP* defined in Chapter 2. This equation is fundamental to international comparisons. To make volume comparisons across economies, it is sufficient if the aggregate, GDP in this case, is converted using PPP for the currency of the economy. These volume measures are referred to as *real expenditures* in ICP.

National Accounts Framework for the International Comparison Program and Expenditure Data

As the objective of ICP is to provide comparable macroeconomic aggregates from the national accounts, the ICP relies on the most detailed level data expenditure data available from the national accounts. For ICP, the GDP expenditures are disaggregated into 155 basic headings. The basic heading is the lowest level aggregate in the GDP breakdown for which expenditure data are available.

Each basic heading comprises homogeneous goods or services for which prices are collected by the participating economies. For example, the Asia and Pacific region includes 20 different items of rice in the *rice basic heading*. Higher-level aggregates are progressively formed using the pyramid approach in Figure 5.3.

Table 5.1 shows details of the composition of various classes, groups, categories, and main aggregates.

While ICP potentially provides PPPs and real expenditures for all the basic headings, classes, groups, categories, including the main aggregates, the six main categories under GDP are of utmost importance for analysts, researchers, users, and policy makers.

Survey Framework and Price Data

Reliable and high-quality data on prices of goods and services that comprise GDP is necessary for producing meaningful PPP estimates. The main steps involved in the ICP are determining list of items (goods and services) to be priced, establishing survey framework, price collection, validation and editing data, and finalizing the national average prices for items priced in each economy for use in the PPP computations.

There are two important considerations in the preparation of lists of items for price collection:

(i) *Consistency with national accounts.* As PPPs are ultimately used for converting expenditure aggregates, it is essential that item prices are consistent with pricing concepts used in the compilation of national accounts final expenditure aggregates by the national statistical agencies.

(ii) *Comparability versus representativity.* Products priced across economies must be as closely aligned as possible with respect to product quality. Comparability is achieved through the use of structured product descriptions

Figure 5.3: Pyramid Structure for Aggregates

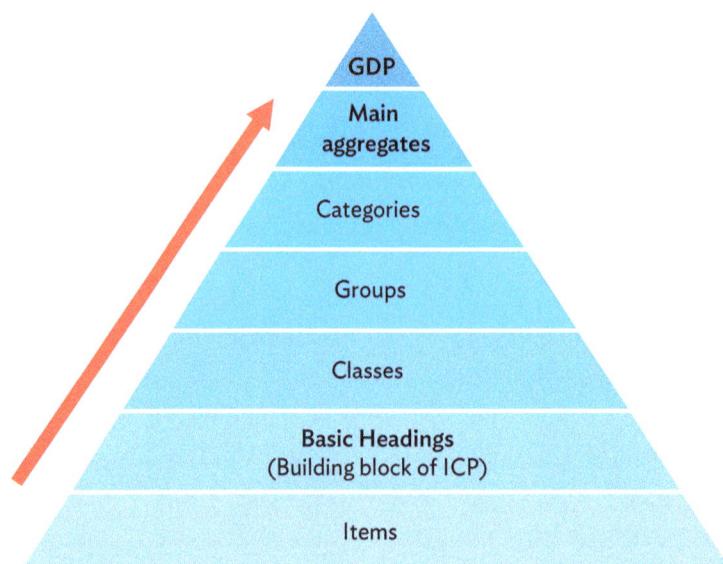

GDP = gross domestic product, ICP = International Comparison Program.
Source: D. S. Prasada Rao. 2013. The Framework of the International Comparison Program. In *Measuring the Real Size of the World Economy*. World Bank.

Table 5.1: Composition of Main Aggregates of Gross Domestic Product

Main Aggregates and Categories		Category	Group	Class	Basic Heading
Gross Domestic Product		28	63	126	155
1100000	Individual Consumption Expenditure by Households	13	44	91	110
1101000	Food and nonalcoholic beverages		2	11	29
1102000	Alcoholic beverages, tobacco and narcotics		3	5	5
1103000	Clothing and footwear		2	5	5
1104000	Housing, water, electricity, gas and other fuels		5	8	8
1105000	Furnishings, household equipment and routine household maintenance		6	12	13
1106000	Health		3	7	7
1107000	Transport		3	13	13
1108000	Communication		3	3	3
1109000	Recreation and culture		6	13	13
1110000	Education		1	1	1
1111000	Restaurants and hotels		2	2	2
1112000	Miscellaneous goods and services		7	10	10
1113000	Net purchases abroad		1	1	1
1200000	Individual Consumption Expenditure by NPISH	5	5	5	5
1201000	Housing		1	1	1
1202000	Health		1	1	1
1203000	Recreation and culture		1	1	1
1204000	Education		1	1	1
1205000	Social protection and other services		1	1	1
1300000	Individual Consumption Expenditure by Government	5	7	16	21
1301000	Housing		1	1	1
1302000	Health		2	7	12
1303000	Recreation and culture		1	1	1
1304000	Education		2	6	6
1305000	Social protection		1	1	1
1400000	Collective Consumption Expenditure by Government	1	1	5	5
1500000	Gross Capital Formation	3	5	8	12
1501000	Gross fixed capital formation		3	6	10
1502000	Changes in inventories		1	1	1
1503000	Acquisitions less disposals of valuables		1	1	1
1600000	Balance of Exports and Imports	1	1	1	2

NPISH = nonprofit institutions serving households.
Source: Asian Development Bank based on World Bank. 2016. *International Comparison Program: Classification of Final Expenditure on GDP.* https://thedocs.worldbank.org/en/doc/708531575560035925-0050022019/original/ICPClassificationdescription20191205.pdf.

describing the quality and characteristics of each product in the item list. However, items priced by each economy from the regional product list must also be representative of the final expenditures in the economies. Otherwise, there would be a mismatch with national accounts. A balance between these competing considerations of comparability versus representativity needs to be achieved.

For a diverse region like Asia and the Pacific, compiling a list of representative products that will take into account the needs of all economies is very challenging. The RIA adopts an inclusive approach through consultations with the economies for compiling the regional product list, which includes items representative of economies. The economies are encouraged to price as many available items, representative of the economy's expenditures, as possible in their price survey.

Regional and Global Product Lists

The product list for pricing by the participating economies is derived by combining product lists prepared at the regional level and a separate list of items identified by the ICP global office at the World Bank. The global list is also known as the global core list of products. Prices of global core list products are used in linking results from different regions.

(i)   *Household consumption (excluding health and education).* This is the biggest component of GDP accounting for approximately 39% of the region's GDP. Consequently, 102 out the 155 basic headings are included in household consumption (excluding health and education). The regional list consists of 691 goods and the global list comprises 414 items, of which 282 are items that overlap with the regional product list.

(ii) *Health and education.* The product list for health includes 159 goods and services and the global core list has 142 items. For education, the regional product list consists of seven items that coincide with the global core list. As there is a diverse mix of government provision and the degree to which these services are subsidized, the basic principle is that prices used for comparisons of health and education should reflect market prices.

(iii) *Housing.* Housing comparisons are undertaken using two recommended alternative approaches, the rental and quantity approaches. For the rental approach, the 2021 ICP in the region included 20 types of dwellings of which 10 were houses (9 from global list and 1 specific to the Asia and Pacific region); and 10 were apartments (9 global and 1 regional). For the quantity approach, the main indicators used are number of dwellings per 100 people and number of rooms per 100 people in the regional comparisons. In addition, quality indicators of facilities of inside water, sanitation, and electricity were collected. The innovative approach for housing comparisons introduced in the 2021 ICP in the region combines the recommended rental and quantity approaches. The housing approach is separately discussed subsequently in this chapter.

(iv) *Government compensation.* A total of 35 occupations, of which 34 are from the global core list, are used for collection of data on compensation paid to the government employees for comparison of government services. After dropping the "senior government official"

occupation, 9 occupations from health, 5 occupations from education, and 20 from collective government services are included. At the time of implementation of the 2005 ICP in the region, it was realized that wages and salaries of government employees were too low in many low-income economies resulting in low PPPs and implausibly very high per capita real expenditures in these economies. This was attributed to the differences in the productivity of government employees in the participating economies, which range from low-income to high-income economies. Consequently, productivity adjustment for wages and salaries was introduced in the 2005 regional comparisons. The 2005 method was further refined during the 2011 and 2017 rounds. Details of these refinements and the exact method used can be found in the report of the 2017 ICP in Asia and the Pacific (ADB 2020). The same methodology is used in the 2021 ICP, but the productivity adjustment factors used for 2017 and 2021 are now based on the latest data available. As a result, productivity adjustment factors used for compiling revised 2017 estimates (described in Chapter 4) are based on these new productivity adjustment factors.

(v)   *Machinery and equipment.* The list for machinery and equipment is basically the global list with 203 items of which 88 are specified and 115 are unspecified items. Based on the recommendation of an Experts Group constituted by the ADB, some of the unspecified items were split using variation in prices submitted for these items.

(vi) *Construction.* Construction consists of residential and nonresidential buildings and civil engineering works. Implementing the input approach to construction, the item list included 33 items for materials, 10 items for equipment rental, and 8 items for labor inputs. There are 50 items from the global core list and 1 regional item. In addition, data on indicators of relevance for material inputs and resource mixes for residential, nonresidential, and civil engineering were collected.

Survey Framework

The ICP global office at the World Bank established the basic survey framework and the RIA in Asia and the Pacific applied the global framework after undertaking modifications suitable for the region. The essential elements are as follows:

(i) *Price data*. Prices used in the ICP are national annual average prices. Thus, it is necessary to take into account the seasonal nature of some of the products involved.

(ii) *National coverage*. As national average prices are used in the ICP, price surveys are nationally representative by covering both rural and urban markets in the participating economies especially for the household consumption items. However, for certain aggregates, the surveys necessarily focused on urban areas or on major cities. For example, in the case of dwellings, survey coverage is largely focused on areas with prevalent rental markets; for machinery and equipment, surveys were limited to capital or major cities.

(iii) *Calendar year*. The ICP requires that prices used in PPP compilation are those observed during the calendar year 2021, thus the prices should be representative of the market transactions during the year.

For the survey design, the participating economies are encouraged to adopt a self-weighting sampling design for the household consumption survey in determining the number of quotations to be collected from urban and rural areas, towns and cities, and outlets from where prices are collected.

Data Editing and Validation

Accurate and reliable price data are critical to providing meaningful estimates of PPPs and real expenditures. The ICP global office at the World Bank and the RIA consider data validation as an important step in the process. ADB, as the RIA, places a very high priority on data quality assurance measures and data validation discussions. It developed tools to be used by economies for intraeconomy data validation and additional tools for intereconomy data validation undertaken by ADB to ensure high quality of input price and GDP data.

(i) *Economy-level validation*. The implementing agencies are responsible for checking price quotations for outliers and ensuring consistency in following the structured product descriptions of each product. The national agencies used the ICP Asia and the Pacific Software Suite software supplied by ADB, which has extensive functionalities including generation of survey questionnaires, data entry, basic data validations, and diagnostics to identify outlier prices and make corrections.

(ii) *Regional-level validation*. The RIA uses a number of diagnostic tools to identify outlier prices:

(a) Price changes in the consumer price index versus price changes in the ICP: These measures are undertaken for intra-economy price validations and to identify potential outlier quotations or unusual prices. For every economy, there are prices for a set of items that are common to the product lists in 2017 and 2021. Using these prices, it is possible to compute a measure of price change over the period 2017–2021, labeled ICP inflation. Validation tests are conducted by comparing the ICP inflation for items in groups of products (food, clothing, etc.) with the consumer price index inflation data from the participating economies. While not expected to be the same, it does help in validating ICP prices when large variations between the two are observed. In addition, the RIA also flags prices exhibiting low minimum–maximum price ratios and/ or very high coefficient of variation.

(b) Dikhanov tables: Dikhanov tables use residuals from the country–product– dummy (CPD) regressions to identify outlier average prices of items through intereconomy validations at the regional level. The CPD regressions are used at the basic heading level and for higher-level aggregates. The intereconomy validation exercises are undertaken in an inclusive manner in regional workshops with the participation of price statisticians from participating economies and a transparent validation process. These regional validation workshops are critical to ensure that the items priced across economies are of comparable quality.

(iii) *Validation of expenditure share data.*
Expenditures and expenditure shares are important inputs into the computation of PPPs and real expenditures. The expenditure share data from the participating economies are scrutinized by assessing differences in expenditure patterns of the 2021 benchmark with patterns in the 2017 ICP cycle. Given the effect of the coronavirus disease (COVID-19) on expenditure patterns, the RIA undertook rigorous examination of the changes in the structure especially for the expenditure aggregates expected to have been severely impacted by the pandemic. The Expert Group conducted an in-depth examination of the expenditure weights and provided recommendations which further helped in validating the levels of expenditures for basic heading and higher levels of expenditure aggregates.

New Approach for Housing Comparisons in Asia and the Pacific

Comparisons of prices and real expenditures for housing have always been problematic. Housing comparisons are classified under *comparison-resistant services.* Comparison of housing across economies is difficult because of varying mixtures of owner-occupied versus rented dwellings. Heston (2013) provides an overview of the problems involved and describes alternative methods for housing comparisons. The recommended approaches for housing comparisons are the *rental* and *quantity or volume approaches.* Choice of approach is largely dictated by whether a sizeable rental market exists in these economies.

Since the 2005 cycle, Asia and the Pacific has been diligently collecting data for both rental and quantity or volume approach and compiling PPPs and real expenditures under both approaches. However, results from the two approaches were found to be implausible (see Chapter 6 in ADB 2020 for detailed discussion). Implausibility of the comparisons is assessed by considering the *"ratio of per capita real expenditure in housing to per capita real household expenditure without housing."* This ratio is generally observed to be in the range of 5%–40% for most of the economies in other regions of the world.

In all cycles—2005, 2011, 2017, and 2021—implementation of both the rental and volume approaches resulted in ratios far above the range of 5%–40% for most economies. In some cases, the ratios were close to or exceeded 100%, which is highly implausible.

As a pragmatic solution, during the 2005, 2011, and 2017 cycles, the **reference volume approach** was used, which assumes that the "ratio of per capita real expenditure on housing to per capita real household expenditure without housing" is the same across all the economies. This is a neutral approach that served the purpose of compiling results for these rounds of the ICP in the absence of reliable PPPs for housing comparisons from the standard approaches.

The reference volume approach, while being a pragmatic solution, has two major deficiencies. First, it ignores all the rental and volume indicator data collected for the purpose of housing comparisons. Second, which is more significant, this approach stipulates that in all these economies, the ratio of per capita real expenditure on housing to per capita real household expenditure without housing is the same for all economies in the comparison. Using the reference volume approach, these ratios are observed to be 16.7 in ICP 2017 and 18.8 in ICP 2021 for all participating economies. These ratios correspond with the ratio observed for the reference economy, which is clearly not satisfactory as the approach depends on the choice of the reference economy.

During the implementation of the 2017 cycle in the region, intensive research was conducted to collect high-quality data and to devise a suitable method for housing comparisons. After considerable experimentation, it was realized that any methodology for housing comparisons must account for the enormous differences in quality of dwellings across economies of the region. These differences are indicative of the diversity of the region: it has the biggest economy (People's Republic of China) and

the very small economies (Brunei Darussalam); it has high-income (Singapore) to low-income (Nepal) economies; high-density (Singapore: 7,585 persons per square kilometer) and low-density (Mongolia: 2 persons per square kilometer)[10] areas; economies with rented accommodations ranging from below 5% in 4 economies to close to 50% in Hong Kong, China; and economies with below 30% urbanization, to fully urbanized economies like Hong Kong, China and Singapore. The estimated PPPs and real expenditures also depend upon the methods and data sources used in the imputation of housing expenditures for owner occupied dwellings. In the region, there are wide variations in the methods applied with rental equivalence method used in nearly half of the economies and either user cost or a combination of both methods in the remaining economies.

Thus, a "hybrid approach" was devised, which is a combination of the recommended rental and quantity approaches for housing comparisons as described in Figure 5.4.

Figure 5.4: The New Hybrid Approach for Comparisons of Prices and Real Expenditures for Housing

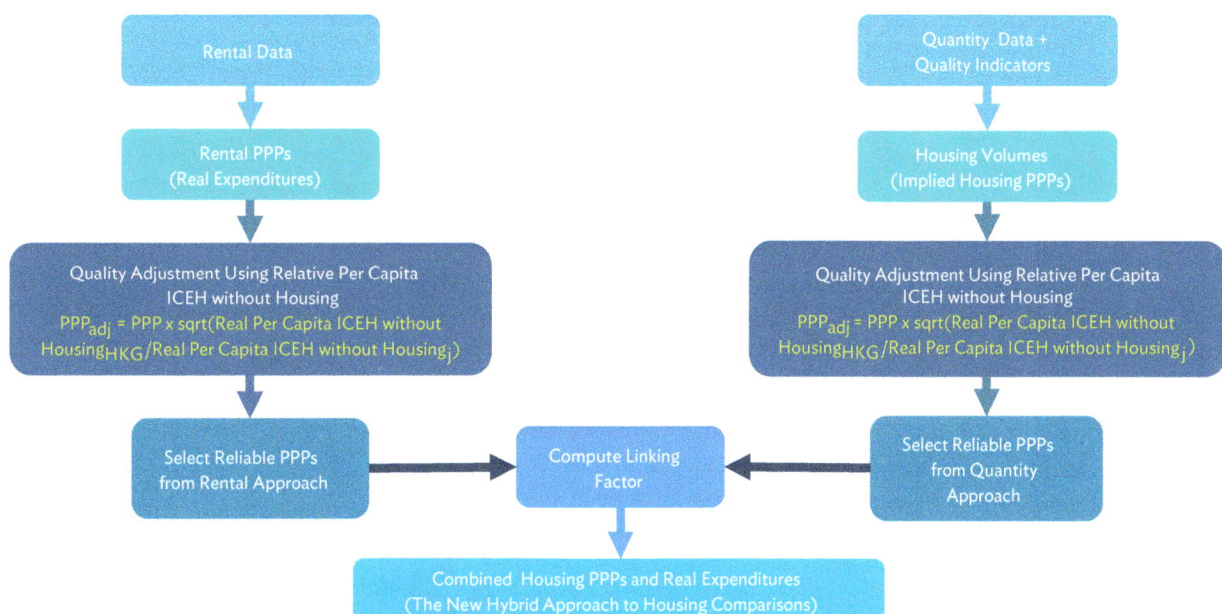

adj = adjusted; HKG = Hong Kong, China; ICEH = individual consumption expenditure by households; PPPs = purchasing power parities; sqrt = square root.
Source: Asian Development Bank (Economic Research and Development Impact Department).

---

[10] Refers to 2021 population density obtained from World Bank Group. World Development Indicators Database. Available: https://data.worldbank.org/indicator/EN.POP.DNST (accessed 7 May 2024).

To adjust for quality differences, the RIA came up with a proposal for quality adjustment, which assumes that quality of dwellings increases with per capita incomes—a phenomenon that is observed in almost all economies. It was found that adjusting for quality differences proportionate to relative per capita income differences may lead to over adjustment. After considering several alternatives, it was recommended by the Expert Group and endorsed first by the Regional Advisory Board, and subsequently by the ICP TAG, to make an adjustment based on the "square root of relative per capita real household expenditure without housing." Under this approach, first PPPs are independently computed using rental and quantity approaches. In the next step, the recommendation is to first apply quality adjustments to the PPPs compiled from both rental and volume approaches using the "square root of relative per capita real household expenditure without housing." Next, assess the "plausibility" of quality adjusted rental and quantity PPPs based on the observed "ratio of per capita real expenditure in housing to per capita real household expenditure without housing." Implausible PPPs (corresponding to the ratios outside the plausibility range of 5%–40%, if any) are then replaced using a linking factor derived from the rental and quantity PPPs of economies with plausible values from both approaches. Finally, the geometric mean of PPPs from both approaches is used for purpose of comparisons.

The new hybrid approach has been subject to extensive testing during 2017 and 2021 ICP and was finally endorsed by the Regional Advisory Board and the ICP TAG for inclusion in the calculation of PPPs in 2021 ICP and for revision of PPPs for 2017 ICP. The effects of the new approach to PPPs for individual consumption expenditure by households (ICEH) and for GDP have been quantified. For the 2021 ICP, the differences in the PPPs for GDP and ICEH from the new hybrid approach and the reference volume approach are provided in Table 5.2. The differences indicate the deviations of the "reference volume" method from the new method, which is

Table 5.2: Percentage Change in Purchasing Power Parities for Gross Domestic Product and Individual Consumption Expenditure by Households—Reference Volume to New Hybrid

Economy	Gross Domestic Product	Individual Consumption Expenditure by Households
(1)	(2)	(3)
Bangladesh	–2.08	–3.21
Bhutan	–2.87	–4.95
Brunei Darussalam	–1.67	–2.92
Cambodia	1.32	1.86
China, People's Republic of	–2.02	–3.49
Fiji	0.33	0.03
Hong Kong, China	–	–
India	–0.65	–1.05
Indonesia	0.50	0.85
Lao People's Democratic Republic	–1.64	–2.74
Malaysia	–2.32	–3.60
Maldives	–1.48	–2.41
Mongolia	1.49	2.36
Nepal	–1.84	–2.79
Pakistan	–2.39	–3.52
Philippines	1.47	1.81
Singapore	–0.14	0.09
Sri Lanka	–2.93	–4.60
Taipei,China	–2.47	–4.31
Thailand	–4.17	–6.81
Viet Nam	1.50	2.44

– = magnitude equals zero.
GDP = gross domestic product, ICEH = individual consumption expenditure by households, NPISH = nonprofit institutions serving households, PPP = purchasing power parity.
Note: Results from the reference volume approach were calculated based on the assumption that housing PPPs from both approaches have the same treatment during the referencing stage. In this table, ICEH includes expenditure by NPISH.
Source: Asian Development Bank estimates based on data supplied by the participating economies.

based on rental and quantity data collected by the economies. It could be seen that the PPPs for GDP and ICEH are revised downward for all economies except for Cambodia, Fiji, Indonesia, Mongolia, the Philippines, and Viet Nam, indicating corresponding increases in real expenditures for housing in these economies.

Following an evaluation of these results, the new approach—which represents a major breakthrough for the ICP in the region—as well as regional results for 2021 ICP and 2017 ICP revisions based on the methodology, are incorporated in the global comparisons. The new approach also brings the Asia and Pacific region in line with the recommended methods for measuring dwelling services with innovations suited to the region's requirements.

Aggregation of Price Data and Compilation of Purchasing Power Parities

To compute PPPs for GDP and corresponding real expenditure aggregates for GDP and its components, first, prices of individual goods and services belonging to the basic headings within that class are aggregated leading to PPPs at the basic heading level. These PPPs calculated for the basic headings are then aggregated upward using their expenditure shares as weights. These weights at the basic heading level are computed as the share of the final expenditure at the basic heading level to the total GDP, based on the national accounts data provided by the implementing agencies of the participating economies. For example, for computing PPPs for the "bread and cereals" class, it is necessary to have (i) PPPs for the five basic headings that make up this class, and (ii) basic heading level expenditures from national accounts for these five classes.

Many index number formulas are available for computing PPPs using price and expenditure data compiled using the methods and steps outlined earlier. Since ICP facilitates comparisons between all pairs of participating economies, for example, comparisons between the People's Republic of China with Singapore; India with Malaysia; Singapore with Viet Nam and so on, it is necessary to use index number methods that satisfy properties of transitivity, base economy invariance, and characteristicity.

Transitivity requires that direct comparison between two economies, say Hong Kong, China and India, would be the same as an indirect comparison through a third economy, say, Malaysia. This means that the method should ensure the following, as expressed in equation (3):

$$PPP_{HKG,India} = PPP_{HKG,Malaysia} \cdot PPP_{Malaysia,India} \quad (3)$$

Base economy invariance requires that the index number method used treats all economies symmetrically and that the PPPs between any two economies are not affected by the choice of the reference economy, which is Hong Kong, China in the case of the Asia and Pacific region.

The characteristicity property advocates that index number methods with PPPs that are transitive must be as close as possible to direct comparisons between pairs of economies.

The TAG for the ICP has recommended the use of the CPD method for calculating PPPs at the basic heading level by aggregating price data for items belonging to a basic heading. At the basic heading level, no expenditure weights are available for this purpose. Rao (2013) provides a detailed description of the CPD methods and their application to compilation of basic heading PPPs. For calculation of PPPs above the basic heading level, for example for classes, groups, categories, main aggregates, and GDP, aggregation is done using expenditure weights available for the basic headings. For aggregation above the basic heading level, the TAG recommends use of the Gini–Èltetö–Köves–Szulc method based on the Fisher bilateral price index. Diewert (2013) provides an overview of the Gini–Èltetö–Köves–Szulc method and compares it with other methods available for this purpose. These methods are described in detail in Chapter 6 of the final report of the 2017 ICP in the region (ADB 2020). Readers are encouraged to delve into the more detailed methodology presented in this 2017 ICP final report.

Reference Purchasing Power Parities

Price data collected by the participating economies are used in compiling basic heading PPPs. However, out of the 155 basic headings used in the ICP, there are some basic headings for which it is difficult to (i) specify the products and (ii) collect product prices that can be used to calculate basic heading PPPs using the CPD method. For such basic headings, PPPs of other basic heading(s) for which price data were collected, and are considered similar are used as proxies or reference PPPs. For example, PPP for the basic heading "maintenance and repair of dwelling" serves as a reference PPP for "repair of household appliance." A list of reference basic headings used in 2021 ICP in Asia and the Pacific is provided in Appendix 4.

CHAPTER 6
Summary and Conclusions

The 2021 International Comparison Program (ICP) in Asia and the Pacific was successfully completed despite significant challenges posed by the unprecedented coronavirus disease (COVID-19) pandemic. This achievement is largely due to the steadfast commitment of the 21 participating economies in the region. The Asian Development Bank (ADB), as the regional implementing agency, devised strategies to ensure high-quality data and the integrity of the ICP exercise, adhering to the core ICP principles and methodology.

The 2021 cycle represents a first step in reducing the 6-year lag between the 2005, 2011, and 2017 rounds of the ICP with the goal of introducing rolling price surveys, ultimately leading to annual implementation of the ICP. After evaluating the 2017 ICP cycle, the United Nations Statistical Commission recommended 2020 as the benchmark year for the subsequent cycle, but the COVID-19 pandemic necessitated a shift to 2021.

This summary report highlights the extensive data on purchasing power parities (PPPs), price levels, and real per capita expenditures from the 2021 ICP cycle. The PPPs and real expenditures for major aggregates and detailed categories, covering several groupings of goods and services, offer a wealth of information for economic analysis. This data is invaluable for national policy makers analyzing the price competitiveness of their economies in relation to subregions of the Asia and Pacific region and globally.

It is hoped that users, after understanding the key results from the 2021 ICP in the region discussed in this report, will be encouraged to explore the detailed results available online for further analyses.[11]

COVID-19 Challenges and Opportunities

The 2021 ICP in Asia and the Pacific holds particular significance due to the pandemic's devastating effects on global economies. The cycle coincided with the first year after COVID-19's severe impact on the region, when regional economies were still grappling with the pandemic while showing signs of recovery. PPPs and real expenditure comparisons from the 2021 cycle offer insights into the pandemic's effects on the region's economies and allow a comparative analysis of the regional results with the 2017 benchmark.

The differential impacts of the COVID-19 pandemic on the ability of implementing agencies in the participating economies to conduct timely and nationwide price surveys posed a significant challenge for the 2021 ICP cycle. Mobility restrictions gave opportunities for exploring alternative means of price data collection, such as websites, web-scraping, telephone calls, and self-administered questionnaires.

---

[11] The public database may be accessed from Asian Development Bank. ICP Data. https://icp.adb.org/data-search-filter.

Through the rigorous intra-economy and intereconomy data validations through a series of regional virtual and face-to-face workshops with the participating economies, guidance from the Regional Advisory Board, and regular monitoring and timely assistance from the ADB team, the 2021 ICP cycle in the region was successfully completed. A comparison of the results from the 2021 cycle with extrapolations from the 2017 cycle showed a higher degree of consistency than observed in previous cycles, further attesting to the quality and reliability of the results.

Methodological Developments

During the 2021 ICP in Asia and the Pacific, a major achievement was ADB's development and implementation of a new methodology for measuring price levels and real expenditures in housing. This new methodology represents a significant advancement over the approach used in the 2005, 2011, and 2017 cycles. It utilizes all rental and quantity indicator data by making innovative adjustments for quality differences in dwellings across economies in the region. The hybrid methodology combines the two standard ICP approaches for housing comparisons namely, rental and quantity approaches, and provides a practical methodology for reliable and data-based housing comparisons in the region. The new housing methodology was implemented for the 2021 ICP as well as in revisions to the 2017 PPP, making the two cycles comparable and replacing the previously used reference volume approach. The World Bank has incorporated the regional estimates based on the new methodology into the PPPs estimated for global comparisons.

The 2021 ICP results include revised estimates of PPPs, price levels, and real expenditures for 2017 accounting mainly for revisions to basic data on gross domestic product (GDP), population, and exchange rates; use of a new, hybrid approach of estimating

actual and imputed rentals for housing; updates to the productivity-adjusted PPPs for government; and uniform treatment of concepts across economies and over the two cycles.

Key Results

The 2021 ICP in Asia and the Pacific facilitates analysis of the pandemic's effects on regional economies' real incomes in comparison to the prepandemic 2017 benchmark. A comparison of the results for 2017 and 2021 highlights the resilience and recovery of the 21 participating economies. Over the period, real GDP in the region increased from HK$243.276 trillion to HK$317.918 trillion, marking a 30.68% increase. More than half of this increase, roughly 19.56% from 2017 to 2021, is attributed to growth in economies of the region. While the ranking of the richest economies in terms of per capita incomes remained the same, there were some shifts in the rankings of economies between the two cycles. These shifts reflect varying levels of recovery among the economies.

The three largest economies by share of real GDP, namely, the People's Republic of China (53.23%), India (20.25%), and Indonesia (6.52%), in per capita real terms are ranked 7th, 17th, and 12th among the 21 economies, respectively. Meanwhile, Singapore (HK$774,311); Brunei Darussalam (HK$470,955); and Hong Kong, China (HK$386,832) have the highest per capita real incomes. The highest per capita real income is 27 times that of the lowest income, and the intereconomy Gini measure of income inequality stands at 0.270, which is much lower than the Gini of 0.414 observed when using GDP based on market exchange rates.

Per capita real actual individual consumption expenditure by households (AICH), which includes household and government expenditure on behalf of households, is an indicator of material well-being. While Singapore has the highest per capita real

GDP; Hong Kong, China (HK$270,778) holds the top rank for per capita real AICH, followed by Singapore (HK$213,002). The People's Republic of China and India are ranked 10th and 17th, respectively. Notably, intereconomy disparities in per capita real AICH are lower, as the highest per capita real AICH for Hong Kong, China is only 13 times higher than that of the lowest level.

For all the participating economies, PPPs of currencies for GDP and other main expenditure aggregates, expressed relative to Hong Kong dollars, are lower than that for exchange rates. Hong Kong, China has the highest price level for GDP followed by Singapore and the People's Republic of China. The lowest price levels are observed in Bhutan, Nepal, and Pakistan. While price level indexes for household consumption and government consumption expenditures are lower than those for GDP, the price levels for gross fixed capital formation are significantly higher.

The regional comparisons compiled as a part of the 2021 ICP cycle are of critical importance in building global comparisons of which the Asia and Pacific region is an important component. Purchasing power parities, GDP expenditures, along with price data for a global list of core items are used by the ICP global office at the World Bank in linking comparisons from different regions, and in calculating global PPPs with the United States dollar as the reference currency to provide comparisons covering 176 economies worldwide.

International comparisons from ICP in this region are pivotal for a comprehensive understanding of its economic significance and global contributions. Though comprising only 21 economies, Asia and the Pacific boasted a population of 3.876 billion in 2021, more than half of the global population. These 21 economies contribute significantly to the global economy, accounting for approximately 27% of the

world's nominal GDP and 35% of the world's real GDP in PPP terms, as per the global 2021 ICP results released by the World Bank.[12] The 2021 global results reveal the economic significance of this region and its resilience in one of the most adverse conditions that prevailed due to COVID-19.

Uses and Limitation of Purchasing Power Parities in Policy Making and Intereconomy Comparisons

Purchasing power parities and internationally comparable national accounts aggregates from the ICP are datasets of public value created through a worldwide partnership among national, regional, and global agencies. The data is increasingly used by policy makers at the national and international levels; international organizations; researchers and analysts; businesses involved in multinational operations; and users interested in the size, structure, and distribution of the world economy. Results from the 2021 ICP cycle provide the users with the most updated numbers for analysis.

The most important use of PPPs from the ICP is in calibrating the international poverty line and measuring the incidence of absolute poverty worldwide. The international poverty line, initially set at $1/day in the 1990s, had been revised to $1.25, $1.90, and $2.15/day following the 2005, 2011, and 2017 ICP cycles, respectively. The PPP-based international poverty line is critical to track the global target of eliminating extreme poverty using comparable data. Additionally, several other Sustainable Development Goal (SDG) targets also require indicators that use PPP-based expenditures for monitoring progress of economies over time; and for making intereconomy comparisons on progress

12 World Bank. DataBank: ICP 2021. https://databank.worldbank.org/source/icp-2021 (accessed 31 May 2024).

using comparable metrics, while identifying factors that contribute to the successes and achievements of these targets. Some of these targets relate to income inequality, zero hunger, quality of education, healthy lives and well-being, affordable and clean energy, labor productivity, clean and environmentally sound technologies, and sustainable cities and communities. The indicators include energy intensity and carbon dioxide emissions in relation to the volumes of economic output in PPP terms, which are critically important in assessing their impact on environment and climate change.

Real per capita incomes are useful in assessing relative standards of living and in understanding inequality in the distribution of income at the regional and global levels. Global inequality measured using the Gini coefficient is based on PPP-converted GDP, reduced from 0.487 in 2011 to 0.474 based on the global 2017 ICP report (World Bank 2020). World inequality has been decreasing since the mid-1990s, the main driver being the reduction in between-economy inequality as driven largely by the strong economic performance of the People's Republic of China and India. The PPPs from ICP make these measurements possible.

International organizations extensively employ PPPs in their policy applications. The United Nations uses PPPs in assessing progress against the SDGs, while the United Nations Development Program uses PPPs for its Human Development Index and Gender Development Index. The International Monetary Fund uses PPPs in its estimation of global and regional growth and inflation in its World Economic Outlook, and for determining quota subscriptions of member countries. The European Commission uses PPPs for allocating Structural Funds to its member states. The World Bank Group incorporates PPPs in the formula used for determining the shareholding rights of member economies of the International

Bank for Reconstruction and Development. The benchmark and extrapolated PPPs are published in the World Bank's World Development Indicators and are used for various research and policy analyses. ADB's *Corporate Results Framework, 2019–2024* (ADB 2019), which integrates SDGs and some indicators related to development progress in Asia and the Pacific, includes indicators whose measurement depends on PPPs. ADB also uses PPP-based GDP as weights in the estimation of regional growth and inflation in its flagship publication, *Asian Development Outlook.*

Additionally, PPPs from the ICP are used for determining cost-of-living adjustments for expatriates and for studying country competitiveness. The PPPs are used in studying economic performance, convergence, and catch-up between economies, and PPP-converted real incomes and investment data are used in measures of labor productivity and total factor productivity across economies of the world. More recently, price data used in compiling PPPs are being utilized for nutrition-based measures of poverty. The ICP PPPs and the metadata including item-level prices are being used in estimating the costs of a healthy diet. According to the *2023 State of Food Security and Nutrition in the World report* (FAO et al. 2023), the cost of a healthy diet in 2021 is around $3.66 per person based on 2017 ICP PPPs, and it estimates that 3.14 billion, or 42% of world's population, cannot afford it.

The contribution of ICP to statistical capacity building in the participating economies cannot be overstated. In addition to contributing to capacity building in the price statistics, the ICP also provides economies the opportunity to improve their estimation of the expenditure side of GDP, as ICP economies are required to provide a detailed breakdown of GDP expenditures by 155 basic headings following the ICP classification.

Despite the numerous uses of PPPs, PPPs should not be used to make any judgment on the overvaluation or undervaluation of a currency, as PPPs from ICP cover both tradable and nontradable goods and services, whereas exchange rates are determined by the total demand for currencies, such as for financing external trade and capital transfers. Further, caution is advised in using the exact rankings of economies based on PPP-converted aggregates when the differences in real expenditures are not significant, as PPPs are subject to sampling and other errors. Finally, PPPs should not be used in making temporal comparisons of PPP-converted GDP or other economic measures, as the PPPs are meant for spatial comparisons for the given benchmark.

Appendixes

Appendix 1: Statistical Tables on Purchasing Power Parities and Real Expenditures, 2021

The tables in this appendix present the key results for 21 participating economies in the 2021 International Comparison Program (ICP) for Asia and the Pacific. Thirty-five expenditure aggregates are presented including gross domestic product (GDP), its main aggregates, and selected expenditure aggregates at levels below the main aggregates. The main aggregates include individual consumption expenditure by households and nonprofit institutions serving households, individual consumption expenditure by government, collective consumption expenditure by government, government final consumption expenditure, gross fixed capital formation, changes in inventories and net acquisitions of valuables, and balance of exports and imports. These expenditure aggregates were derived using the Gini–Eltetö–Köves–Szulc method. Because each real expenditure aggregate is derived by dividing nominal expenditures measured in local currency units by a purchasing power parity specific to the aggregate, the sum of real values of components of GDP will not be equal to the real value of GDP; thus, real expenditures are not additive for a particular economy. For the expenditures in local currency units, participating economies allocated statistical discrepancy (if any) to one or more basic headings based on their best judgment; and for some economies, financial year-based estimates were converted to calendar year. Due to these adjustments, the expenditures in local currency units in the table for some expenditure aggregates may differ from the published expenditure estimates by the economies.

The results presented in these tables are produced by the Asian Development Bank as the ICP regional implementing agency for Asia and the Pacific, based on data supplied by all the participating economies, in accordance with the methodology recommended by the ICP Technical Advisory Group, and endorsed by the Asia and the Pacific Regional Advisory Board. As such, these results are not produced by the participating economies as part of their official statistics.

The following 15 indicator tables in this appendix present data for the 35 expenditure categories.

Table A1.1:   Purchasing Power Parities, 2021 (Hong Kong, China as base)
Table A1.2:   Price Level Indexes, 2021 (Hong Kong, China = 100)
Table A1.3:   Price Level Indexes, 2021 (Asia and the Pacific = 100)
Table A1.4:   Real Expenditure, 2021 (HK$ billion)
Table A1.5:   Economy Shares of Real Expenditure to Asia and the Pacific, 2021 (%)
Table A1.6:   Per Capita Real Expenditure, 2021 (HK$)
Table A1.7:   Per Capita Real Expenditure Index, 2021 (Hong Kong, China = 100)
Table A1.8:   Per Capita Real Expenditure Index, 2021 (Asia and the Pacific = 100)
Table A1.9:   Nominal Expenditure, 2021 (HK$ billion)
Table A1.10:   Economy Shares of Nominal Expenditure to Asia and the Pacific, 2021 (%)
Table A1.11:   Per Capita Nominal Expenditure, 2021 (HK$)
Table A1.12:   Per Capita Nominal Expenditure Index, 2021 (Hong Kong, China = 100)

Table A1.13:   Per Capita Nominal Expenditure Index, 2021 (Asia and the Pacific = 100)

Table A1.14:   Shares of Nominal Expenditure, 2021 (%)

Table A1.15:   Gross Domestic Product, 2021 (billion local currency units)

Table A1.1: Purchasing Power Parities, 2021
(Hong Kong, China as Base)

Expenditure Category	BAN	BHU	BRU	CAM	FIJ	HKG	IND	INO	LAO	MAL	MLD	MON	NEP	PAK	PHI	PRC	SIN	SRI	TAP	THA	VIE
Gross Domestic Product	4.82	3.34	0.09	243.01	0.15	1.00	3.53	818.87	516.29	0.26	1.40	148.19	5.53	7.40	3.30	0.68	0.14	9.46	2.45	1.90	1,212.53
Actual Individual Consumption by Households[a]	4.42	3.06	0.09	235.72	0.15	1.00	3.09	798.84	474.32	0.24	1.48	135.75	5.12	6.60	3.17	0.64	0.16	8.54	2.40	1.78	1,110.77
Food and nonalcoholic beverages	5.55	4.33	0.10	279.88	0.15	1.00	3.29	972.67	651.04	0.26	1.21	164.94	6.01	7.36	3.47	0.64	0.13	11.56	3.00	2.07	1,392.40
Food	5.49	4.32	0.10	275.82	0.15	1.00	3.23	961.80	645.45	0.26	1.20	160.86	5.90	7.26	3.45	0.63	0.13	11.37	2.99	2.02	1,383.23
Bread and cereals	6.58	4.53	0.09	294.50	0.16	1.00	3.68	1,071.32	764.32	0.29	1.34	193.03	6.93	8.26	3.96	0.76	0.14	11.49	3.55	2.48	1,519.19
Meat and Fish	5.77	4.48	0.10	274.71	0.13	1.00	3.61	829.81	580.51	0.23	0.72	123.76	6.31	6.86	2.94	0.58	0.13	9.16	2.80	1.71	1,412.72
Fruits and Vegetables	3.44	3.84	0.13	256.23	0.15	1.00	2.45	925.37	588.49	0.28	2.04	276.52	4.38	4.62	3.81	0.52	0.13	10.79	3.05	1.93	1,204.51
Other food and nonalcoholic beverages	6.12	4.54	0.10	295.52	0.16	1.00	3.63	697.11	697.11	0.26	1.26	193.92	4.43	8.76	3.54	0.74	0.12	13.46	2.72	2.30	1,393.80
Alcoholic beverages, tobacco and narcotics	6.07	3.34	0.11	156.03	0.31	1.00	7.58	1,083.35	492.28	0.47	2.31	116.56	10.03	5.39	3.35	0.72	0.30	31.67	2.86	3.00	1,107.04
Clothing and footwear	6.97	5.18	0.13	306.91	0.18	1.00	3.53	1,296.08	677.54	0.32	2.48	221.26	6.67	8.93	4.81	1.38	0.16	9.83	2.73	2.75	1,543.31
Clothing	6.64	4.82	0.12	294.22	0.17	1.00	3.41	1,220.86	670.27	0.30	2.52	196.32	6.69	8.74	4.30	1.38	0.16	9.41	2.63	2.73	1,468.66
Housing, water, electricity, gas and other fuels[a]	2.52	1.39	0.06	224.51	0.09	1.00	2.02	504.18	322.17	0.14	1.99	131.68	3.52	5.12	2.70	0.42	0.17	4.05	1.88	0.79	825.51
Furnishings, household equipment and routine household maintenance	4.81	4.91	0.10	288.86	0.20	1.00	3.90	1,035.14	645.80	0.29	1.47	232.01	6.88	8.11	3.52	0.84	0.16	12.31	3.06	2.82	1,589.65
Health and Education[a]	2.32	1.46	0.07	115.01	0.10	1.00	1.84	503.53	153.67	0.21	0.80	59.02	2.19	3.90	1.90	0.53	0.15	3.43	1.60	1.13	597.29
Health[a]	2.15	1.50	0.06	115.71	0.09	1.00	1.60	571.79	197.40	0.17	0.76	60.58	2.32	4.27	2.29	0.39	0.16	3.48	1.35	1.20	646.51
Education[a]	2.52	1.45	0.07	115.51	0.10	1.00	2.11	465.29	131.01	0.26	0.84	57.25	2.12	3.63	1.69	0.72	0.14	3.41	1.97	1.07	557.41
Transportation and Communication	6.46	5.23	0.11	372.91	0.18	1.00	4.29	1,023.59	753.44	0.33	1.88	201.42	8.07	8.94	4.64	0.61	0.24	14.64	2.56	2.69	1,495.41
Transportation	6.34	4.61	0.09	363.98	0.16	1.00	4.60	904.85	816.78	0.26	1.57	165.04	10.19	8.95	3.78	0.54	0.23	13.16	2.45	2.21	1,635.00
Communication	5.73	6.54	0.19	329.51	0.21	1.00	2.74	1,323.76	528.33	0.46	2.54	312.11	4.82	7.96	7.30	0.77	0.24	22.24	2.64	4.72	1,263.10
Recreation and culture[a]	6.74	4.75	0.15	323.48	0.21	1.00	4.82	1,125.94	659.65	0.36	1.98	224.47	6.57	8.46	4.37	0.77	0.16	10.51	3.10	2.76	1,511.03
Restaurants and hotels	4.67	2.89	0.12	265.47	0.25	1.00	4.02	889.45	646.08	0.18	1.47	172.37	6.00	7.99	3.28	0.76	0.13	9.56	2.42	1.85	1,157.01
Miscellaneous goods and services[a]	5.63	3.68	0.10	268.23	0.18	1.00	4.02	945.11	622.34	0.28	1.56	166.14	6.80	8.66	3.65	0.82	0.17	9.68	2.80	2.22	1,349.20
Individual Consumption Expenditure by Government	3.40	1.62	0.06	152.51	0.12	1.00	3.88	502.69	207.37	0.22	0.83	57.38	3.81	6.38	2.62	0.68	0.15	4.58	1.89	1.33	655.66
Collective Consumption Expenditure by Government	4.40	1.86	0.06	228.04	0.14	1.00	4.55	645.36	328.81	0.25	1.03	88.52	5.87	8.84	3.03	0.74	0.12	6.38	2.13	1.59	894.69
Gross fixed capital formation	5.74	5.07	0.10	245.34	0.16	1.00	4.23	845.84	656.39	0.28	1.33	195.57	7.35	10.02	3.39	0.71	0.14	12.47	2.70	2.13	1,459.47
Machinery and equipment	11.84	10.19	0.17	498.03	0.28	1.00	8.59	1,860.12	1,246.01	0.53	2.09	356.11	14.18	19.60	6.01	1.01	0.19	26.19	4.07	4.21	2,839.69
Construction	3.47	2.95	0.06	141.90	0.11	1.00	2.53	484.64	403.81	0.17	0.99	124.98	4.48	5.90	2.20	0.54	0.12	7.25	2.17	1.21	899.14
Other products	11.60	10.35	0.17	515.63	0.29	1.00	7.93	1,901.52	1,244.62	0.54	2.23	358.10	14.33	19.57	6.14	1.03	0.19	26.21	4.02	4.23	2,869.54
Changes in inventories and Acquisitions less disposals of valuables	7.06	5.87	0.13	340.21	0.20	1.00	5.83	1,219.59	796.24	0.35	1.64	215.55	8.25	10.08	4.51	0.80	0.17	15.51	3.04	2.81	1,804.30
Balance of Exports and Imports	10.95	9.51	0.17	527.23	0.27	1.00	9.51	1,840.51	1,247.48	0.53	1.98	366.52	15.20	20.92	6.34	0.83	0.17	25.58	3.60	4.11	2,979.15
Individual Consumption Expenditure by Households[b]	4.57	3.34	0.09	246.92	0.15	1.00	3.05	838.02	510.34	0.24	1.60	149.94	5.30	6.66	3.25	0.63	0.17	9.13	2.46	1.83	1,175.71
Individual Consumption Expenditure by Households without Housing[b]	5.09	3.80	0.10	260.13	0.16	1.00	3.30	925.77	555.53	0.27	1.51	156.52	5.74	6.98	3.48	0.67	0.17	10.42	2.55	2.15	1,279.31
Government Final Consumption Expenditure	3.96	1.75	0.06	186.24	0.13	1.00	4.22	579.82	283.34	0.24	0.94	73.79	4.88	7.69	2.84	0.71	0.13	5.49	2.01	1.47	779.40
Domestic Absorption	4.73	3.36	0.09	237.14	0.15	1.00	3.46	796.53	506.62	0.25	1.38	144.81	5.64	7.35	3.21	0.67	0.15	9.34	2.44	1.85	1,182.67
Total Consumption	4.40	2.82	0.08	233.34	0.14	1.00	3.22	781.01	449.13	0.24	1.42	129.52	5.14	6.83	3.15	0.66	0.16	8.28	2.37	1.76	1,085.03

BAN = Bangladesh; BHU = Bhutan; BRU = Brunei Darussalam; CAM = Cambodia; FIJ = Fiji; HKG = Hong Kong, China; IND = India; INO = Indonesia; LAO = Lao People's Democratic Republic; MAL = Malaysia; MLD = Maldives; MON = Mongolia; NEP = Nepal; PAK = Pakistan; PHI = Philippines; PRC = People's Republic of China; SIN = Singapore; SRI = Sri Lanka; TAP = Taipei,China; THA = Thailand; VIE = Viet Nam.

a Includes individual consumption expenditure by households, nonprofit institutions serving households, and government.

b Includes expenditure by nonprofit institutions serving households.

Source: Asian Development Bank estimates based on data supplied by the participating economies.

Table A1.2: Price Level Indexes, 2021

(Hong Kong, China = 100)

Expenditure Category	BAN	BHU	BRU	CAM	FIJ	HKG	IND	INO	LAO	MAL	MLD	MON	NEP	PAK	PHI	PRC	SIN	SRI	TAP	THA	VIE
Gross Domestic Product	44	35	52	46	58	100	37	44	41	48	71	40	36	35	52	82	80	37	68	46	41
Actual Individual Consumption by Households[a]	40	32	52	45	54	100	33	43	38	45	75	37	34	32	50	77	95	33	67	43	37
Food and nonalcoholic beverages	51	46	60	53	56	100	35	53	52	49	61	45	40	35	55	77	77	45	83	50	47
Food	50	45	60	52	54	100	34	52	52	49	60	44	39	35	54	76	76	44	83	49	46
Bread and cereals	60	48	51	56	59	100	39	58	61	54	68	53	46	39	62	91	82	45	99	60	51
Meat and Fish	53	47	61	52	50	100	38	45	47	44	37	34	42	33	46	70	77	36	78	42	47
Fruits and Vegetables	31	40	74	49	56	100	26	50	47	52	103	75	29	22	60	63	78	42	85	47	40
Other food and nonalcoholic beverages	56	48	59	56	61	100	38	59	56	49	64	53	42	42	56	89	71	53	75	56	47
Alcoholic beverages, tobacco and narcotics	55	35	63	30	117	100	80	59	39	88	117	32	66	26	53	87	175	124	79	73	37
Clothing and footwear	64	54	76	58	68	100	37	70	54	59	125	60	44	43	76	167	95	38	76	67	52
Clothing	61	51	70	56	65	100	36	66	54	57	127	54	44	42	68	166	91	37	73	66	49
Housing, water, electricity, gas and other fuels[a]	23	15	34	43	32	100	21	27	26	25	101	36	23	24	43	51	99	16	52	19	28
Furnishings, household equipment and routine household maintenance	44	52	55	55	74	100	41	56	52	55	74	63	45	39	56	102	91	48	85	68	53
Health and Education[a]	21	15	38	22	37	100	19	27	12	40	40	16	14	19	30	64	87	13	44	27	20
Health[a]	20	16	37	22	35	100	17	31	16	32	38	17	14	20	36	47	95	14	37	29	22
Education[a]	23	15	40	22	39	100	22	25	11	49	42	16	15	17	27	86	81	13	55	26	19
Transportation and Communication	59	55	61	71	66	100	45	56	60	61	95	55	53	43	73	73	139	57	71	65	50
Transportation	58	48	50	69	59	100	48	49	65	49	79	45	67	43	60	65	136	51	68	54	55
Communication	52	69	110	62	79	100	29	72	42	87	128	85	32	38	115	93	138	87	73	115	42
Recreation and culture[a]	62	50	86	61	78	100	51	61	53	68	100	61	43	40	69	93	90	41	86	67	51
Restaurants and hotels	43	30	71	50	94	100	42	48	33	33	74	47	39	38	52	91	75	37	67	45	39
Miscellaneous goods and services[a]	51	39	60	51	67	100	42	51	50	53	79	45	45	41	58	99	99	38	78	54	45
Individual Consumption Expenditure by Government	31	17	35	29	46	100	41	27	17	41	42	16	25	31	41	82	88	18	52	32	22
Collective Consumption Expenditure by Government	40	20	33	43	53	100	48	35	26	48	52	24	39	42	48	89	72	25	59	39	30
Gross fixed capital formation	52	53	56	47	61	100	45	46	53	52	67	53	48	48	53	85	79	49	75	52	49
Machinery and equipment	108	107	100	94	104	100	90	101	100	100	106	97	93	94	95	122	112	102	113	102	95
Construction	32	31	37	27	41	100	27	26	32	31	50	34	29	28	35	65	69	28	60	29	30
Other products	106	109	99	98	108	100	83	103	100	101	113	98	94	94	97	124	110	102	112	103	96
Changes in inventories and Acquisitions less disposals of valuables	65	62	73	65	76	100	61	66	64	65	83	59	54	48	71	96	98	61	84	68	61
Balance of Exports and Imports	100	100	100	100	100	100	100	100	100	100	100	100	100	100	100	100	100	100	100	100	100
Individual Consumption Expenditure by Households[b]	42	35	55	47	56	100	32	46	41	46	81	41	35	32	51	76	96	36	68	45	39
Individual Consumption Expenditure by Households without Housing[b]	47	40	58	49	62	100	35	50	45	51	76	43	38	33	55	81	97	41	71	52	43
Government Final Consumption Expenditure	36	18	33	35	50	100	44	32	23	45	47	20	32	37	45	86	77	21	56	36	26
Domestic Absorption	43	35	51	45	56	100	36	43	41	47	70	40	37	35	51	80	86	36	68	45	40
Total Consumption	40	30	48	44	54	100	34	42	36	45	72	35	34	33	50	80	92	32	66	43	36

BAN = Bangladesh; BHU = Bhutan; BRU = Brunei Darussalam; CAM = Cambodia; FIJ = Fiji; HKG = Hong Kong, China; IND = India; INO = Indonesia; LAO = Lao People's Democratic Republic; MAL = Malaysia; MLD = Maldives; MON = Mongolia; NEP = Nepal; PAK = Pakistan; PHI = Philippines; PRC = People's Republic of China; SIN = Singapore; SRI = Sri Lanka; TAP = Taipei,China; THA = Thailand; VIE = Viet Nam.

[a] Includes individual consumption expenditure by households, nonprofit institutions serving households, and government.

[b] Includes expenditure by nonprofit institutions serving households.

Source: Asian Development Bank estimates based on data supplied by the participating economies.

Table A1.3: Price Level Indexes, 2021
(Asia and the Pacific = 100)

Expenditure Category	BAN	BHU	BRU	CAM	FIJ	HKG	IND	INO	LAO	MAL	MLD	MON	NEP	PAK	PHI	PRC	SIN	SRI	TAP	THA	VIE
Gross Domestic Product	68	55	82	72	90	155	58	69	64	75	110	63	57	55	81	127	124	57	106	72	63
Actual Individual Consumption by Households[a]	72	57	93	80	97	178	58	77	68	81	133	66	60	56	89	138	170	60	119	77	66
Food and nonalcoholic beverages	94	85	112	99	104	186	64	98	97	91	114	84	74	65	102	144	142	84	155	94	87
Food	95	86	113	99	103	189	64	99	98	92	114	83	74	66	103	144	145	84	157	93	88
Bread and cereals	105	83	90	97	102	174	67	101	107	94	118	92	79	69	109	159	142	78	172	105	89
Meat and Fish	90	81	104	89	85	171	65	77	80	75	63	58	71	56	79	120	132	61	133	71	81
Fruits and Vegetables	74	94	174	114	131	234	60	118	110	121	242	177	67	52	141	148	183	99	198	110	95
Other food and nonalcoholic beverages	103	88	109	103	113	184	70	109	103	89	117	97	78	77	103	164	131	97	139	103	86
Alcoholic beverages, tobacco and narcotics	75	47	85	40	157	135	107	79	53	118	157	43	89	35	71	117	235	167	107	98	50
Clothing and footwear	77	66	92	70	82	121	45	85	65	71	151	73	53	51	92	201	115	46	91	81	62
Clothing	76	63	87	70	81	125	45	83	67	71	159	67	55	52	85	208	113	46	91	83	62
Housing, water, electricity, gas and other fuels[a]	60	38	89	110	83	259	55	71	67	66	261	93	60	63	110	132	257	41	135	49	72
Furnishings, household equipment and routine household maintenance	59	69	74	73	99	134	55	75	69	74	100	85	61	52	75	136	122	65	114	92	72
Health and Education[a]	49	36	88	51	86	232	45	63	29	93	94	37	33	43	70	149	203	31	103	64	46
Health[a]	54	44	103	61	98	278	47	86	44	89	107	46	39	57	100	129	263	38	104	81	60
Education[a]	45	30	78	43	77	198	44	50	21	96	84	31	30	34	53	171	160	26	108	51	37
Transportation and Communication	95	89	99	114	106	161	73	90	97	99	153	89	86	69	118	118	224	92	115	105	81
Transportation	100	84	87	119	103	173	84	85	113	85	137	78	116	74	103	112	235	89	118	93	95
Communication	77	102	163	92	117	148	42	106	63	128	189	126	47	56	170	137	204	128	108	169	63
Recreation and culture[a]	79	64	110	78	99	128	65	78	67	87	128	78	55	52	88	118	115	52	110	85	65
Restaurants and hotels	61	43	102	72	135	142	60	69	74	47	106	67	56	54	74	130	107	53	96	64	55
Miscellaneous goods and services[a]	69	52	81	68	90	134	56	69	67	71	105	61	60	55	77	133	132	51	104	72	61
Individual Consumption Expenditure by Government	49	27	56	46	74	159	65	44	26	66	67	25	40	49	66	131	141	29	84	52	35
Collective Consumption Expenditure by Government	56	27	45	60	73	139	66	49	37	66	72	33	54	59	66	124	100	35	82	54	42
Gross fixed capital formation	71	73	77	63	83	136	61	63	72	71	92	73	66	65	73	116	108	66	102	70	67
Machinery and equipment	95	94	88	83	91	88	79	89	88	88	93	85	82	82	83	107	98	90	99	90	84
Construction	61	60	71	52	79	192	51	51	62	60	96	66	57	54	67	125	132	55	116	57	58
Other products	90	93	85	83	92	85	71	88	85	86	96	83	80	80	83	106	94	87	95	88	82
Changes in inventories and Acquisitions less disposals of valuables	82	78	92	82	97	127	78	84	81	83	105	75	69	61	90	121	124	77	107	87	77
Balance of Exports and Imports	100	100	100	100	100	100	100	100	100	100	100	100	100	100	100	100	100	100	100	100	100
Individual Consumption Expenditure by Households[b]	76	64	100	85	101	182	58	83	74	83	147	74	63	58	93	137	174	65	124	81	72
Individual Consumption Expenditure by Households without Housing[b]	79	68	97	83	104	169	59	85	75	86	129	72	64	56	93	137	164	69	120	88	73
Government Final Consumption Expenditure	53	27	49	52	73	148	66	46	34	66	70	30	47	54	66	127	114	32	82	53	39
Domestic Absorption	69	56	81	72	89	160	58	69	65	75	112	63	59	56	81	128	137	58	108	72	63
Total Consumption	69	51	83	76	93	172	58	73	62	78	123	61	58	56	85	137	158	56	113	73	63

BAN = Bangladesh; BHU = Bhutan; BRU = Brunei Darussalam; CAM = Cambodia; FIJ = Fiji; HKG = Hong Kong, China; IND = India; INO = Indonesia; LAO = Lao People's Democratic Republic; MAL = Malaysia; MLD = Maldives; MON = Mongolia; NEP = Nepal; PAK = Pakistan; PHI = Philippines; PRC = People's Republic of China; SIN = Singapore; SRI = Sri Lanka; TAP = Taipei,China; THA = Thailand; VIE = Viet Nam.

[a] Includes individual consumption expenditure by households, nonprofit institutions serving households, and government.

[b] Includes expenditure by nonprofit institutions serving households.

Source: Asian Development Bank estimates based on data supplied by the participating economies.

Table A1.4: Real Expenditure, 2021
(HK$ billion)

Expenditure Category	BAN	BHU	BRU	CAM	FIJ	HKG	IND	INO	LAO	MAL	MLD	MON	NEP	PAK	PHI	PRC	SIN	SRI	TAP	THA	VIE	AP
Gross Domestic Product	7,783.9	61.3	207.6	454.7	57.5	2,867.6	64,376.0	20,732.0	358.3	6,004.3	57.8	293.9	821.3	8,276.7	5,882.8	169,241.9	4,222.8	1,861.3	8,836.2	8,527.0	6,993.4	317,918.1
Actual Individual Consumption by Households[a]	5,902.0	40.7	62.9	330.9	55.4	2,007.3	47,711.0	12,657.4	191.5	4,179.7	30.7	188.5	765.8	8,221.8	4,940.7	79,662.2	1,161.6	1,365.5	4,713.0	5,684.4	4,561.7	184,434.6
Food and nonalcoholic beverages	2,410.8	10.0	7.5	128.1	17.0	178.9	13,022.6	3,091.4	62.3	929.6	6.8	55.6	382.5	2,492.1	1,625.0	12,888.4	105.7	311.8	460.8	1,147.2	864.4	40,198.4
Food	2,428.9	9.2	6.7	125.0	16.8	167.6	13,085.1	2,776.1	56.0	885.6	6.0	52.2	384.2	2,405.6	1,505.9	12,618.1	96.9	296.4	436.4	1,038.2	837.1	39,233.9
Bread and cereals	902.9	2.5	1.7	35.8	3.3	19.2	2,607.2	650.6	14.4	133.4	0.5	5.1	119.5	391.5	464.9	1,465.1	16.5	83.3	81.4	181.9	213.9	7,394.5
Meat and Fish	443.9	1.1	2.3	39.9	3.6	88.3	1,250.2	965.3	25.7	287.6	2.5	31.4	54.3	420.2	613.5	5,754.6	31.7	36.9	148.6	286.8	341.7	10,829.9
Fruits and Vegetables	525.9	2.8	0.9	20.8	5.0	29.0	4,453.7	473.0	8.4	189.7	0.9	1.8	107.9	549.3	168.3	3,720.5	22.0	42.0	137.3	413.6	134.5	11,007.3
Other food and nonalcoholic beverages	502.6	3.7	2.7	30.5	4.9	42.4	4,923.7	988.3	13.9	326.3	3.1	19.6	102.0	1,105.5	380.3	2,483.0	36.0	137.9	94.3	277.9	167.9	11,646.5
Alcoholic beverages, tobacco and narcotics	86.5	1.1	0.1	17.5	4.2	11.9	422.5	735.7	18.7	36.0	0.5	12.3	17.9	89.4	90.2	1,652.5	11.2	4.9	87.9	92.7	103.1	3,496.7
Clothing and footwear	225.3	1.2	1.1	5.9	1.5	83.9	2,324.0	246.8	1.9	85.1	0.6	4.0	17.8	417.2	53.8	1,670.7	30.1	45.7	173.2	106.2	87.0	5,582.8
Clothing	210.8	0.9	1.0	3.7	1.2	55.9	1,959.4	226.0	1.5	78.8	0.4	3.3	15.0	366.8	40.4	1,348.1	25.9	44.3	157.5	97.4	68.8	4,707.2
Housing, water, electricity, gas and other fuels[a]	1,698.7	9.5	13.9	47.5	6.1	338.1	9,179.9	2,106.0	36.5	1,109.2	6.0	21.5	143.5	2,292.6	693.9	20,161.2	173.1	266.2	1,009.2	1,138.2	741.3	41,192.0
Furnishings, household equipment and routine household maintenance	176.5	0.9	4.4	4.7	2.0	104.0	1,029.3	379.3	8.2	147.2	1.5	2.7	10.5	221.5	117.5	2,217.7	48.4	19.5	163.6	127.5	156.7	4,943.6
Health and Education[a]	931.9	15.1	15.5	110.9	13.3	343.1	11,419.1	2,536.3	47.7	640.9	11.6	72.5	171.0	1,635.2	1,121.1	21,137.0	264.4	358.7	1,280.0	1,897.5	1,531.9	45,555.0
Health[a]	386.6	6.0	5.1	64.3	4.8	202.6	5,594.1	879.6	14.0	356.3	6.1	26.1	93.0	799.7	367.0	12,979.6	136.9	220.6	920.6	1,004.7	729.3	24,799.7
Education[a]	530.5	9.0	10.1	46.0	8.4	140.5	5,712.6	1,663.8	34.9	294.5	5.6	47.2	77.0	815.2	765.1	8,682.8	125.3	133.4	411.4	877.9	795.7	21,186.9
Transportation and Communication	189.1	2.7	8.0	14.4	4.8	148.8	5,894.1	1,482.5	9.6	541.8	3.0	15.0	20.2	486.2	342.7	9,456.2	93.7	163.1	495.1	471.2	601.8	20,443.7
Transportation	173.0	1.9	8.0	14.2	3.4	84.1	4,760.3	1,249.6	7.1	341.7	1.5	12.3	10.5	378.3	305.3	8,077.9	70.4	172.4	407.0	483.9	318.5	16,881.4
Communication	22.0	0.8	0.8	0.5	1.4	64.7	1,238.8	292.2	2.7	189.1	1.3	3.1	11.5	120.5	59.9	1,836.9	25.2	5.3	102.8	41.6	300.2	4,321.4
Recreation and culture[a]	62.0	0.9	2.1	5.3	0.3	172.1	260.9	312.9	2.8	80.8	0.3	1.8	12.7	253.8	42.8	1,909.7	102.1	81.5	216.3	163.7	136.5	3,821.4
Restaurants and hotels	130.1	1.2	1.7	12.0	0.1	132.4	446.1	1,022.2	7.6	396.6	1.3	0.9	8.6	168.9	264.8	3,732.4	101.9	36.6	375.6	390.3	229.1	7,460.3
Miscellaneous goods and services[a]	183.8	2.8	8.5	6.2	4.1	494.2	5,214.2	504.6	17.7	355.4	2.1	10.2	13.5	454.6	653.8	9,295.9	237.1	140.3	674.1	597.1	283.5	19,153.6
Individual Consumption Expenditure by Government	62.9	11.0	16.6	34.2	6.0	144.0	2,258.5	1,327.4	18.7	500.0	8.9	43.7	37.0	371.0	393.8	10,423.3	142.3	195.1	844.4	1,177.7	628.2	18,653.9
Collective Consumption Expenditure by Government	444.3	15.3	57.1	12.1	9.7	219.5	3,542.4	1,398.5	63.8	344.2	7.5	45.0	40.3	472.9	656.1	14,933.7	323.9	121.0	632.1	887.3	450.6	24,677.4
Gross fixed capital formation	2,062.9	17.8	60.1	103.0	10.7	483.0	15,434.6	6,180.6	128.2	1,079.7	17.2	59.8	182.9	823.2	1,276.1	68,222.7	950.5	371.3	2,111.2	1,802.0	1,821.3	103,198.9
Machinery and equipment	173.0	4.5	16.3	23.5	2.2	108.9	2,617.9	452.3	19.1	174.6	5.3	13.3	33.2	161.2	178.1	10,960.5	184.5	45.5	572.1	503.3	242.9	16,492.1
Construction	2,691.7	14.7	38.7	93.9	8.9	310.4	14,573.5	8,115.2	92.3	930.6	9.7	44.5	165.2	560.2	1,218.7	57,109.9	427.9	417.6	951.7	989.0	2,107.1	90,871.5
Other products	39.0	0.1	3.3	0.5	0.5	63.7	759.0	238.5	18.6	92.0	1.0	3.9	9.4	91.2	93.1	6,262.5	229.1	15.6	321.8	123.7	25.7	8,392.2
Changes in inventories and Acquisitions less disposals of valuables	51.7	0.1	12.6	17.6	1.0	-1.9	639.9	236.9	-0.0	126.5	-1.9	14.6	71.6	103.9	-48.9	1,724.3	59.5	118.4	80.9	298.3	189.4	3,694.5
Balance of Exports and Imports	-248.6	-4.1	14.4	-2.9	-9.1	159.7	-576.2	242.4	-8.8	210.1	3.9	-2.4	-102.0	-309.5	-367.0	3,604.5	1,224.9	-50.9	853.0	-1.6	3.3	4,633.2
Individual Consumption Expenditure by Households[b]	5,654.1	31.9	49.3	294.8	49.3	1,863.3	45,533.6	11,269.4	170.4	3,687.6	23.8	154.0	713.7	7,790.6	4,498.4	69,971.9	1,022.1	1,180.3	3,948.9	4,656.4	3,959.4	166,523.1
Individual Consumption Expenditure by Households without Housing[b]	4,651.5	25.8	40.5	253.3	42.0	1,580.5	38,207.9	9,362.6	140.6	3,020.5	19.5	133.4	588.8	6,375.6	3,877.7	57,320.6	865.1	959.2	3,167.5	3,706.2	3,434.3	137,773.2
Government Final Consumption Expenditure	547.6	26.5	73.7	42.8	15.9	363.5	5,893.0	2,707.5	87.7	828.7	16.1	88.0	77.5	851.1	1,066.0	25,563.8	465.7	303.0	1,462.5	2,027.7	1,045.7	43,554.0
Domestic Absorption	8,509.0	72.5	185.8	472.5	76.1	2,707.9	67,279.2	20,753.3	386.8	5,741.1	52.8	306.8	1,079.7	9,206.1	6,761.8	167,651.2	2,501.9	2,024.2	7,622.9	8,746.1	7,161.7	319,299.3
Total Consumption	6,364.8	54.3	107.0	346.1	64.9	2,226.8	50,796.3	14,102.0	248.9	4,524.2	37.6	228.4	809.0	8,551.7	5,592.8	94,219.4	1,454.2	1,502.1	5,337.6	6,555.6	5,041.4	208,165.0

0.0 = magnitude is less than half of the unit employed.

AP = Asia and the Pacific; BAN = Bangladesh; BHU = Bhutan; BRU = Brunei Darussalam; CAM = Cambodia; FIJ = Fiji; HKG = Hong Kong, China; IND = India; INO = Indonesia; LAO = Lao People's Democratic Republic; MAL = Malaysia; MLD = Maldives; MON = Mongolia; NEP = Nepal; PAK = Pakistan; PHI = Philippines; PRC = People's Republic of China; SIN = Singapore; SRI = Sri Lanka; TAP = Taipei,China; THA = Thailand; VIE = Viet Nam.

Note: Each real aggregate value is derived by using a purchasing power parity that is specific to that aggregate, so real aggregates may not sum up to the total of their real components for an economy.

[a] Includes individual consumption expenditure by households, nonprofit institutions serving households, and government.

[b] Includes expenditure by nonprofit institutions serving households.

Source: Asian Development Bank estimates based on data supplied by the participating economies.

Table A1.5: Economy Shares of Real Expenditure to Asia and the Pacific, 2021

(%)

Expenditure Category	BAN	BHU	BRU	CAM	FIJ	HKG	IND	INO	LAO	MAL	MLD	MON	NEP	PAK	PHI	PRC	SIN	SRI	TAP	THA	VIE	AP
Gross Domestic Product	2.45	0.02	0.07	0.14	0.02	0.90	20.25	6.52	0.11	1.89	0.02	0.09	0.26	2.60	1.85	53.23	1.33	0.59	2.78	2.68	2.20	100.00
Actual Individual Consumption by Households[a]	3.20	0.02	0.03	0.18	0.03	1.09	25.87	6.86	0.10	2.27	0.02	0.10	0.42	4.46	2.68	43.19	0.63	0.74	2.56	3.08	2.47	100.00
Food and nonalcoholic beverages	6.00	0.02	0.02	0.32	0.04	0.44	32.40	7.69	0.15	2.31	0.02	0.14	0.95	6.20	4.04	32.06	0.26	0.78	1.15	2.85	2.15	100.00
Food	6.19	0.02	0.02	0.32	0.04	0.43	33.35	7.08	0.14	2.26	0.02	0.13	0.98	6.13	3.84	32.16	0.25	0.76	1.11	2.65	2.13	100.00
Bread and cereals	12.21	0.03	0.02	0.48	0.04	0.26	35.26	8.80	0.19	1.80	0.01	0.07	1.62	5.29	6.29	19.81	0.22	1.13	1.10	2.46	2.89	100.00
Meat and Fish	4.10	0.01	0.02	0.37	0.03	0.82	11.54	8.91	0.24	2.66	0.02	0.29	0.50	3.88	5.66	53.14	0.29	0.34	1.37	2.65	3.16	100.00
Fruits and Vegetables	4.78	0.03	0.01	0.19	0.05	0.26	40.46	4.30	0.08	1.72	0.01	0.02	0.98	4.99	1.53	33.80	0.20	0.38	1.25	3.76	1.22	100.00
Other food and nonalcoholic beverages	4.32	0.03	0.02	0.26	0.04	0.36	42.28	8.49	0.08	2.80	0.01	0.02	0.88	9.49	3.27	21.32	0.31	1.18	0.81	2.39	1.44	100.00
Alcoholic beverages, tobacco and narcotics	2.47	0.03	0.00	0.50	0.12	0.34	12.08	21.04	0.54	1.03	0.01	0.35	0.51	2.56	2.58	47.26	0.32	0.14	2.51	2.65	2.95	100.00
Clothing and footwear	4.04	0.02	0.02	0.11	0.03	1.50	41.63	4.42	0.03	1.52	0.01	0.07	0.32	7.47	0.96	29.93	0.54	0.82	3.10	1.90	1.56	100.00
Clothing	4.48	0.02	0.02	0.08	0.03	1.19	41.63	4.80	0.03	1.67	0.01	0.07	0.32	7.79	0.86	28.64	0.55	0.94	3.35	2.07	1.46	100.00
Housing, water, electricity, gas and other fuels[a]	4.12	0.02	0.03	0.12	0.01	0.82	22.29	5.11	0.09	2.69	0.01	0.05	0.35	5.57	1.68	48.94	0.42	0.65	2.45	2.76	1.80	100.00
Furnishings, household equipment and routine household maintenance	3.57	0.02	0.09	0.09	0.04	2.10	20.82	7.67	0.17	2.98	0.03	0.05	0.21	4.48	2.38	44.86	0.98	0.39	3.31	2.58	3.17	100.00
Health and Education[a]	2.05	0.03	0.03	0.24	0.03	0.75	25.07	5.57	0.10	1.41	0.03	0.16	0.38	3.59	2.46	46.40	0.58	0.79	2.81	4.17	3.36	100.00
Health[a]	1.56	0.02	0.02	0.26	0.02	0.82	22.56	3.55	0.06	1.44	0.02	0.11	0.37	3.22	1.48	52.34	0.55	0.90	3.71	4.05	2.94	100.00
Education[a]	2.50	0.04	0.05	0.22	0.04	0.66	26.96	7.85	0.16	1.39	0.03	0.22	0.36	3.85	3.61	40.98	0.59	0.63	1.94	4.14	3.76	100.00
Transportation and Communication	0.93	0.01	0.04	0.07	0.02	0.73	28.83	7.25	0.05	2.65	0.01	0.07	0.10	2.36	1.68	46.25	0.46	0.80	2.42	2.30	2.94	100.00
Transportation	1.02	0.01	0.05	0.08	0.02	0.50	28.20	7.40	0.04	2.02	0.01	0.07	0.06	2.24	1.81	47.85	0.42	1.02	2.41	2.87	1.89	100.00
Communication	0.51	0.02	0.02	0.01	0.03	1.50	28.67	6.76	0.06	4.38	0.03	0.07	0.27	2.79	1.39	42.51	0.58	0.12	2.38	0.96	6.95	100.00
Recreation and culture[a]	1.62	0.02	0.06	0.14	0.01	4.50	6.83	8.19	0.07	2.12	0.01	0.05	0.33	6.64	1.12	49.97	2.67	2.13	5.66	4.28	3.57	100.00
Restaurants and hotels	1.74	0.02	0.02	0.16	0.00	1.77	5.98	13.70	0.10	5.32	0.02	0.01	0.12	2.26	3.55	50.03	1.37	0.49	5.03	5.23	3.07	100.00
Miscellaneous goods and services[a]	0.96	0.01	0.04	0.03	0.02	2.58	27.22	2.63	0.09	1.86	0.01	0.05	0.07	2.37	3.41	48.53	1.24	0.73	3.52	3.12	1.48	100.00
Individual Consumption Expenditure by Government	0.34	0.06	0.09	0.18	0.03	0.77	12.11	7.12	0.10	2.68	0.05	0.23	0.20	1.99	2.11	55.93	0.76	1.05	4.53	6.31	3.37	100.00
Collective Consumption Expenditure by Government	1.80	0.06	0.23	0.05	0.04	0.89	14.35	5.67	0.26	1.39	0.03	0.18	0.16	1.92	2.66	60.52	1.31	0.49	2.56	3.60	1.83	100.00
Gross fixed capital formation	2.00	0.02	0.06	0.10	0.01	0.47	14.96	5.99	0.12	1.05	0.03	0.06	0.18	0.80	1.24	66.11	0.92	0.36	2.05	1.75	1.76	100.00
Machinery and equipment	1.05	0.03	0.10	0.14	0.01	0.66	15.87	2.74	0.12	1.06	0.03	0.08	0.20	0.98	1.08	66.46	1.12	0.28	3.05	1.47	1.76	100.00
Construction	2.96	0.02	0.04	0.01	0.01	0.34	16.04	8.93	0.10	1.02	0.01	0.05	0.18	0.62	1.34	62.85	0.47	0.46	1.05	1.09	2.32	100.00
Other products	0.46	0.00	0.04	0.01	0.01	0.76	9.04	2.84	0.22	1.10	0.01	0.05	0.11	1.09	1.11	74.62	2.73	0.19	3.84	1.47	0.31	100.00
Changes in inventories and Acquisitions less disposals of valuables	1.40	0.00	0.34	0.48	0.03	-0.05	17.32	6.41	-0.00	3.42	-0.05	0.40	1.94	2.81	-1.32	46.67	1.61	3.21	2.19	8.07	5.13	100.00
Balance of Exports and Imports	-5.37	-0.09	0.31	-0.06	-0.20	3.45	-12.44	5.23	-0.19	4.53	0.08	-0.05	-2.20	-6.68	-7.92	77.80	26.44	-1.10	18.41	-0.03	0.07	100.00
Individual Consumption Expenditure by Households[b]	3.40	0.02	0.03	0.18	0.03	1.12	27.34	6.77	0.10	2.21	0.01	0.09	0.43	4.68	2.70	42.02	0.61	0.71	2.37	2.80	2.38	100.00
Individual Consumption Expenditure by Households without Housing[b]	3.38	0.02	0.03	0.18	0.03	1.15	27.73	6.80	0.10	2.19	0.01	0.10	0.43	4.63	2.81	41.61	0.63	0.70	2.30	2.69	2.49	100.00
Government Final Consumption Expenditure	1.26	0.06	0.17	0.10	0.04	0.83	13.53	6.22	0.20	1.90	0.04	0.20	0.18	1.95	2.45	58.69	1.07	0.70	3.36	4.66	2.40	100.00
Domestic Absorption	2.66	0.02	0.06	0.15	0.02	0.85	21.07	6.50	0.12	1.80	0.02	0.10	0.34	2.88	2.12	52.51	0.78	0.63	2.39	2.74	2.24	100.00
Total Consumption	3.06	0.03	0.05	0.17	0.03	1.07	24.40	6.77	0.12	2.17	0.02	0.11	0.39	4.11	2.69	45.26	0.70	0.72	2.56	3.15	2.42	100.00

0.00 = magnitude is less than half of the unit employed.

AP = Asia and the Pacific; BAN = Bangladesh; BHU = Bhutan; BRU = Brunei Darussalam; CAM = Cambodia; FIJ = Fiji; HKG = Hong Kong, China; IND = India; INO = Indonesia; LAO = Lao People's Democratic Republic; MAL = Malaysia; MLD = Maldives; MON = Mongolia; NEP = Nepal; PAK = Pakistan; PHI = Philippines; PRC = People's Republic of China; SIN = Singapore; SRI = Sri Lanka; TAP = Taipei,China; THA = Thailand; VIE = Viet Nam.

Note: Each real aggregate value is derived by using a purchasing power parity that is specific to that aggregate, so real aggregates may not sum up to the total of their real components for an economy.

a Includes individual consumption expenditure by households, nonprofit institutions serving households, and government.

b Includes expenditure by nonprofit institutions serving households.

Source: Asian Development Bank estimates based on data supplied by the participating economies.

Table A1.6: Per Capita Real Expenditure, 2021
(HK$)

Expenditure Category	BAN	BHU	BRU	CAM	FIJ	HKG	IND	INO	LAO	MAL	MLD	MON	NEP	PAK	PHI	PRC	SIN	SRI	TAP	THA	VIE	AP
Gross Domestic Product	45,717	81,049	470,955	27,407	64,376	386,832	47,087	76,030	48,828	184,316	101,638	89,532	28,263	36,821	53,383	119,829	774,311	84,007	376,515	122,360	70,994	82,030
Actual Individual Consumption by Households[a]	34,664	53,772	142,700	19,946	62,029	270,778	34,898	46,418	26,096	128,303	54,102	57,434	26,353	36,577	44,835	56,404	213,002	61,629	200,823	81,569	46,308	47,588
Food and nonalcoholic beverages	14,160	13,259	17,059	7,721	19,055	24,129	9,525	11,337	8,491	28,535	11,914	16,930	13,163	11,087	14,746	9,125	19,373	14,074	19,633	16,462	8,775	10,372
Food	14,266	12,220	15,111	7,531	18,750	22,604	9,571	10,181	7,637	27,187	10,615	15,909	13,221	10,702	13,665	8,934	17,759	13,376	18,594	14,898	8,498	10,123
Bread and cereals	5,303	3,242	3,858	2,157	3,683	2,587	1,907	2,386	1,960	4,096	831	1,569	4,113	1,742	4,219	1,037	3,029	3,759	3,467	2,610	2,172	1,908
Meat and Fish	2,607	1,405	5,130	2,403	4,084	11,916	914	3,540	3,502	8,828	4,354	9,561	1,867	1,869	5,567	4,074	5,806	1,666	6,334	4,116	3,469	2,794
Fruits and Vegetables	3,089	3,670	2,055	1,256	5,645	3,907	3,258	1,735	1,147	5,824	1,586	535	3,712	2,444	1,527	2,634	4,035	1,894	5,852	5,935	1,365	2,840
Other food and nonalcoholic beverages	2,952	4,921	6,210	1,840	5,445	5,719	3,601	3,624	1,897	10,017	5,493	5,974	3,510	4,918	3,451	1,758	6,606	6,223	4,018	3,988	1,704	3,005
Alcoholic beverages, tobacco and narcotics	508	1,404	190	1,056	4,749	1,605	1,700	2,698	2,552	1,105	870	3,742	616	398	819	1,170	2,050	223	3,746	1,330	1,046	902
Clothing and footwear	1,324	1,553	2,571	356	1,695	11,318	309	905	255	2,612	974	1,218	612	1,856	488	1,183	5,518	2,061	7,379	1,524	883	1,440
Clothing	1,238	1,199	2,338	222	1,386	7,546	1,433	829	205	2,418	712	1,000	515	1,632	366	954	4,747	2,000	6,715	1,398	698	1,215
Housing, water, electricity, gas and other fuels[a]	9,977	12,591	31,546	2,861	6,854	45,603	6,714	7,723	4,975	34,048	10,496	6,547	4,939	10,199	6,297	14,275	31,737	12,014	43,004	16,333	7,525	10,628
Furnishings, household equipment and routine household maintenance	1,037	1,171	10,082	280	2,219	14,032	753	1,391	1,118	4,517	2,635	816	363	985	1,066	1,570	8,869	881	6,970	1,830	1,591	1,276
Health and Education[a]	5,473	20,029	35,187	6,682	14,940	46,285	8,352	9,301	6,502	19,673	20,410	22,100	5,886	7,275	10,174	14,966	48,488	16,191	54,540	27,229	15,552	11,754
Health[a]	2,270	7,996	11,675	3,877	5,416	27,326	4,092	3,226	1,904	10,939	10,657	7,946	3,199	3,558	3,331	9,190	25,099	10,077	39,229	14,417	7,403	6,399
Education[a]	3,116	11,937	22,955	2,769	9,352	18,959	4,178	6,102	4,757	9,040	9,783	14,374	2,651	3,627	6,943	6,148	22,967	6,022	17,531	12,598	8,078	5,467
Transportation and Communication	1,111	3,508	18,250	866	5,385	20,066	4,311	5,437	1,303	16,632	5,246	4,558	694	2,163	3,110	6,695	17,180	7,362	21,095	6,762	6,109	5,275
Transportation	1,016	2,477	18,138	859	3,853	11,343	3,482	4,582	966	10,488	2,603	3,762	363	1,683	2,771	5,719	12,916	7,782	17,342	6,944	3,233	4,356
Communication	129	1,058	1,873	32	1,600	8,723	906	1,072	365	5,806	2,274	952	397	536	543	1,301	4,616	240	4,380	598	3,048	1,115
Recreation and culture[a]	364	1,137	4,811	317	337	23,214	191	1,148	388	2,482	520	552	438	1,129	389	1,352	18,717	3,677	9,218	2,348	1,386	986
Restaurants and hotels	764	1,604	3,889	724	143	17,861	326	3,749	1,032	12,176	2,218	277	297	751	2,403	2,643	16,003	1,650	16,003	5,601	2,325	1,925
Miscellaneous goods and services[a]	1,080	3,695	19,327	371	4,582	66,663	3,814	1,851	2,409	10,910	3,725	3,115	464	2,022	5,933	6,582	43,479	6,333	28,722	8,568	2,878	4,942
Individual Consumption Expenditure by Government	369	14,598	37,627	2,062	6,716	19,431	1,652	4,868	2,549	15,348	15,592	13,316	1,274	1,650	3,574	7,386	26,085	8,806	35,982	16,900	6,378	4,813
Collective Consumption Expenditure by Government	2,610	20,275	129,647	728	10,857	29,610	2,591	5,129	8,696	10,565	13,222	13,720	1,388	2,104	5,954	10,574	59,393	5,460	26,933	12,732	4,574	6,367
Gross fixed capital formation	12,116	23,479	136,314	6,210	11,966	65,157	11,289	22,666	17,469	33,145	30,309	18,205	6,295	3,662	11,580	48,304	174,296	16,757	89,960	25,858	18,489	26,628
Machinery and equipment	1,016	5,984	36,894	1,414	2,487	14,687	1,915	1,659	2,597	5,359	9,330	4,045	1,141	717	1,616	7,760	33,838	2,055	24,377	7,222	2,466	4,255
Construction	15,809	19,385	87,811	5,661	9,962	41,876	10,660	29,761	12,574	28,567	17,033	13,568	5,686	2,492	11,059	40,436	78,470	18,849	40,552	14,192	21,390	23,447
Other products	229	82	7,450	31	582	8,594	555	874	2,533	2,824	1,778	1,185	323	406	844	4,434	42,009	703	13,714	1,775	261	2,165
Changes in inventories and Acquisitions less disposals of valuables	304	184	1,064	1,064	1,143	-258	468	869	-0	3,882	-3,303	4,462	2,463	462	-444	1,221	10,905	5,345	3,447	4,280	1,923	953
Balance of Exports and Imports	-1,460	-5,460	32,654	-176	-10,196	21,545	-421	889	-1,197	6,449	6,870	-724	-3,511	-1,377	-3,331	2,552	224,613	-2,295	36,348	-23	33	1,195
Individual Consumption Expenditure by Households[b]	33,209	42,194	111,819	17,767	55,233	251,347	33,305	41,328	23,218	113,199	41,808	46,902	24,560	34,658	40,821	49,543	187,411	53,273	168,267	66,819	40,194	42,967
Individual Consumption Expenditure by Households without Housing[b]	27,320	34,091	91,865	15,265	46,990	213,206	27,947	34,335	19,163	92,721	34,348	40,632	20,260	28,364	35,188	40,585	158,638	43,294	134,971	53,183	34,863	35,548
Government Final Consumption Expenditure	3,216	35,085	167,259	2,580	17,794	49,041	4,310	9,929	11,956	25,439	28,346	26,815	2,666	3,786	9,674	18,100	85,388	13,676	62,320	29,097	10,616	11,238
Domestic Absorption	49,976	95,876	421,491	28,477	85,193	365,287	49,210	76,108	52,709	176,235	92,836	93,456	37,153	40,956	61,360	118,703	458,766	91,361	324,816	125,504	72,703	82,386
Total Consumption	37,383	71,771	242,684	20,860	72,631	300,388	37,154	51,716	33,925	138,881	66,120	69,571	27,840	38,045	50,752	66,711	266,647	67,796	227,437	94,071	51,179	53,711

0 = magnitude is less than half of the unit employed.

AP = Asia and the Pacific; BAN = Bangladesh; BHU = Bhutan; BRU = Brunei Darussalam; CAM = Cambodia; FIJ = Fiji; HKG = Hong Kong, China; IND = India; INO = Indonesia; LAO = Lao People's Democratic Republic; MAL = Malaysia; MLD = Maldives; MON = Mongolia; NEP = Nepal; PAK = Pakistan; PHI = Philippines; PRC = People's Republic of China; SIN = Singapore; SRI = Sri Lanka; TAP = Taipei,China; THA = Thailand; VIE = Viet Nam.

Note: Each real aggregate value is derived by using a purchasing power parity that is specific to that aggregate, so real aggregates may not sum up to the total of their real components for an economy.

a Includes individual consumption expenditure by households, nonprofit institutions serving households, and government.

b Includes expenditure by nonprofit institutions serving households.

Source: Asian Development Bank estimates based on data supplied by the participating economies.

Table A1.7: Per Capita Real Expenditure Index, 2021
(Hong Kong, China = 100)

Expenditure Category	BAN	BHU	BRU	CAM	FIJ	HKG	IND	INO	LAO	MAL	MLD	MON	NEP	PAK	PHI	PRC	SIN	SRI	TAP	THA	VIE	AP
Gross Domestic Product	12	21	122	7	17	100	12	20	13	48	26	23	7	10	14	31	200	22	97	32	18	21
Actual Individual Consumption by Households a	13	20	53	7	23	100	13	17	10	47	20	21	10	14	17	21	79	23	74	30	17	18
Food and nonalcoholic beverages	59	55	71	32	79	100	39	47	35	118	49	70	55	46	61	38	80	58	81	68	36	43
Food	63	54	67	33	83	100	42	45	34	120	47	70	58	47	60	40	79	59	82	66	38	45
Bread and cereals	205	125	149	83	142	100	74	92	76	158	32	61	159	67	163	40	117	145	134	101	84	74
Meat and Fish	22	12	43	20	34	100	8	30	29	74	37	80	16	16	47	34	49	14	53	35	29	23
Fruits and Vegetables	79	94	53	32	144	100	83	44	29	149	41	14	95	63	39	67	103	48	150	152	35	73
Other food and nonalcoholic beverages	52	86	109	32	95	100	63	63	33	175	96	104	61	86	60	31	116	109	70	70	30	53
Alcoholic beverages, tobacco and narcotics	32	87	12	66	296	100	19	168	159	69	54	233	38	25	51	73	128	14	233	83	65	56
Clothing and footwear	12	14	23	3	18	100	15	8	2	23	9	11	5	5	4	10	14	18	65	13	8	13
Clothing	16	16	31	3	18	100	19	11	3	32	9	13	7	22	5	13	63	26	89	19	9	16
Housing, water, electricity, gas and other fuels a	22	28	69	6	15	100	15	17	11	75	23	14	11	22	14	31	70	26	94	36	17	23
Furnishings, household equipment and routine household maintenance	7	8	72	2	16	100	5	10	8	32	19	6	3	7	8	11	63	6	50	13	11	9
Health and Education a	12	43	76	14	32	100	18	20	14	43	44	48	13	16	22	32	105	35	118	59	34	25
Health a	8	29	43	14	20	100	15	12	7	40	39	29	12	13	12	34	92	37	144	53	27	23
Education a	16	63	121	15	49	100	22	32	25	48	52	76	14	19	37	32	121	32	92	66	43	29
Transportation and Communication	6	17	91	15	27	100	21	27	6	83	26	23	3	11	15	33	86	37	105	34	30	26
Transportation	9	22	160	8	34	100	31	40	9	92	23	33	3	15	24	50	114	69	153	61	29	38
Communication	1	12	21	0	18	100	10	12	4	67	26	11	5	6	6	15	53	3	50	7	35	13
Recreation and culture a	2	5	21	1	1	100	1	5	2	11	2	2	2	5	2	6	81	16	40	10	6	4
Restaurants and hotels	4	9	22	4	1	100	2	21	6	68	12	2	2	4	13	15	105	9	90	31	13	11
Miscellaneous goods and services a	2	6	29	1	7	100	6	3	4	16	6	5	1	3	9	10	65	9	43	13	4	7
Individual Consumption Expenditure by Government	2	75	194	11	35	100	9	25	13	79	80	69	7	8	18	38	134	45	185	87	33	25
Collective Consumption Expenditure by Government	9	68	438	2	37	100	9	17	29	36	45	46	5	7	20	36	201	18	91	43	15	22
Gross fixed capital formation	19	36	209	10	18	100	17	35	27	51	47	28	10	6	18	74	268	26	138	40	28	41
Machinery and equipment	7	41	251	10	17	100	13	11	18	36	64	28	8	5	11	53	230	14	166	49	17	29
Construction	38	46	210	14	24	100	25	71	30	68	41	32	14	6	26	97	187	45	97	34	51	56
Other products	3	1	87	0	7	100	6	10	29	33	21	14	4	5	10	52	489	8	160	21	3	25
Changes in inventories and Acquisitions less disposals of valuables	-118	-71	-11,062	-413	-444	100	-182	-337	0	-1,508	1,283	-1,733	-957	-179	172	-474	-4,235	-2,076	-1,339	-1,662	-747	-370
Balance of Exports and Imports	-7	-25	152	-1	-47	100	-2	4	-6	30	32	-3	-16	-6	-15	12	1,043	-11	169	-0	0	6
Individual Consumption Expenditure by Households b	13	17	44	7	22	100	13	16	9	45	17	19	10	14	16	20	75	21	67	27	16	17
Individual Consumption Expenditure by Households without Housing b	13	16	43	7	22	100	13	16	9	43	16	19	10	13	17	19	74	20	63	25	16	17
Government Final Consumption Expenditure	7	72	341	5	36	100	9	20	24	52	58	55	5	8	20	37	174	28	127	59	22	23
Domestic Absorption	14	26	115	8	23	100	13	21	14	48	25	26	10	11	17	32	126	25	89	34	20	23
Total Consumption	12	24	81	7	24	100	12	17	11	46	22	23	9	13	17	22	89	23	76	31	17	18

0 = magnitude is less than half of the unit employed.

AP = Asia and the Pacific; BAN = Bangladesh; BHU = Bhutan; BRU = Brunei Darussalam; CAM = Cambodia; FIJ = Fiji; HKG = Hong Kong, China; IND = India; INO = Indonesia; LAO = Lao People's Democratic Republic; MAL = Malaysia; MLD = Maldives; MON = Mongolia; NEP = Nepal; PAK = Pakistan; PHI = Philippines; PRC = People's Republic of China; SIN = Singapore; SRI = Sri Lanka; TAP = Taipei,China; THA = Thailand; VIE = Viet Nam.

Note: Each real aggregate value is derived by using a purchasing power parity that is specific to that aggregate, so real aggregates may not sum up to the total of their real components for an economy.

a Includes individual consumption expenditure by households, nonprofit institutions serving households, and government.

b Includes expenditure by nonprofit institutions serving households.

Source: Asian Development Bank estimates based on data supplied by the participating economies.

Table A1.8: Per Capita Real Expenditure Index, 2021

(Asia and the Pacific = 100)

Expenditure Category	BAN	BHU	BRU	CAM	FIJ	HKG	IND	INO	LAO	MAL	MLD	MON	NEP	PAK	PHI	PRC	SIN	SRI	TAP	THA	VIE	AP
Gross Domestic Product	56	99	574	33	78	472	57	93	60	225	124	109	34	45	65	146	944	102	459	149	87	100
Actual Individual Consumption by Households[a]	73	113	300	42	130	569	73	98	55	270	114	121	55	77	94	119	448	130	422	171	97	100
Food and nonalcoholic beverages	137	128	164	74	184	233	92	109	82	275	115	163	127	107	142	88	187	136	189	159	85	100
Food	141	121	149	74	185	223	95	101	75	269	105	157	131	106	135	88	175	132	184	147	84	100
Bread and cereals	278	170	202	113	193	136	100	125	103	215	44	82	216	91	221	54	159	197	182	137	114	100
Meat and Fish	93	50	184	86	146	426	33	127	125	316	156	342	67	67	199	146	208	60	227	147	124	100
Fruits and Vegetables	109	129	72	44	199	138	115	61	40	205	56	19	131	86	54	93	142	67	206	209	48	100
Other food and nonalcoholic beverages	98	164	207	61	181	190	120	121	63	333	183	199	117	164	115	59	220	207	134	133	57	100
Alcoholic beverages, tobacco and narcotics	56	156	21	117	526	178	34	299	283	123	96	415	68	44	91	130	227	25	415	147	116	100
Clothing and footwear	92	108	178	25	118	786	118	63	18	181	68	85	42	129	34	82	383	143	512	106	61	100
Clothing	102	99	192	18	114	621	118	68	17	199	59	82	42	134	30	79	391	165	553	115	57	100
Housing, water, electricity, gas and other fuels[a]	94	118	297	27	64	429	63	73	47	320	99	62	46	96	59	134	299	113	405	154	71	100
Furnishings, household equipment and routine household maintenance	81	92	790	22	174	1,100	59	109	88	354	207	64	28	77	84	123	695	69	546	143	125	100
Health and Education[a]	47	170	299	57	127	394	71	79	55	167	174	188	50	62	87	127	413	138	464	232	132	100
Health[a]	35	125	182	61	85	427	64	50	30	171	167	124	50	56	52	144	392	157	613	225	116	100
Education[a]	57	218	420	51	171	347	76	112	87	165	179	263	48	66	127	112	420	110	321	230	148	100
Transportation and Communication	21	67	346	16	102	380	82	103	25	315	99	86	13	41	59	127	326	140	400	128	116	100
Transportation	23	57	416	20	88	260	80	105	22	241	60	86	8	39	64	131	297	179	398	159	74	100
Communication	12	95	168	3	143	782	81	96	33	521	204	85	36	48	49	117	414	21	393	54	273	100
Recreation and culture[a]	37	115	488	32	34	2,354	19	116	39	252	53	56	44	115	39	137	1,898	373	935	238	141	100
Restaurants and hotels	40	83	202	38	7	928	17	195	54	633	115	14	15	39	125	137	970	86	831	291	121	100
Miscellaneous goods and services[a]	22	75	391	8	93	1,349	77	37	49	221	75	63	9	41	120	133	880	128	581	173	58	100
Individual Consumption Expenditure by Government	8	303	782	43	140	404	34	101	53	319	324	277	26	34	74	153	542	183	748	351	133	100
Collective Consumption Expenditure by Government	41	318	2,036	11	171	465	41	81	137	166	208	215	22	33	94	166	933	86	423	200	72	100
Gross fixed capital formation	46	88	512	23	45	245	42	85	66	124	114	68	24	14	43	181	655	63	338	97	69	100
Machinery and equipment	24	141	867	33	58	345	45	39	61	126	219	95	27	17	38	182	795	48	573	170	58	100
Construction	67	83	375	24	42	179	45	127	54	122	73	58	24	11	47	172	335	80	173	61	91	100
Other products	11	4	344	1	27	397	26	40	117	130	82	55	15	19	39	205	1,940	32	633	82	12	100
Changes in inventories and Acquisitions less disposals of valuables	32	19	2,988	112	120	-27	49	91	-0	407	-347	468	258	48	-47	128	1,144	561	362	449	202	100
Balance of Exports and Imports	-122	-457	2,732	-15	-853	1,802	-35	74	-100	539	575	-61	-294	-115	-279	213	18,789	-192	3,040	-2	3	100
Individual Consumption Expenditure by Households[b]	77	98	260	41	129	585	78	96	54	263	97	109	57	81	95	115	436	124	392	156	94	100
Individual Consumption Expenditure by Households without Housing[b]	77	96	258	43	132	600	79	97	54	261	97	114	57	80	99	114	446	122	380	150	98	100
Government Final Consumption Expenditure	29	312	1,488	23	158	436	38	88	106	226	252	239	24	34	86	161	760	122	555	259	94	100
Domestic Absorption	61	116	512	35	103	443	60	92	64	214	113	113	45	50	74	144	557	111	394	152	88	100
Total Consumption	70	134	452	39	135	559	69	96	63	259	123	130	52	71	94	124	496	126	423	175	95	100

0 = magnitude is less than half of the unit employed.

AP = Asia and the Pacific; BAN = Bangladesh; BHU = Bhutan; BRU = Brunei Darussalam; CAM = Cambodia; FIJ = Fiji; HKG = Hong Kong, China; IND = India; INO = Indonesia; LAO = Lao People's Democratic Republic; MAL = Malaysia; MLD = Maldives; MON = Mongolia; NEP = Nepal; PAK = Pakistan; PHI = Philippines; PRC = People's Republic of China; SRI = Sri Lanka; SIN = Singapore; TAP = Taipei,China; THA = Thailand; VIE = Viet Nam.

Note: Each real aggregate value is derived by using a purchasing power parity that is specific to that aggregate, so real aggregates may not sum up to the total of their real components for an economy.

[a] Includes individual consumption expenditure by households, nonprofit institutions serving households, and government.

[b] Includes expenditure by nonprofit institutions serving households.

Source: Asian Development Bank estimates based on data supplied by the participating economies.

Table A1.9: Nominal Expenditure, 2021
(HK$ billion)

Expenditure Category	BAN	BHU	BRU	CAM	FIJ	HKG	IND	INO	LAO	MAL	MLD	MON	NEP	PAK	PHI	PRC	SIN	SRI	TAP	THA	VIE	AP
Gross Domestic Product	3,426.5	21.5	108.9	209.6	33.5	2,867.6	23,899.3	9,223.9	148.3	2,906.2	40.8	118.8	299.0	2,927.0	3,063.6	138,482.0	3,373.5	688.0	6,009.9	3,935.2	2,846.3	204,629.5
Actual Individual Consumption by Households[a]	2,381.6	13.1	32.9	148.0	30.2	2,007.3	15,517.0	5,493.7	72.8	1,889.6	23.0	69.8	258.0	2,592.4	2,468.9	61,568.4	1,105.6	455.9	3,135.3	2,456.3	1,700.8	103,420.5
Food and nonalcoholic beverages	1,223.2	4.6	4.5	68.0	9.5	178.9	4,509.7	1,633.7	32.5	454.3	4.1	25.0	151.3	876.5	888.9	9,948.3	80.9	140.9	382.9	578.4	404.0	21,600.2
Food	1,218.2	4.2	4.0	65.4	9.1	167.6	4,446.3	1,450.7	29.0	429.8	3.6	22.9	149.2	834.4	819.4	9,612.6	74.0	131.7	361.9	510.7	388.7	20,733.3
Bread and cereals	543.0	1.2	0.9	20.0	1.9	19.2	1,008.5	378.7	8.8	72.2	0.3	2.7	54.5	154.6	290.6	1,337.3	13.5	37.4	80.2	109.7	109.1	4,244.4
Meat and Fish	234.1	0.5	1.4	20.8	1.8	88.3	475.1	435.2	12.0	125.5	0.9	10.6	22.5	137.7	284.9	4,045.7	24.5	13.2	115.4	119.3	162.0	6,331.4
Fruits and Vegetables	165.3	1.1	0.7	10.1	2.8	29.0	1,146.8	237.8	4.0	98.2	0.9	1.3	31.1	121.4	212.3	2,352.7	17.2	17.7	116.2	194.0	54.4	4,703.8
Other food and nonalcoholic beverages	280.8	1.8	1.6	17.1	3.0	42.4	1,879.4	582.0	7.8	158.3	2.0	10.4	43.2	462.9	212.3	2,212.5	25.7	72.6	71.0	155.4	78.5	6,320.6
Alcoholic beverages, tobacco and narcotics	48.0	0.4	0.1	5.2	4.9	11.9	337.0	433.0	7.4	31.6	0.6	3.9	11.8	23.0	47.7	1,431.3	19.5	6.1	69.9	67.6	38.3	2,599.0
Clothing and footwear	143.4	0.6	0.9	3.4	1.0	83.9	863.4	173.8	1.0	50.3	0.7	2.4	7.8	178.1	40.9	2,785.9	28.6	17.5	131.2	71.0	45.0	4,631.1
Clothing	127.8	0.5	0.7	2.1	0.8	55.9	702.5	149.9	0.8	44.8	0.5	1.8	6.6	153.3	27.4	2,239.5	23.5	16.3	114.9	64.7	33.9	3,768.1
Housing, water, electricity, gas and other fuels[a]	391.6	1.4	4.8	20.2	2.0	338.1	1,948.7	576.9	9.4	281.2	6.0	7.7	33.2	561.3	295.8	10,271.4	172.0	42.1	527.1	217.3	205.4	15,913.6
Furnishings, household equipment and routine household maintenance	77.6	0.5	2.5	2.5	1.5	104.0	422.3	213.3	4.2	81.2	1.1	1.7	4.8	85.8	65.4	2,253.7	44.2	9.4	138.8	87.3	83.6	3,685.3
Health and Education[a]	197.8	2.3	5.9	24.2	5.0	343.1	2,207.2	693.9	5.9	257.0	4.7	11.7	24.7	304.6	336.0	13,543.1	230.9	48.2	569.4	520.1	307.1	19,642.8
Health[a]	75.8	1.0	1.9	14.1	1.7	202.6	939.6	273.3	2.2	113.7	2.3	4.3	12.9	163.2	132.5	6,036.3	129.8	30.4	345.0	292.4	158.3	8,933.3
Education[a]	122.0	1.4	4.0	10.1	3.3	140.5	1,267.6	420.6	3.7	143.3	2.4	7.4	11.7	141.4	203.5	7,506.8	101.1	17.8	224.4	227.7	148.9	10,709.5
Transportation and Communication	111.7	1.5	4.9	10.2	3.2	148.8	2,661.1	824.5	5.8	332.8	2.8	8.2	10.7	207.7	251.0	6,913.8	130.4	93.3	352.2	307.8	302.1	12,684.3
Transportation	100.1	0.9	4.0	9.8	2.0	84.1	2,304.7	614.3	4.6	168.3	1.2	5.6	7.1	161.8	182.0	5,211.5	95.6	88.7	276.9	260.0	174.8	9,758.2
Communication	11.5	0.6	0.9	0.3	1.1	64.7	356.5	210.2	1.1	164.5	1.7	2.7	3.7	45.9	69.0	1,702.3	34.7	4.6	75.2	47.7	127.3	2,926.1
Recreation and culture[a]	38.2	0.4	1.8	3.2	0.2	172.1	132.3	191.4	1.5	55.3	0.3	1.1	5.5	102.6	29.6	1,769.6	92.0	33.5	186.0	109.6	69.2	2,995.7
Restaurants and hotels	55.5	0.4	1.2	6.0	0.1	132.4	188.5	494.0	3.9	130.4	0.9	0.4	3.4	64.5	137.1	3,413.3	76.6	13.7	252.2	175.4	89.0	5,239.0
Miscellaneous goods and services[a]	94.6	1.1	5.1	3.1	2.8	494.2	2,204.7	259.1	8.8	187.6	1.7	4.6	6.0	188.1	376.5	9,238.0	233.7	53.1	523.7	321.9	128.4	14,336.8
Individual Consumption Expenditure by Government	19.5	1.9	5.8	9.9	2.8	144.0	922.8	362.6	3.1	205.5	3.7	6.8	9.3	113.2	163.1	8,605.8	125.6	34.9	442.7	381.2	138.3	11,702.4
Collective Consumption Expenditure by Government	178.7	3.0	18.7	5.2	5.1	219.5	1,694.1	490.4	16.8	164.0	3.9	10.9	15.6	199.8	314.1	13,361.3	232.8	30.2	374.3	343.2	135.3	17,817.0
Gross fixed capital formation	1,081.4	9.5	33.9	48.0	6.5	483.0	6,871.8	2,840.4	67.4	560.0	11.6	31.9	88.5	394.3	682.6	58,295.5	752.0	181.0	1,579.0	933.4	892.2	75,843.7
Machinery and equipment	187.1	4.8	16.3	22.2	2.3	108.9	2,366.0	457.2	19.0	175.0	5.6	12.9	31.0	151.0	169.1	13,383.1	206.0	46.6	645.7	515.3	231.5	18,756.5
Construction	853.0	4.5	14.3	25.3	3.6	310.4	3,872.4	2,136.9	29.9	292.2	4.8	15.2	48.7	157.9	423.3	37,140.5	294.6	118.4	574.1	290.8	635.9	47,246.7
Other products	41.4	0.1	3.3	0.5	0.6	63.7	633.4	246.4	18.5	92.8	1.1	3.8	8.9	85.3	90.2	7,772.0	251.4	16.0	359.3	127.3	24.8	9,840.5
Changes in inventories and Acquisitions less disposals of valuables	33.4	0.1	9.1	11.4	0.8	-1.9	392.6	157.0	-0.0	82.5	-1.6	8.6	38.9	50.1	-34.9	1,652.3	58.2	71.8	68.2	203.9	114.7	2,915.1
Balance of Exports and Imports	-248.6	-4.1	14.4	-2.9	-9.1	159.7	-576.2	242.4	-8.8	210.1	3.9	-2.4	-102.0	-309.5	-367.0	3,604.5	1,224.9	-50.9	853.0	-1.6	3.3	4,633.2
Individual Consumption Expenditure by Households[b]	2,362.1	11.2	27.1	138.1	27.4	1,863.3	14,594.2	5,131.2	69.7	1,684.1	19.3	63.0	248.7	2,479.2	2,305.7	52,962.7	979.9	421.0	2,692.6	2,075.2	1,562.5	91,718.1
Individual Consumption Expenditure by Households without Housing[b]	2,164.3	10.3	23.3	125.0	25.9	1,580.5	13,280.4	4,709.3	62.6	1,540.8	14.9	57.0	222.4	2,127.6	2,129.3	46,562.8	837.4	390.6	2,240.7	1,937.2	1,474.7	81,516.9
Government Final Consumption Expenditure	198.2	4.9	24.5	15.1	7.9	363.5	2,616.9	852.9	19.9	369.5	7.6	17.7	24.9	313.0	477.3	21,967.0	358.5	65.1	817.0	724.3	273.6	29,519.4
Domestic Absorption	3,675.1	25.6	94.5	212.5	42.6	2,707.9	24,475.5	8,981.5	157.1	2,696.1	36.9	121.2	401.0	3,236.5	3,430.7	134,877.5	2,148.5	738.8	5,156.8	3,936.8	2,843.1	199,996.3
Total Consumption	2,560.3	16.1	51.5	153.2	35.3	2,226.8	17,211.1	5,984.1	89.6	2,053.6	26.9	80.7	273.6	2,792.2	2,783.0	74,929.7	1,338.4	486.1	3,509.6	2,799.5	1,836.1	121,237.5

0.0 = magnitude is less than half of the unit employed.
AP = Asia and the Pacific; BAN = Bangladesh; BHU = Bhutan; BRU = Brunei Darussalam; CAM = Cambodia; FIJ = Fiji; HKG = Hong Kong, China; IND = India; INO = Indonesia; LAO = Lao People's Democratic Republic; MAL = Malaysia; MLD = Maldives;
MON = Mongolia; NEP = Nepal; PAK = Pakistan; PHI = Philippines; PRC = People's Republic of China; SIN = Singapore; SRI = Sri Lanka; TAP = Taipei,China; THA = Thailand; VIE = Viet Nam.
[a] Includes individual consumption expenditure by households, nonprofit institutions serving households, and government.
[b] Includes expenditure by nonprofit institutions serving households.
Source: Asian Development Bank estimates based on data supplied by the participating economies.

Table A1.10: Economy Shares of Nominal Expenditure to Asia and the Pacific, 2021

(%)

Expenditure Category	BAN	BHU	BRU	CAM	FIJ	HKG	IND	INO	LAO	MAL	MLD	MON	NEP	PAK	PHI	PRC	SIN	SRI	TAP	THA	VIE	AP
Gross Domestic Product	1.67	0.01	0.05	0.10	0.02	1.40	11.68	4.51	0.07	1.42	0.02	0.06	0.15	1.43	1.50	67.67	1.65	0.34	2.94	1.92	1.39	100.00
Actual Individual Consumption by Households[a]	2.30	0.01	0.03	0.14	0.03	1.94	15.00	5.31	0.07	1.83	0.02	0.07	0.25	2.51	2.39	59.53	1.07	0.44	3.03	2.38	1.64	100.00
Food and nonalcoholic beverages	5.66	0.02	0.02	0.31	0.04	0.83	20.88	7.56	0.15	2.10	0.02	0.12	0.70	4.06	4.12	46.06	0.37	0.65	1.77	2.68	1.87	100.00
Food	5.88	0.02	0.02	0.32	0.04	0.81	21.45	7.00	0.14	2.07	0.02	0.11	0.72	4.02	3.95	46.36	0.36	0.64	1.75	2.46	1.87	100.00
Bread and cereals	12.79	0.03	0.02	0.47	0.05	0.45	23.76	8.92	0.21	1.70	0.01	0.06	1.28	3.64	6.85	31.51	0.32	0.88	1.89	2.58	2.57	100.00
Meat and Fish	3.70	0.01	0.02	0.33	0.03	1.40	7.50	6.87	0.19	1.98	0.01	0.17	0.36	2.18	4.50	63.90	0.39	0.21	1.82	1.88	2.56	100.00
Fruits and Vegetables	3.51	0.02	0.01	0.22	0.06	0.62	24.38	5.06	0.08	2.09	0.02	0.03	0.66	2.58	2.15	50.02	0.36	0.38	2.47	4.13	1.16	100.00
Other food and nonalcoholic beverages	4.44	0.03	0.03	0.27	0.05	0.67	29.73	9.21	0.12	2.51	0.03	0.16	0.68	7.32	3.36	35.01	0.41	1.15	1.12	2.46	1.24	100.00
Alcoholic beverages, tobacco and narcotics	1.85	0.01	0.00	0.20	0.19	0.46	12.96	16.66	0.28	1.22	0.02	0.15	0.45	0.89	1.83	55.07	0.75	0.24	2.69	2.60	1.47	100.00
Clothing and footwear	3.10	0.01	0.02	0.07	0.02	1.81	18.64	3.75	0.02	1.09	0.01	0.05	0.17	3.85	0.88	60.16	0.62	0.38	2.83	1.53	0.97	100.00
Clothing	3.39	0.01	0.02	0.05	0.02	1.48	18.64	3.98	0.02	1.19	0.01	0.05	0.17	4.07	0.73	59.43	0.62	0.43	3.05	1.72	0.90	100.00
Housing, water, electricity, gas and other fuels[a]	2.46	0.01	0.03	0.13	0.01	2.12	12.25	3.63	0.06	1.77	0.04	0.05	0.21	3.53	1.86	64.54	1.08	0.26	3.31	1.37	1.29	100.00
Furnishings, household equipment and routine household maintenance	2.11	0.01	0.07	0.07	0.04	2.82	11.46	5.79	0.12	2.20	0.03	0.05	0.13	2.33	1.77	61.15	1.20	0.25	3.77	2.37	2.27	100.00
Health and Education[a]	1.01	0.01	0.03	0.12	0.03	1.75	11.24	3.53	0.03	1.31	0.02	0.06	0.13	1.55	1.71	68.95	1.18	0.25	2.90	2.65	1.56	100.00
Health[a]	0.85	0.01	0.02	0.16	0.02	2.27	10.52	3.06	0.02	1.27	0.03	0.05	0.14	1.83	1.48	67.57	1.45	0.34	3.86	3.27	1.77	100.00
Education[a]	1.14	0.01	0.04	0.09	0.03	1.31	11.84	3.93	0.03	1.34	0.02	0.07	0.11	1.32	1.90	70.10	0.94	0.17	2.10	2.13	1.39	100.00
Transportation and Communication	0.88	0.01	0.04	0.08	0.03	1.17	20.98	6.50	0.05	2.62	0.02	0.06	0.08	1.64	1.98	54.51	1.03	0.74	2.78	2.43	2.38	100.00
Transportation	1.03	0.01	0.04	0.10	0.02	0.86	23.62	6.30	0.05	1.72	0.01	0.06	0.07	1.66	1.86	53.41	0.98	0.91	2.84	2.66	1.79	100.00
Communication	0.39	0.02	0.03	0.01	0.04	2.21	12.18	7.18	0.04	5.62	0.06	0.09	0.12	1.57	2.36	58.18	1.19	0.16	2.57	1.63	4.35	100.00
Recreation and culture[a]	1.28	0.01	0.06	0.11	0.01	5.74	4.42	6.39	0.05	1.85	0.01	0.04	0.18	3.42	0.99	59.07	3.07	1.12	6.21	3.66	2.31	100.00
Restaurants and hotels	1.06	0.01	0.02	0.12	0.00	2.53	3.60	9.43	0.07	2.49	0.02	0.01	0.07	1.23	2.62	65.15	1.46	0.26	4.81	3.35	1.70	100.00
Miscellaneous goods and services[a]	0.66	0.01	0.04	0.02	0.02	3.45	15.38	1.81	0.06	1.31	0.01	0.03	0.04	1.31	2.63	64.44	1.63	0.37	3.65	2.24	0.90	100.00
Individual Consumption Expenditure by Government	0.17	0.02	0.05	0.08	0.02	1.23	7.89	3.10	0.03	1.76	0.03	0.06	0.08	0.97	1.39	73.54	1.07	0.30	3.78	3.26	1.18	100.00
Collective Consumption Expenditure by Government	1.00	0.02	0.10	0.03	0.03	1.23	9.51	2.75	0.09	0.92	0.02	0.06	0.09	1.12	1.76	74.99	1.31	0.17	2.10	1.93	0.76	100.00
Gross fixed capital formation	1.43	0.01	0.04	0.06	0.01	0.64	9.06	3.75	0.09	0.74	0.03	0.04	0.12	0.52	0.90	76.86	0.99	0.24	2.08	1.23	1.18	100.00
Machinery and equipment	1.00	0.03	0.09	0.12	0.01	0.58	12.61	2.44	0.10	0.93	0.03	0.07	0.17	0.81	0.90	71.35	1.10	0.25	3.44	2.75	1.23	100.00
Construction	1.81	0.01	0.03	0.05	0.01	0.66	8.20	4.52	0.06	0.62	0.01	0.03	0.10	0.33	0.92	78.61	0.62	0.25	1.22	0.62	1.35	100.00
Other products	0.42	0.00	0.03	0.01	0.01	0.65	6.44	2.50	0.19	0.94	0.01	0.04	0.09	0.87	0.92	78.98	2.55	0.16	3.65	1.29	0.25	100.00
Changes in inventories and Acquisitions less disposals of valuables	1.14	0.00	0.31	0.39	0.03	-0.07	13.47	5.38	-0.00	2.83	-0.05	0.30	1.33	1.72	-1.20	56.68	2.00	2.46	2.34	6.99	3.94	100.00
Balance of Exports and Imports	-5.37	-0.09	0.31	-0.06	-0.20	3.45	-12.44	5.23	-0.19	4.53	0.08	-0.05	-2.20	-6.68	-7.92	77.80	26.44	-1.10	18.41	-0.03	0.07	100.00
Individual Consumption Expenditure by Households[b]	2.58	0.01	0.03	0.15	0.03	2.03	15.91	5.59	0.08	1.84	0.02	0.07	0.27	2.70	2.51	57.75	1.07	0.46	2.94	2.26	1.70	100.00
Individual Consumption Expenditure by Households without Housing[b]	2.65	0.01	0.03	0.15	0.03	1.94	16.29	5.78	0.08	1.89	0.02	0.07	0.27	2.61	2.61	57.12	1.03	0.48	2.75	2.38	1.81	100.00
Government Final Consumption Expenditure	0.67	0.02	0.08	0.05	0.03	1.23	8.86	2.89	0.07	1.25	0.03	0.06	0.08	1.06	1.62	74.42	1.21	0.22	2.77	2.45	0.93	100.00
Domestic Absorption	1.84	0.01	0.05	0.11	0.02	1.35	12.24	4.49	0.08	1.35	0.02	0.06	0.20	1.62	1.72	67.44	1.07	0.37	2.58	1.97	1.42	100.00
Total Consumption	2.11	0.01	0.04	0.13	0.03	1.84	14.20	4.94	0.07	1.69	0.02	0.07	0.23	2.30	2.30	61.80	1.10	0.40	2.89	2.31	1.51	100.00

0.00 = magnitude is less than half of the unit employed.

AP = Asia and the Pacific; BAN = Bangladesh; BHU = Bhutan; BRU = Brunei Darussalam; CAM = Cambodia; FIJ = Fiji; HKG = Hong Kong, China; IND = India; INO = Indonesia; LAO = Lao People's Democratic Republic; MAL = Malaysia; MLD = Maldives; MON = Mongolia; NEP = Nepal; PAK = Pakistan; PHI = Philippines; PRC = People's Republic of China; SIN = Singapore; SRI = Sri Lanka; TAP = Taipei,China; THA = Thailand; VIE = Viet Nam.

[a] Includes individual consumption expenditure by households, nonprofit institutions serving households, and government.

[b] Includes expenditure by nonprofit institutions serving households.

Source: Asian Development Bank estimates based on data supplied by the participating economies.

Table A1.11: Per Capita Nominal Expenditure, 2021
(HK$)

Expenditure Category	BAN	BHU	BRU	CAM	FIJ	HKG	IND	INO	LAO	MAL	MLD	MON	NEP	PAK	PHI	PRC	SIN	SRI	TAP	THA	VIE	AP
Gross Domestic Product	20,125	28,458	247,106	12,632	37,458	386,832	17,481	33,827	20,208	89,211	71,856	36,200	10,288	13,021	27,801	98,050	618,583	31,051	256,084	56,469	28,895	52,799
Actual Individual Consumption by Households[a]	13,988	17,316	74,608	8,917	33,792	270,778	11,350	20,147	9,922	58,004	40,422	21,272	8,879	11,533	22,404	43,593	202,723	20,578	133,598	35,248	17,266	26,685
Food and nonalcoholic beverages	7,184	6,038	10,303	4,098	10,683	24,129	3,299	5,991	4,431	13,946	7,292	7,619	5,205	3,899	8,066	7,044	14,829	6,359	16,316	8,301	4,101	5,573
Food	7,155	5,548	9,008	3,940	10,217	22,604	3,252	5,320	3,951	13,194	6,420	6,982	5,135	3,712	7,436	6,806	13,564	5,945	15,421	7,329	3,946	5,350
Bread and cereals	3,189	1,546	1,987	1,205	2,162	2,587	738	1,389	1,201	2,217	562	826	1,875	688	2,637	947	2,476	1,689	3,419	1,574	1,107	1,095
Meat and Fish	1,375	662	3,104	1,252	2,035	11,916	347	1,596	1,630	3,853	1,595	3,228	775	613	2,585	2,865	4,495	596	4,916	1,712	1,645	1,634
Fruits and Vegetables	971	1,480	1,531	611	3,158	3,907	839	872	541	3,015	1,638	403	1,070	540	918	1,666	3,148	799	4,953	2,784	552	1,214
Other food and nonalcoholic beverages	1,649	2,350	3,682	1,031	3,328	5,719	1,375	2,134	1,060	4,861	3,497	3,161	1,485	2,059	1,927	1,567	4,711	3,275	3,027	2,230	797	1,631
Alcoholic beverages, tobacco and narcotics	282	493	120	312	5,538	1,605	246	1,588	1,007	970	1,018	1,190	407	102	432	1,013	3,585	276	2,977	970	389	671
Clothing and footwear	842	845	1,955	207	1,154	11,318	632	637	138	1,545	1,221	735	268	792	371	1,973	5,249	792	5,591	1,019	457	1,195
Clothing	751	608	1,636	124	900	7,546	514	550	110	1,376	907	536	226	682	249	1,586	4,301	735	4,895	928	344	972
Housing, water, electricity, gas and other fuels[a]	2,300	1,841	10,853	1,218	2,197	45,603	1,425	2,116	1,285	8,633	10,579	2,352	1,144	2,497	2,684	7,273	31,539	1,900	22,459	3,118	2,085	4,106
Furnishings, household equipment and routine household maintenance	456	604	5,586	154	1,642	14,032	309	782	579	2,492	1,962	516	164	382	593	1,596	8,099	424	5,913	1,252	849	951
Health and Education[a]	1,162	3,079	13,411	1,458	5,552	46,285	1,614	2,545	801	7,889	8,257	3,559	850	1,355	3,049	9,589	42,344	2,174	24,262	7,463	3,118	5,068
Health[a]	445	1,263	4,318	851	1,904	27,326	687	1,002	301	3,491	4,102	1,313	445	726	1,203	4,274	23,806	1,372	14,699	4,195	1,607	2,305
Education[a]	717	1,816	9,093	607	3,649	18,959	927	1,543	500	4,398	4,155	2,245	404	629	1,847	5,315	18,538	802	9,564	3,267	1,511	2,763
Transportation and Communication	656	1,928	11,203	613	3,549	20,066	1,946	3,024	787	10,215	4,983	2,505	369	924	2,277	4,895	23,902	4,212	15,006	4,417	3,067	3,273
Transportation	588	1,201	9,140	593	2,285	11,343	1,686	2,253	632	5,165	2,068	1,694	243	720	1,651	3,690	17,538	4,004	11,800	3,732	1,774	2,518
Communication	68	728	2,063	20	1,265	8,723	261	771	155	5,050	2,915	811	126	204	626	1,205	6,364	208	3,206	685	1,292	755
Recreation and culture[a]	224	567	4,156	194	262	23,214	97	702	205	1,699	520	338	189	456	268	1,253	16,879	1,511	7,926	1,573	703	773
Restaurants and hotels	326	488	2,774	364	135	17,861	138	1,812	535	5,758	1,651	130	117	287	1,244	2,417	14,047	617	10,747	2,517	903	1,352
Miscellaneous goods and services[a]	556	1,431	11,650	189	3,078	66,663	1,613	950	1,202	2,938	2,245	1,412	208	837	3,417	6,541	42,856	2,396	22,315	4,618	1,303	3,699
Individual Consumption Expenditure by Government	115	2,483	13,198	597	3,121	19,431	675	1,330	424	6,307	6,510	2,085	320	504	1,480	6,093	23,037	1,575	18,864	5,469	1,404	3,019
Collective Consumption Expenditure by Government	1,050	3,970	42,320	315	5,722	29,610	1,239	1,798	2,292	5,036	6,910	3,314	536	889	2,851	9,460	42,693	1,362	15,949	4,924	1,374	4,597
Gross fixed capital formation	6,352	12,519	76,811	2,890	7,268	65,157	5,026	10,417	9,192	17,189	20,395	9,714	3,046	1,754	6,194	41,275	137,889	8,167	67,283	13,394	9,058	19,569
Machinery and equipment	1,099	6,414	37,041	1,336	2,575	14,687	1,731	1,677	2,594	5,371	9,876	3,930	1,065	672	1,534	9,476	37,780	2,104	27,513	7,394	2,350	4,840
Construction	5,010	6,016	32,385	1,524	4,066	41,876	2,832	7,837	4,070	8,970	8,515	4,627	1,676	703	3,841	26,297	54,012	5,342	24,461	4,172	6,456	12,191
Other products	243	89	7,385	30	627	8,594	463	903	2,528	2,847	2,004	1,158	305	380	819	5,503	46,097	721	15,310	1,827	252	2,539
Changes in inventories and Acquisitions less disposals of valuables	196	114	20,712	686	872	-258	287	576	-0	-2,533	-2,742	2,624	1,338	223	-317	1,170	10,666	3,240	2,905	2,926	1,165	752
Balance of Exports and Imports	-1,460	-5,460	32,654	-176	-10,196	21,545	-421	889	-1,197	6,449	6,870	-724	-3,511	-1,377	-3,331	2,552	224,613	-2,295	36,348	-23	33	1,195
Individual Consumption Expenditure by Households[b]	13,873	14,834	61,410	8,321	30,671	251,347	10,675	18,817	9,499	51,697	33,912	19,187	8,559	11,029	20,923	37,499	179,685	19,002	114,735	29,778	15,862	23,665
Individual Consumption Expenditure by Households without Housing[b]	12,712	13,620	52,901	7,532	29,003	213,206	9,714	17,270	8,534	47,298	26,276	17,352	7,651	9,465	19,322	32,968	153,545	17,629	95,476	27,799	14,971	21,033
Government Final Consumption Expenditure	1,164	6,452	55,517	911	8,843	49,041	1,914	3,128	2,716	11,343	13,420	5,398	856	1,393	4,331	15,553	65,731	2,937	34,813	10,394	2,777	7,617
Domestic Absorption	21,585	33,918	214,452	12,808	47,654	365,287	17,902	32,938	21,406	82,762	64,986	36,924	13,799	14,399	31,132	95,498	393,971	33,347	219,737	56,492	28,862	51,603
Total Consumption	15,038	21,286	116,928	9,232	39,514	300,388	12,589	21,945	12,214	63,040	47,332	24,585	9,415	12,422	25,254	53,053	245,416	21,939	149,548	40,172	18,640	31,282

0 = magnitude is less than half of the unit employed.

AP = Asia and the Pacific; BAN = Bangladesh; BHU = Bhutan; BRU = Brunei Darussalam; CAM = Cambodia; FIJ = Fiji; HKG = Hong Kong, China; IND = India; INO = Indonesia; LAO = Lao People's Democratic Republic; MAL = Malaysia; MLD = Maldives; MON = Mongolia; NEP = Nepal; PAK = Pakistan; PHI = Philippines; PRC = People's Republic of China; SIN = Singapore; SRI = Sri Lanka; TAP = Taipei,China; THA = Thailand; VIE = Viet Nam.

a Includes individual consumption expenditure by households, nonprofit institutions serving households, and government.

b Includes expenditure by nonprofit institutions serving households.

Source: Asian Development Bank estimates based on data supplied by the participating economies.

Table A1.12: Per Capita Nominal Expenditure Index, 2021

(Hong Kong, China = 100)

Expenditure Category	BAN	BHU	BRU	CAM	FIJ	HKG	IND	INO	LAO	MAL	MLD	MON	NEP	PAK	PHI	PRC	SIN	SRI	TAP	THA	VIE	AP
Gross Domestic Product	5	7	64	3	10	100	5	9	5	23	19	9	3	3	7	25	160	8	66	15	7	14
Actual Individual Consumption by Households[a]	5	6	28	3	12	100	4	7	4	21	15	8	3	4	8	16	75	8	49	13	6	10
Food and nonalcoholic beverages	30	25	43	17	44	100	14	25	18	58	30	32	22	16	33	29	61	26	68	34	17	23
Food	32	25	40	17	45	100	14	24	17	58	28	31	23	16	33	30	60	26	68	32	17	24
Bread and cereals	123	60	77	47	84	100	29	54	46	86	22	32	72	27	102	37	96	65	132	61	43	42
Meat and Fish	12	6	26	11	17	100	3	13	14	32	13	27	7	5	22	24	38	5	41	14	14	14
Fruits and Vegetables	25	38	39	16	81	100	21	22	14	77	42	10	27	14	23	43	81	20	127	71	14	31
Other food and nonalcoholic beverages	29	41	64	18	58	100	24	37	19	85	61	55	26	36	34	27	82	57	53	39	14	29
Alcoholic beverages, tobacco and narcotics	18	31	7	19	345	100	15	99	63	60	63	74	25	6	27	63	223	17	185	60	24	42
Clothing and footwear	7	7	17	2	10	100	6	6	1	14	11	6	2	7	3	17	46	7	49	9	4	11
Clothing	10	8	22	2	12	100	7	7	1	18	12	7	3	9	3	21	57	10	65	12	5	13
Housing, water, electricity, gas and other fuels[a]	5	4	24	3	5	100	3	5	3	19	23	5	3	5	6	16	69	4	49	7	5	9
Furnishings, household equipment and routine household maintenance	3	4	40	1	12	100	2	6	4	18	14	4	1	3	4	11	58	3	42	9	6	7
Health and Education[a]	3	7	29	3	12	100	3	5	2	17	18	8	2	3	7	21	91	5	52	16	7	11
Health[a]	2	5	16	3	7	100	3	4	1	13	15	5	2	3	4	16	87	5	54	15	6	8
Education[a]	4	10	48	3	19	100	5	8	3	23	22	12	2	3	10	28	98	4	50	17	8	15
Transportation and Communication	3	10	56	3	18	100	10	15	4	51	25	12	2	5	11	24	119	21	75	22	15	16
Transportation	5	11	81	5	20	100	15	20	6	46	18	15	2	6	15	33	155	35	104	33	16	22
Communication	1	8	24	0	14	100	5	9	2	58	33	9	1	2	7	14	73	2	37	8	15	9
Recreation and culture[a]	1	2	18	1	1	100	0	3	3	7	2	1	1	2	1	5	73	7	34	7	3	3
Restaurants and hotels	2	3	16	2	1	100	1	10	3	22	9	1	1	2	7	14	79	3	60	14	5	8
Miscellaneous goods and services[a]	1	2	17	0	5	100	2	1	2	9	4	2	0	1	5	10	64	4	33	7	2	6
Individual Consumption Expenditure by Government	1	13	68	3	16	100	3	7	2	32	34	11	2	3	8	31	119	8	97	28	7	16
Collective Consumption Expenditure by Government	4	13	143	1	19	100	4	6	8	17	23	11	2	3	10	32	144	5	54	17	5	16
Gross fixed capital formation	10	19	118	4	11	100	8	16	14	26	31	15	5	3	10	63	212	13	103	21	14	30
Machinery and equipment	7	44	252	9	18	100	12	11	18	37	67	27	7	5	10	65	257	14	187	50	16	33
Construction	12	14	77	4	10	100	7	19	10	21	20	11	4	2	9	63	129	13	58	10	15	29
Other products	3	1	86	0	7	100	5	11	29	33	23	13	4	4	10	64	536	8	178	21	15	30
Changes in inventories and Acquisitions less disposals of valuables	-76	-44	-8,043	-267	-339	100	-112	-224	0	-984	1,065	-1,019	-520	-86	123	-454	-4,142	-1,258	-1,128	-1,136	-452	-292
Balance of Exports and Imports	-7	-25	152	-1	-47	100	-2	4	-6	30	32	-3	-16	-6	-15	12	1,043	-11	169	-0	0	6
Individual Consumption Expenditure by Households[b]	6	6	24	3	12	100	4	7	4	21	13	8	3	4	8	15	71	8	46	12	6	9
Individual Consumption Expenditure by Households without Housing[b]	6	6	25	4	14	100	5	8	4	22	12	8	4	4	9	15	72	8	45	13	7	10
Government Final Consumption Expenditure	2	13	113	2	18	100	4	6	6	23	27	11	2	3	9	32	134	6	71	21	6	16
Domestic Absorption	6	9	59	4	13	100	5	9	6	23	18	10	4	4	9	26	108	9	60	15	8	14
Total Consumption	5	7	39	3	13	100	4	7	4	21	16	8	3	4	8	18	82	7	50	13	6	10

0 = magnitude is less than half of the unit employed.

AP = Asia and the Pacific; BAN = Bangladesh; BHU = Bhutan; BRU = Brunei Darussalam; CAM = Cambodia; FIJ = Fiji; HKG = Hong Kong, China; IND = India; INO = Indonesia; LAO = Lao People's Democratic Republic; MAL = Malaysia; MLD = Maldives; MON = Mongolia; NEP = Nepal; PAK = Pakistan; PHI = Philippines; PRC = People's Republic of China; SIN = Singapore; SRI = Sri Lanka; TAP = Taipei,China; THA = Thailand; VIE = Viet Nam.

[a] Includes individual consumption expenditure by households, nonprofit institutions serving households, and government.

[b] Includes expenditure by nonprofit institutions serving households.

Source: Asian Development Bank estimates based on data supplied by the participating economies.

Table A1.13: Per Capita Nominal Expenditure Index, 2021
(Asia and the Pacific = 100)

Expenditure Category	BAN	BHU	BRU	CAM	FIJ	HKG	IND	INO	LAO	MAL	MLD	MON	NEP	PAK	PHI	PRC	SIN	SRI	TAP	THA	VIE	AP
Gross Domestic Product	38	54	468	24	71	733	33	64	38	169	136	69	19	25	53	186	1,172	59	485	107	55	100
Actual Individual Consumption by Households[a]	52	65	280	33	127	1,015	43	75	37	217	151	80	33	43	84	163	760	77	501	132	65	100
Food and nonalcoholic beverages	129	108	185	74	192	433	59	107	80	250	131	137	93	70	145	126	266	114	293	149	74	100
Food	134	104	168	74	191	423	61	99	74	247	120	131	96	69	139	127	254	111	288	137	74	100
Bread and cereals	291	141	181	110	197	236	67	127	110	202	51	75	171	63	241	86	226	154	312	144	101	100
Meat and Fish	84	41	190	77	125	729	21	98	100	236	98	198	47	38	158	175	275	36	301	105	101	100
Fruits and Vegetables	80	122	126	50	260	322	69	72	45	248	135	33	88	44	76	137	259	66	408	229	45	100
Other food and nonalcoholic beverages	101	144	226	63	204	351	84	131	65	298	214	194	91	126	118	96	289	201	186	137	49	100
Alcoholic beverages, tobacco and narcotics	42	74	18	47	826	239	37	237	150	145	152	177	61	15	64	151	535	41	444	145	58	100
Clothing and footwear	71	71	164	17	97	947	53	53	12	129	102	62	22	66	31	165	439	66	468	85	38	100
Clothing	77	63	168	13	93	776	53	57	11	142	93	55	23	70	26	163	442	76	503	95	35	100
Housing, water, electricity, gas and other fuels[a]	56	45	264	30	54	1,111	35	52	31	210	258	57	28	61	65	177	768	46	547	76	51	100
Furnishings, household equipment and routine household maintenance	48	64	587	16	173	1,476	32	82	61	262	206	54	17	40	62	168	852	45	622	132	89	100
Health and Education[a]	23	61	265	29	110	913	32	50	16	156	163	70	17	27	60	189	835	43	479	147	62	100
Health[a]	19	55	187	37	83	1,186	30	43	13	151	178	57	19	32	52	185	1,033	60	638	182	70	100
Education[a]	26	66	329	22	132	686	34	56	18	159	150	81	15	23	67	192	671	29	346	118	55	100
Transportation and Communication	20	59	342	19	108	613	59	92	24	312	152	77	11	28	70	150	730	129	459	135	94	100
Transportation	23	48	363	24	91	451	67	89	25	205	82	67	10	29	66	147	697	159	469	148	70	100
Communication	9	96	273	3	168	1,155	35	102	20	669	386	107	17	27	83	160	843	28	425	91	171	100
Recreation and culture[a]	29	73	538	25	34	3,003	13	91	27	220	67	44	25	59	35	162	2,184	195	1,025	204	91	100
Restaurants and hotels	24	36	205	27	10	1,321	10	134	40	296	122	10	9	21	92	179	1,039	46	795	186	67	100
Miscellaneous goods and services[a]	15	39	315	5	83	1,802	44	26	32	156	79	38	6	23	92	177	1,159	65	603	125	35	100
Individual Consumption Expenditure by Government	4	82	437	20	103	644	22	44	14	209	216	69	11	17	49	202	763	52	625	181	46	100
Collective Consumption Expenditure by Government	23	86	921	7	124	644	27	39	50	110	150	72	12	19	62	206	929	30	347	107	30	100
Gross fixed capital formation	32	64	393	15	37	333	26	53	47	88	104	50	16	9	32	211	705	42	344	68	46	100
Machinery and equipment	23	133	765	28	53	303	36	35	54	111	204	81	22	14	32	196	781	43	568	153	49	100
Construction	41	49	266	12	33	344	23	64	33	74	70	38	14	6	32	216	443	44	201	34	53	100
Other products	10	4	291	1	25	338	18	36	100	112	79	46	12	15	32	217	1,816	28	603	72	10	100
Changes in inventories and Acquisitions less disposals of valuables	26	15	2,754	91	116	-34	38	77	-0	337	-365	349	178	30	-42	156	1,418	431	386	389	155	100
Balance of Exports and Imports	-122	-457	2,732	-15	-853	1,802	-35	74	-100	539	575	-61	-294	-115	-279	213	18,789	-192	3,040	-2	3	100
Individual Consumption Expenditure by Households[b]	59	63	259	35	130	1,062	45	80	40	218	143	81	36	47	88	158	759	80	485	126	67	100
Individual Consumption Expenditure by Households without Housing[b]	60	65	252	36	138	1,014	46	82	41	225	125	83	36	45	92	157	730	84	454	132	71	100
Government Final Consumption Expenditure	15	85	729	12	116	644	25	41	36	149	176	71	11	18	57	204	863	39	457	136	36	100
Domestic Absorption	42	66	416	25	92	708	35	64	41	160	126	72	27	28	60	185	763	65	426	109	56	100
Total Consumption	48	68	374	30	126	960	40	70	39	202	151	79	30	40	81	170	785	70	478	128	60	100

0 = magnitude is less than half of the unit employed.

AP = Asia and the Pacific; BAN = Bangladesh; BHU = Bhutan; BRU = Brunei Darussalam; CAM = Cambodia; FIJ = Fiji; HKG = Hong Kong, China; IND = India; INO = Indonesia; LAO = Lao People's Democratic Republic; MAL = Malaysia; MLD = Maldives; MON = Mongolia; NEP = Nepal; PAK = Pakistan; PHI = Philippines; PRC = People's Republic of China; SIN = Singapore; SRI = Sri Lanka; TAP = Taipei,China; THA = Thailand; VIE = Viet Nam.

[a] Includes individual consumption expenditure by households, nonprofit institutions serving households, and government.

[b] Includes expenditure by nonprofit institutions serving households.

Source: Asian Development Bank estimates based on data supplied by the participating economies.

Table A1.14: Shares of Nominal Expenditure, 2021

(%)

Expenditure Category	BAN	BHU	BRU	CAM	FIJ	HKG	IND	INO	LAO	MAL	MLD	MON	NEP	PAK	PHI	PRC	SIN	SRI	TAP	THA	VIE	AP
Gross Domestic Product	100.00	100.00	100.00	100.00	100.00	100.00	100.00	100.00	100.00	100.00	100.00	100.00	100.00	100.00	100.00	100.00	100.00	100.00	100.00	100.00	100.00	100.00
Actual Individual Consumption by Households[a]	69.50	60.85	30.19	70.59	90.21	70.00	64.93	59.56	49.10	65.02	56.25	58.76	86.30	88.57	80.59	44.46	32.77	66.27	52.17	62.42	59.75	50.54
Food and nonalcoholic beverages	35.70	21.22	4.17	32.44	28.52	6.24	18.87	17.71	21.93	15.63	10.15	21.05	50.59	29.95	29.01	7.18	2.40	20.48	6.37	14.70	14.19	10.56
Food	35.55	19.50	3.65	31.19	27.27	5.84	18.60	15.73	19.55	14.79	8.93	19.29	49.92	28.51	26.75	6.94	2.19	19.14	6.02	12.98	13.66	10.13
Bread and cereals	15.85	5.43	0.80	9.54	5.77	0.67	4.22	4.11	5.94	2.49	0.78	2.28	18.22	5.28	9.48	0.97	0.40	5.44	1.34	2.79	3.83	2.07
Meat and Fish	6.83	2.33	1.26	9.91	5.43	3.08	1.99	4.72	8.06	4.32	2.22	8.92	7.53	4.70	9.30	2.92	0.73	1.92	1.92	3.03	5.69	3.09
Fruits and Vegetables	4.82	5.20	0.62	4.83	8.43	1.01	4.80	2.58	2.68	3.38	2.28	1.11	10.40	4.15	3.30	1.70	0.51	2.57	1.93	4.93	1.91	2.30
Other food and nonalcoholic beverages	8.20	8.26	1.49	8.16	8.88	1.48	7.86	6.31	5.24	5.45	4.87	8.73	14.44	15.81	6.93	1.60	0.76	10.55	1.18	3.95	2.76	3.09
Alcoholic beverages, tobacco and narcotics	1.40	1.73	0.05	2.47	14.78	0.41	1.41	1.88	4.98	1.09	1.42	3.29	3.95	6.09	1.56	1.03	0.58	0.89	1.16	1.72	1.35	1.27
Clothing and footwear	4.19	2.97	0.79	1.64	3.08	2.93	3.61	1.63	0.68	1.73	1.70	2.61	2.20	5.24	1.33	2.01	0.85	2.55	2.18	1.80	1.58	2.26
Clothing	3.73	2.14	0.66	0.98	2.40	1.95	2.94	1.43	0.55	1.54	1.26	1.48	2.20	5.24	0.89	1.62	0.70	2.37	1.91	1.64	1.19	1.84
Housing, water, electricity, gas and other fuels[a]	11.43	6.47	4.39	9.64	5.87	11.79	8.15	6.25	6.36	9.68	14.72	6.50	11.12	19.18	9.66	7.42	5.10	6.12	8.77	5.52	7.22	7.78
Furnishings, household equipment and routine household maintenance	2.27	2.12	2.26	1.22	4.38	3.63	1.77	2.31	2.86	2.79	2.73	1.43	1.60	2.93	2.13	1.63	1.31	1.36	2.31	2.22	2.94	1.80
Health and Education[a]	5.77	10.82	5.43	11.54	14.82	11.97	9.24	7.52	3.96	8.84	11.49	9.83	8.26	10.41	10.97	9.78	6.85	7.00	9.47	13.22	10.79	9.60
Health[a]	2.21	4.44	1.75	6.74	5.08	7.06	3.93	2.96	1.49	3.91	5.71	3.63	4.33	5.58	4.33	4.36	3.85	4.42	5.74	7.43	5.56	4.37
Education[a]	3.56	6.38	3.68	4.80	9.74	4.90	5.30	4.56	2.47	4.93	5.78	6.20	3.93	4.83	6.64	5.42	3.00	2.58	3.73	5.79	5.23	5.23
Transportation and Communication	3.26	6.78	4.53	4.85	9.48	5.19	11.13	8.94	3.89	11.45	6.93	6.92	3.58	7.10	8.19	4.99	3.86	13.56	5.86	7.82	10.61	6.20
Transportation	2.92	4.22	3.70	4.69	6.10	2.93	9.64	6.66	3.13	5.79	2.88	4.68	2.36	5.53	5.94	3.76	2.84	12.89	4.61	6.61	6.14	4.77
Communication	0.34	2.56	0.83	0.16	3.38	2.26	1.49	2.28	0.76	5.66	4.06	2.24	1.22	1.57	2.25	1.23	1.03	0.67	1.25	1.21	4.47	1.43
Recreation and culture[a]	1.11	1.99	1.68	1.54	0.70	6.00	0.55	2.08	1.02	1.90	0.72	0.93	1.84	3.50	0.97	1.28	2.73	4.87	3.10	2.79	2.43	1.46
Restaurants and hotels	1.62	1.71	1.12	2.88	0.36	4.62	0.79	5.36	2.65	4.49	2.30	0.36	1.14	2.20	4.48	2.46	2.27	1.99	4.20	4.46	3.13	2.56
Miscellaneous goods and services[a]	2.76	5.03	4.71	1.49	8.22	17.23	9.22	2.81	5.95	6.45	4.09	3.90	2.02	6.43	12.29	6.67	6.93	7.72	8.71	8.18	4.51	7.01
Individual Consumption Expenditure by Government	0.57	8.72	5.34	4.72	8.33	5.02	3.86	3.93	2.10	7.07	9.06	5.76	3.11	3.87	5.33	6.21	3.72	5.07	7.37	9.69	4.86	5.72
Collective Consumption Expenditure by Government	5.22	13.95	17.13	2.49	15.27	7.65	7.09	5.32	11.34	5.64	9.62	9.15	5.21	6.83	10.25	9.65	6.90	4.39	6.23	8.72	4.75	8.71
Gross fixed capital formation	31.56	43.99	31.08	22.88	19.40	16.84	28.75	30.79	45.48	19.27	28.38	26.84	29.60	13.47	22.28	42.10	22.29	26.30	26.27	23.72	31.35	37.06
Machinery and equipment	5.46	22.54	14.99	12.06	6.87	10.83	9.90	4.96	12.83	6.02	13.74	10.86	10.35	5.16	5.52	9.66	6.11	6.78	10.74	13.09	8.13	9.17
Construction	24.89	21.14	13.11	10.86	10.86	2.22	16.20	23.17	20.14	10.05	11.85	12.78	16.29	5.40	13.82	26.82	8.73	17.20	9.55	7.39	22.34	23.09
Other products	1.21	0.31	2.99	0.24	1.67	3.79	2.65	2.67	12.51	3.19	2.79	3.20	2.96	2.91	2.94	5.61	7.45	2.32	5.98	3.24	0.87	4.81
Changes in inventories and Acquisitions less disposals of valuables	0.97	0.40	8.38	5.43	2.33	-0.07	1.64	1.70	-0.00	2.84	-3.82	7.25	13.00	1.71	-1.14	1.19	1.72	10.43	1.13	5.18	4.03	1.42
Balance of Exports and Imports	-7.25	-19.18	13.21	-1.39	-27.22	5.57	-2.41	2.63	-5.92	7.23	9.56	-2.00	-34.13	-10.58	-11.98	2.60	36.31	-7.39	14.19	-0.04	0.12	2.26
Individual Consumption Expenditure by Households[b]	68.93	52.12	24.85	65.87	81.88	64.98	61.07	55.63	47.00	57.95	47.19	53.00	83.20	84.70	75.26	38.25	29.05	61.20	44.80	52.73	54.90	44.82
Individual Consumption Expenditure by Households without Housing[b]	63.16	47.86	21.41	59.62	77.43	55.12	55.57	51.06	42.23	53.02	36.57	47.93	74.37	72.69	69.50	33.62	24.82	56.78	37.28	49.23	51.81	39.84
Government Final Consumption Expenditure	5.79	22.67	22.47	7.21	23.61	12.68	10.95	9.25	13.44	12.71	18.68	14.91	8.32	10.69	15.58	15.86	10.63	9.46	13.59	18.41	9.61	14.43
Domestic Absorption	107.25	119.18	86.79	101.39	127.22	94.43	102.41	97.37	105.92	92.77	90.44	102.00	134.13	110.58	111.98	97.40	63.69	107.39	85.81	100.04	99.88	97.74
Total Consumption	74.72	74.80	47.32	73.08	105.49	77.65	72.02	64.88	60.44	70.66	65.87	67.92	91.52	95.40	90.84	54.11	39.67	70.66	58.40	71.14	64.51	59.25

0.00 = magnitude is less than half of the unit employed.

AP = Asia and the Pacific; BAN = Bangladesh; BHU = Bhutan; BRU = Brunei Darussalam; CAM = Cambodia; FIJ = Fiji; HKG = Hong Kong, China; IND = India; INO = Indonesia; LAO = Lao People's Democratic Republic; MAL = Malaysia; MLD = Maldives; MON = Mongolia; NEP = Nepal; PAK = Pakistan; PHI = Philippines; PRC = People's Republic of China; SIN = Singapore; SRI = Sri Lanka; TAP = Taipei,China; THA = Thailand; VIE = Viet Nam.

a Includes individual consumption expenditure by households, nonprofit institutions serving households, and government.

b Includes expenditure by nonprofit institutions serving households.

Source: Asian Development Bank estimates based on data supplied by the participating economies.

Table A1.15: Gross Domestic Product, 2021
(billion local currency units)

Expenditure Category	BAN	BHU	BRU	CAM	FIJ	HKG	IND	INO	LAO	MAL	MLD	MON	NEP	PAK	PHI	PRC	SIN	SRI	TAP	THA	VIE
Gross Domestic Product	37,509.51	204.66	18.82	110,505.92	8.91	2,867.62	227,242.95	16,976,751.40	184,982.07	1,548.90	80.77	43,555.48	4,543.22	61,229.90	19,410.61	114,923.70	583.22	17,600.19	21,663.23	16,188.61	8,479,666.50
Actual Individual Consumption by Households[a]	26,070.79	124.53	5.68	78,008.46	8.04	2,007.30	147,541.10	10,111,243.17	90,825.71	1,007.08	45.44	25,593.91	3,920.95	54,230.23	15,642.22	51,094.51	191.13	11,663.57	11,301.63	10,104.92	5,066,959.22
Food and nonalcoholic beverages	13,390.41	43.42	0.78	35,853.22	2.54	178.87	42,879.74	3,006,879.01	40,564.03	242.14	8.20	9,166.77	2,298.42	18,336.10	5,631.92	8,255.87	13.98	3,604.21	1,380.22	2,379.63	1,203,613.25
Food	13,335.10	39.90	0.69	34,464.86	2.43	167.56	42,276.83	2,670,091.00	36,169.64	229.07	7.22	8,400.86	2,267.78	17,454.13	5,191.63	7,977.30	12.79	3,369.47	1,304.53	2,101.00	1,157,938.28
Bread and cereals	5,944.57	11.12	0.15	10,539.52	0.51	19.18	9,589.10	696,977.75	10,991.77	38.49	0.63	993.95	827.88	3,234.08	1,841.01	1,109.83	2.33	957.20	289.25	451.32	324,980.43
Meat and Fish	2,562.58	4.76	0.24	10,951.55	0.48	88.34	4,517.26	801,018.55	14,916.77	66.90	1.79	3,884.17	342.23	2,880.84	1,804.81	3,357.46	4.24	337.97	415.90	490.88	482,703.86
Fruits and Vegetables	1,809.03	10.65	0.12	5,340.82	0.75	28.96	10,903.80	437,733.80	4,954.09	52.35	1.84	485.42	472.40	2,538.69	640.96	1,952.43	2.97	452.63	419.03	798.22	161,974.07
Other food and nonalcoholic beverages	3,074.22	16.90	0.28	9,021.33	0.79	42.39	17,869.58	1,071,148.91	9,701.40	84.39	3.93	3,803.24	655.92	9,682.50	1,345.14	1,836.15	4.44	1,856.41	256.04	639.21	233,954.89
Alcoholic beverages, tobacco and narcotics	524.95	3.55	0.01	2,733.22	1.32	11.90	3,203.95	796,974.37	9,218.03	16.83	1.14	1,431.84	179.53	481.93	301.92	1,187.81	3.38	156.59	251.81	277.95	114,084.04
Clothing and footwear	1,570.22	6.08	0.15	1,814.81	0.27	83.90	8,209.89	319,886.33	1,266.62	26.82	1.37	884.47	118.45	3,726.03	259.08	2,311.97	4.95	448.74	472.93	292.17	134,191.57
Clothing	1,399.20	4.37	0.12	1,085.80	0.21	55.94	6,679.49	275,935.27	1,010.20	23.89	1.02	644.68	100.00	3,206.44	173.62	1,858.53	4.06	416.79	414.10	265.96	100,995.81
Housing, water, electricity, gas and other fuels[a]	4,286.26	13.24	0.83	10,657.26	0.52	338.06	18,528.71	1,061,804.65	11,761.35	149.90	11.89	2,830.18	505.25	11,742.43	1,874.14	8,524.06	29.74	1,076.82	1,899.94	893.97	611,942.36
Furnishings, household equipment and routine household maintenance	849.97	4.35	0.43	1,343.90	0.39	104.02	4,015.28	392,666.89	5,295.75	43.27	2.21	621.16	72.48	1,795.74	414.18	1,870.28	7.64	240.16	500.19	358.97	249,119.06
Health and Education[a]	2,165.52	22.14	1.02	12,751.42	1.32	343.12	20,986.45	1,277,094.35	7,331.03	136.97	9.28	4,281.63	375.23	6,372.27	2,128.99	11,239.20	39.92	1,232.24	2,052.46	2,139.41	915,014.47
Health[a]	830.10	9.08	0.33	7,443.63	0.45	202.57	8,933.86	502,930.97	2,758.00	60.61	4.61	1,580.17	196.67	3,414.33	839.69	5,009.43	22.44	777.68	1,243.41	1,202.76	471,479.34
Education[a]	1,335.42	13.06	0.69	5,307.79	0.87	140.55	12,052.59	774,163.39	4,573.03	76.36	4.67	2,701.46	178.55	2,957.94	1,289.30	6,229.77	17.48	454.56	809.05	936.65	443,535.13
Transportation and Communication	1,222.68	13.87	0.85	5,360.63	0.84	148.75	25,302.95	1,517,461.90	7,202.77	177.36	5.60	3,013.81	162.87	4,345.04	1,590.12	5,737.65	22.54	2,387.46	1,269.43	1,266.20	899,941.24
Transportation	1,096.29	8.63	0.70	5,186.03	0.54	84.09	21,913.55	1,130,666.00	5,787.82	89.68	2.32	2,038.02	107.35	3,385.62	1,152.84	4,324.95	16.54	2,269.43	998.23	1,069.77	520,732.21
Communication	126.39	5.23	0.16	174.60	0.30	64.66	3,389.40	386,795.91	1,414.95	87.67	3.28	975.79	55.52	959.41	437.28	1,412.71	6.00	118.03	271.20	196.43	379,209.03
Recreation and culture[a]	418.13	4.08	0.32	1,700.00	0.06	172.09	1,258.09	352,249.09	1,878.42	29.50	0.58	406.79	83.64	2,145.93	187.42	1,468.58	15.91	856.38	670.48	451.07	206,250.33
Restaurants and hotels	607.05	3.51	0.21	3,187.94	0.03	132.41	1,792.01	909,182.31	4,894.03	69.52	1.86	156.60	51.82	1,348.96	868.81	2,832.66	13.24	349.55	909.12	721.51	265,038.04
Miscellaneous goods and services[a]	1,035.61	10.29	0.89	1,650.90	0.73	494.18	20,963.01	476,944.26	11,000.76	99.96	3.30	1,698.85	91.76	3,935.80	2,385.64	7,666.42	40.41	1,358.14	1,887.70	1,324.04	382,512.90
Individual Consumption Expenditure by Government	213.66	17.85	1.01	5,218.56	0.74	144.04	8,773.98	667,277.85	3,878.44	109.51	7.32	2,508.38	141.12	2,367.73	1,033.67	7,141.76	21.72	892.77	1,595.76	1,568.00	411,902.06
Collective Consumption Expenditure by Government	1,956.44	28.55	3.22	2,752.75	1.36	219.50	16,108.19	902,552.44	20,980.09	87.43	7.77	3,986.93	236.90	4,180.44	1,990.35	11,088.26	40.25	771.86	1,349.23	1,411.68	403,114.00
Gross fixed capital formation	11,838.10	90.03	5.85	25,280.92	1.73	483.01	65,339.45	5,227,853.94	84,137.37	298.44	22.93	11,688.26	1,344.96	8,247.37	4,324.55	48,378.38	130.01	4,629.24	5,691.78	3,839.68	2,658,068.80
Machinery and equipment	2,047.85	46.12	2.82	11,687.05	0.61	108.88	22,496.62	841,405.96	23,742.32	93.26	11.10	4,728.49	470.42	3,158.65	1,071.21	11,106.37	35.62	1,192.73	2,327.41	2,119.75	689,690.08
Construction	9,337.49	43.27	2.47	13,329.64	0.97	310.43	36,820.62	3,933,012.08	37,258.57	155.74	9.57	5,566.75	740.00	3,304.08	2,681.78	30,822.20	50.92	3,028.10	2,069.26	1,196.10	1,894,545.15
Other products	452.76	0.64	0.56	264.24	0.15	63.71	6,022.21	453,435.90	23,136.48	49.44	2.25	1,393.02	134.54	1,784.64	571.55	6,449.81	43.46	408.41	1,295.11	523.82	73,833.57
Changes in inventories and Acquisitions less disposals of valuables	365.33	0.82	1.58	6,004.07	0.21	-1.91	3,733.11	288,892.89	-1.02	43.97	-3.08	3,157.64	590.83	1,047.03	-221.00	1,371.21	10.06	1,836.57	245.79	838.81	341,762.62
Balance of Exports and Imports	-2,721.15	-39.26	2.49	-1,540.29	-2.43	159.71	-5,478.91	446,208.96	-10,960.09	111.97	7.72	-871.26	-1,550.41	-6,475.18	-2,325.50	2,991.34	211.77	-1,301.05	3,074.80	-6.48	9,761.87
Individual Consumption Expenditure by Households[b]	25,857.13	106.68	4.68	72,789.90	7.30	1,863.26	138,767.13	9,443,965.32	86,947.27	897.57	38.12	23,085.53	3,779.83	51,862.49	14,608.55	43,952.75	169.41	10,770.80	9,705.88	8,536.92	4,655,057.16
Individual Consumption Expenditure by Households without Housing[b]	23,691.66	97.95	4.03	65,886.13	6.90	1,580.52	126,274.38	8,667,573.46	78,117.04	821.19	29.54	20,878.19	3,378.87	44,507.45	13,490.71	38,641.62	144.77	9,992.51	8,076.74	7,969.44	4,393,478.13
Government Final Consumption Expenditure	2,170.10	46.40	4.23	7,971.31	2.10	363.55	24,882.16	1,569,830.29	24,858.53	196.94	15.09	6,495.31	378.01	6,548.17	3,024.02	18,230.02	61.97	1,664.63	2,944.99	2,979.68	815,016.06
Domestic Absorption	40,230.66	243.93	16.33	112,046.20	11.34	2,707.91	232,721.85	16,530,542.44	195,942.16	1,436.92	73.05	44,426.75	6,093.63	67,705.07	21,736.11	111,932.36	371.45	18,901.24	18,588.43	16,195.09	8,469,904.63
Total Consumption	28,027.23	153.08	8.91	80,761.21	9.40	2,226.80	163,649.29	11,013,795.61	111,805.81	1,094.51	53.21	29,580.84	4,157.84	58,410.67	17,632.56	62,182.77	231.39	12,435.43	12,650.87	11,516.60	5,470,073.22

BAN = Bangladesh; BHU = Bhutan; BRU = Brunei Darussalam; CAM = Cambodia; FIJ = Fiji; HKG = Hong Kong, China; IND = India; INO = Indonesia; LAO = Lao People's Democratic Republic; MAL = Malaysia; MLD = Maldives; MON = Mongolia; NEP = Nepal; PAK = Pakistan; PHI = Philippines; PRC = People's Republic of China; SIN = Singapore; SRI = Sri Lanka; TAP = Taipei,China; THA = Thailand; VIE = Viet Nam.

Note: Expenditure aggregates in local currency units presented are the best possible estimates provided by the participating economies, using most recent available data sources, and some of these aggregates may be different from the published expenditure estimates by the economies.

a Includes individual consumption expenditure by households, nonprofit institutions serving households, and government.

b Includes expenditure by nonprofit institutions serving households.

Source: Asian Development Bank estimates.

Appendix 2: Statistical Tables on Purchasing Power Parities and Real Expenditures, 2017 Revised

The tables in this appendix present the revised key results for 22 participating economies[1] in the 2017 International Comparison Program (ICP) for Asia and the Pacific. Thirty-five expenditure aggregates are presented including gross domestic product (GDP), its main aggregates, and selected expenditure aggregates at levels below the main aggregates. The main aggregates include individual consumption expenditure by households and nonprofit institutions serving households, individual consumption expenditure by government, collective consumption expenditure by government, government final consumption expenditure, gross fixed capital formation, changes in inventories and net acquisitions of valuables, and balance of exports and imports. These expenditure aggregates were derived using the Gini–Eltetö–Köves–Szulc method. Because each real expenditure aggregate is derived by dividing nominal expenditures measured in local currency units by a purchasing power parity specific to the aggregate, the sum of real values of components of GDP will not be equal to the real value of GDP; thus, real expenditures are not additive for a particular economy. For the expenditures in local currency units, participating economies allocated statistical discrepancy (if any) to one or more basic headings based on their best judgment; and for some economies, financial year-based estimates were converted to calendar year. Due to these adjustments, the expenditures in local currency units in the table for some expenditure aggregates may differ from the published expenditure estimates by the economies.

The results are based on (i) revisions in the 2017 estimates of GDP, population, and exchange rates; (ii) implementation of a new, hybrid approach of estimating actual and imputed rentals for housing; (iii) updates to the productivity-adjusted PPPs for government; and (iv) uniform treatment of concepts across economies and over the two cycles.

The results presented in these tables are produced by the Asian Development Bank as the ICP regional implementing agency for Asia and the Pacific, based on data supplied by all the participating economies, in accordance with the methodology recommended by the ICP Technical Advisory Group, and approved by the Asia and the Pacific Regional Advisory Board. As such, these results are not produced by participating economies as part of their official statistics.

The following 15 indicator tables in this appendix present data for the 35 expenditure categories.

Table A2.1:   Purchasing Power Parities, 2017 Revised (Hong Kong, China as base)
Table A2.2:   Price Level Indexes, 2017 Revised (Hong Kong, China = 100)
Table A2.3:   Price Level Indexes, 2017 Revised (Asia and the Pacific = 100)
Table A2.4:   Real Expenditure, 2017 Revised (HK$ billion)
Table A2.5:   Economy Shares of Real Expenditure to Asia and the Pacific, 2017 Revised (%)
Table A2.6:   Per Capita Real Expenditure, 2017 Revised (HK$)
Table A2.7:   Per Capita Real Expenditure Index, 2017 Revised (Hong Kong, China = 100)
Table A2.8:   Per Capita Real Expenditure Index, 2017 Revised (Asia and the Pacific = 100)
Table A2.9:   Nominal Expenditure, 2017 Revised (HK$ billion)

---

[1]   Twenty-two economies participated in the 2017 ICP in Asia and the Pacific. These include the 21 economies that participated in the 2021 ICP with the then-participation of Myanmar.

Table A2.10:   Economy Shares of Nominal Expenditure to Asia and the Pacific, 2017 Revised (%)

Table A2.11:   Per Capita Nominal Expenditure, 2017 Revised (HK$)

Table A2.12:   Per Capita Nominal Expenditure Index, 2017 Revised (Hong Kong, China = 100)

Table A2.13:   Per Capita Nominal Expenditure Index, 2017 Revised (Asia and the Pacific = 100)

Table A2.14:   Shares of Nominal Expenditure, 2017 Revised (%)

Table A2.15:   Gross Domestic Product, 2017 Revised (billion local currency units)

Table A2.1: Purchasing Power Parities, 2017 Revised
(Hong Kong, China as Base)

Expenditure Category	BAN	BHU	BRU	CAM	FIJ	HKG	IND	INO	LAO	MAL	MLD	MON	MYA	NEP	PAK	PHI	PRC	SIN	SRI	TAP	THA	VIE
Gross Domestic Product	4.84	3.16	0.10	241.32	0.15	1.00	3.37	783.50	462.58	0.26	1.35	132.06	60.40	5.02	5.48	3.25	0.67	0.15	8.12	2.57	2.04	1,187.99
Actual Individual Consumption by Households[a]	4.41	2.91	0.10	232.87	0.15	1.00	3.12	782.91	460.69	0.26	1.46	127.28	59.78	4.60	5.07	3.06	0.63	0.17	7.51	2.51	1.91	1,107.69
Food and nonalcoholic beverages	5.42	3.92	0.12	274.64	0.17	1.00	3.30	1,029.62	594.71	0.28	1.22	145.29	77.42	5.79	6.38	3.34	0.67	0.15	11.15	3.21	2.31	1,399.67
Food	5.39	3.83	0.12	271.10	0.17	1.00	3.23	1,021.44	581.25	0.28	1.19	141.19	76.51	5.68	6.29	3.37	0.66	0.15	11.01	3.21	2.28	1,387.08
Bread and cereals	6.16	4.50	0.12	277.28	0.18	1.00	3.51	1,209.42	628.95	0.30	1.26	177.29	89.65	6.06	6.65	4.01	0.79	0.16	10.66	3.68	2.52	1,512.57
Meat and Fish	5.56	3.57	0.11	288.27	0.17	1.00	3.61	879.72	577.86	0.27	0.76	108.70	73.71	6.73	5.85	2.78	0.61	0.16	10.25	3.10	2.06	1,348.45
Fruits and Vegetables	3.90	3.92	0.16	269.11	0.15	1.00	2.65	1,111.97	552.32	0.30	2.02	231.16	70.09	4.37	5.55	3.66	0.58	0.15	10.77	3.44	2.42	1,341.61
Other food and nonalcoholic beverages	5.74	3.78	0.12	270.63	0.18	1.00	3.55	1,000.20	614.54	0.27	1.27	158.56	78.09	6.03	6.78	3.25	0.72	0.12	11.89	2.73	2.28	1,439.75
Alcoholic beverages, tobacco and narcotics	6.12	3.72	0.12	190.78	0.27	1.00	6.95	970.90	503.06	0.59	1.85	127.33	58.72	8.88	3.95	2.54	0.76	0.32	27.32	2.88	3.26	1,048.38
Clothing and footwear	5.73	3.88	0.19	290.92	0.20	1.00	3.13	1,068.43	518.13	0.33	1.40	183.03	78.17	5.73	7.10	4.88	1.29	0.17	8.81	2.59	2.14	1,398.50
Clothing	5.54	3.48	0.18	295.15	0.19	1.00	3.04	1,089.08	502.38	0.31	1.33	170.25	75.59	5.63	6.86	4.31	1.27	0.16	8.46	2.49	2.03	1,341.42
Housing, water, electricity, gas and other fuels[a]	2.55	1.36	0.06	246.24	0.08	1.00	2.78	483.63	323.63	0.13	2.08	124.86	38.71	2.99	3.10	2.76	0.37	0.18	3.24	2.12	0.85	871.29
Furnishings, household equipment and routine household maintenance	5.81	4.57	0.11	286.42	0.21	1.00	3.84	1,005.98	578.47	0.28	1.70	200.89	74.17	5.70	6.76	3.21	0.88	0.18	10.05	3.24	2.68	1,580.34
Health and Education[a]	2.83	1.34	0.07	96.41	0.11	1.00	1.64	448.94	143.80	0.21	0.77	55.70	25.69	1.96	2.89	1.79	0.48	0.16	2.56	1.60	1.28	562.95
Health[a]	2.47	1.19	0.08	114.42	0.09	1.00	1.38	423.82	191.12	0.20	0.66	58.00	26.61	2.04	3.10	2.10	0.36	0.17	3.25	1.27	1.28	629.90
Education[a]	3.20	1.48	0.06	83.59	0.12	1.00	1.94	469.81	120.49	0.22	0.88	54.06	25.27	1.95	2.75	1.63	0.64	0.14	2.09	2.10	1.30	521.75
Transportation and Communication	5.04	4.42	0.16	304.17	0.15	1.00	3.72	931.70	703.05	0.32	1.95	165.75	88.96	6.74	6.03	3.79	0.56	0.21	10.11	2.49	2.49	1,328.95
Transportation	5.14	4.03	0.14	313.32	0.16	1.00	3.93	902.43	709.26	0.28	1.80	154.11	82.77	8.28	6.38	3.53	0.52	0.22	10.48	2.59	2.41	1,623.25
Communication	4.68	5.83	0.28	272.57	0.13	1.00	2.93	1,073.36	710.27	0.42	2.36	215.53	111.76	3.97	5.27	5.00	0.66	0.21	8.80	2.21	2.95	950.98
Recreation and culture[a]	6.27	5.02	0.19	350.63	0.20	1.00	4.52	1,170.26	730.18	0.39	2.28	201.77	86.37	5.48	7.90	4.05	0.89	0.15	12.88	3.27	3.24	1,654.33
Restaurants and hotels	4.75	3.17	0.10	242.70	0.19	1.00	3.98	787.36	703.73	0.24	1.13	204.05	72.48	4.50	6.39	3.54	0.73	0.15	10.65	2.47	1.97	1,139.15
Miscellaneous goods and services[a]	5.38	3.46	0.11	270.73	0.18	1.00	3.93	912.63	551.11	0.30	1.37	148.82	71.78	6.10	6.84	3.44	0.80	0.18	8.45	2.81	2.28	1,319.31
Individual Consumption Expenditure by Government	3.93	1.48	0.07	143.76	0.12	1.00	3.21	541.87	183.20	0.22	0.78	51.52	30.45	3.57	4.96	2.59	0.63	0.15	3.67	1.87	1.49	647.97
Collective Consumption Expenditure by Government	4.52	1.76	0.06	225.14	0.13	1.00	3.78	614.77	274.54	0.23	0.87	76.24	42.56	5.50	5.90	2.98	0.71	0.12	5.14	2.21	1.84	806.68
Gross fixed capital formation	6.09	4.52	0.12	275.52	0.17	1.00	3.92	825.98	562.58	0.29	1.28	166.28	70.95	7.08	7.05	3.84	0.73	0.14	10.54	2.94	2.32	1,491.83
Machinery and equipment	12.73	9.46	0.20	521.37	0.27	1.00	7.06	1,655.46	1,090.05	0.50	2.26	293.56	137.08	11.52	12.42	6.49	1.00	0.21	19.00	4.32	4.15	2,659.03
Construction	3.59	2.61	0.08	163.97	0.12	1.00	2.53	497.58	330.18	0.19	0.83	107.06	42.13	4.86	4.51	2.58	0.57	0.12	6.77	2.35	1.46	963.34
Other products	12.44	9.49	0.21	508.88	0.26	1.00	6.48	1,647.49	1,077.38	0.49	2.28	290.07	130.88	11.96	12.43	6.36	0.98	0.20	18.54	4.22	4.08	2,635.93
Changes in inventories and Acquisitions less disposals of valuables	6.85	5.01	0.16	336.67	0.22	1.00	4.59	1,167.20	706.74	0.37	1.63	186.42	91.59	7.35	7.83	4.32	0.81	0.18	13.32	3.26	2.97	1,725.84
Balance of Exports and Imports	10.32	8.35	0.18	519.70	0.27	1.00	8.36	1,716.81	1,057.84	0.55	1.97	313.03	174.54	13.41	13.51	6.47	0.87	0.18	19.56	3.91	4.35	2,870.38
Individual Consumption Expenditure by Households[b]	4.51	3.13	0.10	242.75	0.16	1.00	3.13	808.34	495.16	0.26	1.56	139.24	63.03	4.72	5.10	3.12	0.62	0.17	7.99	2.57	1.95	1,162.98
Individual Consumption Expenditure by Households without Housing[b]	5.00	3.47	0.11	250.99	0.17	1.00	3.25	883.48	531.89	0.29	1.51	143.29	67.23	5.06	5.37	3.32	0.67	0.17	9.10	2.64	2.27	1,245.75
Government Final Consumption Expenditure	4.20	1.64	0.06	177.69	0.12	1.00	3.52	582.88	241.43	0.22	0.83	64.95	37.98	4.60	5.46	2.80	0.67	0.13	4.45	2.03	1.68	735.70
Domestic Absorption	4.83	3.23	0.10	240.82	0.15	1.00	3.37	778.81	462.55	0.26	1.34	130.90	60.94	5.21	5.52	3.24	0.67	0.16	8.14	2.59	2.01	1,178.57
Total Consumption	4.42	2.71	0.09	229.94	0.15	1.00	3.19	764.21	428.33	0.25	1.37	120.47	57.40	4.64	5.17	3.05	0.65	0.16	7.24	2.48	1.92	1,071.62

BAN = Bangladesh; BHU = Bhutan; BRU = Brunei Darussalam; CAM = Cambodia; FIJ = Fiji; HKG = Hong Kong, China; IND = India; INO = Indonesia; LAO = Lao People's Democratic Republic; MAL = Malaysia; MLD = Maldives; MON = Mongolia; MYA = Myanmar; NEP = Nepal; PAK = Pakistan; PHI = Philippines; PRC = People's Republic of China; SIN = Singapore; SRI = Sri Lanka; TAP = Taipei,China; THA = Thailand; VIE = Viet Nam.

[a] Includes individual consumption expenditure by households, nonprofit institutions serving households, and government.

[b] Includes expenditure by nonprofit institutions serving households.

Source: Asian Development Bank estimates based on data supplied by the participating economies.

Table A2.2: Price Level Indexes, 2017 Revised
(Hong Kong, China = 100)

Expenditure Category	BAN	BHU	BRU	CAM	FIJ	HKG	IND	INO	LAO	MAL	MLD	MON	MYA	NEP	PAK	PHI	PRC	SIN	SRI	TAP	THA	VIE
Gross Domestic Product	47	38	58	46	58	100	40	46	44	48	68	42	35	37	41	50	77	82	41	66	47	41
Actual Individual Consumption by Households[a]	43	35	57	45	57	100	37	46	44	46	74	41	34	34	38	47	72	96	38	64	44	39
Food and nonalcoholic beverages	53	47	69	53	64	100	39	60	56	51	62	46	44	43	47	52	77	83	57	82	53	49
Food	52	46	68	52	63	100	39	59	55	51	60	45	44	42	47	52	76	84	56	82	52	48
Bread and cereals	60	54	70	53	68	100	42	70	59	54	64	57	51	45	49	62	92	92	54	94	58	53
Meat and Fish	54	43	62	55	64	100	43	51	55	49	39	35	42	50	43	43	70	91	52	79	47	47
Fruits and Vegetables	38	47	90	52	58	100	32	65	52	55	102	74	40	33	41	57	67	84	55	88	56	47
Other food and nonalcoholic beverages	56	45	65	52	68	100	42	58	58	48	64	51	40	45	50	50	83	69	61	70	52	50
Alcoholic beverages, tobacco and narcotics	59	45	70	37	101	100	83	57	48	107	93	41	34	66	29	39	88	180	140	74	75	37
Clothing and footwear	55	46	110	56	75	100	37	62	49	60	71	58	45	43	53	76	149	98	45	66	49	49
Clothing	54	42	101	57	70	100	36	63	47	57	67	54	43	42	51	67	147	91	43	64	47	47
Housing, water, electricity, gas and other fuels[a]	25	16	33	47	32	100	33	28	31	24	105	40	22	22	23	43	43	104	17	54	20	30
Furnishings, household equipment and routine household maintenance	56	55	60	55	81	100	46	59	55	50	86	64	42	42	50	50	102	104	51	83	62	55
Health and Education[a]	27	16	40	19	41	100	20	26	14	39	39	18	15	15	21	28	55	88	13	41	29	20
Health[a]	24	14	47	22	34	100	16	25	18	37	33	19	15	15	23	32	41	97	17	33	29	22
Education[a]	31	18	34	16	46	100	23	27	11	41	44	17	14	15	20	25	73	81	11	54	30	18
Transportation and Communication	49	53	92	59	56	100	44	54	66	57	99	53	51	50	45	59	64	120	52	64	57	46
Transportation	50	48	80	60	60	100	47	53	67	51	91	49	47	62	47	55	61	122	54	66	55	57
Communication	45	70	156	52	49	100	35	63	67	76	120	69	64	30	39	77	76	116	45	57	68	33
Recreation and culture[a]	61	60	105	67	74	100	54	68	69	71	116	64	49	41	58	63	103	84	66	84	74	58
Restaurants and hotels	46	38	57	47	71	100	48	46	67	44	57	52	42	34	47	55	84	79	54	63	45	40
Miscellaneous goods and services[a]	52	41	62	52	67	100	47	53	52	54	69	48	41	45	51	53	92	102	43	72	52	46
Individual Consumption Expenditure by Government	38	18	37	28	44	100	38	32	17	39	40	16	17	27	37	40	73	86	19	48	34	23
Collective Consumption Expenditure by Government	44	21	34	43	48	100	45	36	26	41	44	24	24	41	44	46	82	70	26	56	42	28
Gross fixed capital formation	59	54	68	53	62	100	47	48	53	52	65	53	41	53	52	59	84	82	54	75	53	52
Machinery and equipment	123	113	115	100	100	100	84	96	103	91	115	94	79	86	92	100	115	118	97	111	95	93
Construction	35	31	46	32	44	100	30	29	31	34	42	34	24	36	33	40	66	68	35	60	34	34
Other products	121	114	117	98	97	100	78	96	102	89	115	93	75	89	92	98	114	110	95	108	94	92
Changes in inventories and Acquisitions less disposals of valuables	66	60	88	65	81	100	55	68	67	67	83	60	52	55	58	67	94	103	68	84	68	60
Balance of Exports and Imports	100	100	100	100	100	100	100	100	100	100	100	100	100	100	100	100	100	100	100	100	100	100
Individual Consumption Expenditure by Households[b]	44	37	59	47	58	100	37	47	47	47	79	44	36	35	38	48	71	96	41	66	45	41
Individual Consumption Expenditure by Households without Housing[b]	48	42	60	48	66	100	39	51	50	53	77	46	39	38	40	51	78	97	47	67	52	43
Government Final Consumption Expenditure	41	20	35	34	46	100	42	34	23	40	42	21	22	34	40	43	77	75	23	52	39	26
Domestic Absorption	47	39	58	46	58	100	40	45	44	47	68	42	35	39	41	50	77	88	42	66	46	41
Total Consumption	43	33	53	44	56	100	38	45	40	46	70	38	33	35	38	47	75	93	37	63	44	37

BAN = Bangladesh; BHU = Bhutan; BRU = Brunei Darussalam; CAM = Cambodia; FIJ = Fiji; HKG = Hong Kong, China; IND = India; INO = Indonesia; LAO = Lao People's Democratic Republic; MAL = Malaysia; MLD = Maldives; MON = Mongolia; MYA = Myanmar; NEP = Nepal; PAK = Pakistan; PHI = Philippines; PRC = People's Republic of China; SIN = Singapore; SRI = Sri Lanka; TAP = Taipei,China; THA = Thailand; VIE = Viet Nam.

a Includes individual consumption expenditure by households, nonprofit institutions serving households, and government.

b Includes expenditure by nonprofit institutions serving households.

Source: Asian Development Bank estimates based on data supplied by the participating economies.

Table A2.3: Price Level Indexes, 2017 Revised

(Asia and the Pacific = 100)

Expenditure Category	BAN	BHU	BRU	CAM	FIJ	HKG	IND	INO	LAO	MAL	MLD	MON	MYA	NEP	PAK	PHI	PRC	SIN	SRI	TAP	THA	VIE
Gross Domestic Product	76	61	94	75	94	161	65	74	71	77	110	68	56	60	65	81	124	132	67	106	76	67
Actual Individual Consumption by Households[a]	77	63	102	80	102	179	67	82	78	83	133	73	61	61	67	85	130	171	69	115	79	69
Food and nonalcoholic beverages	92	82	121	93	113	176	69	105	99	90	108	82	78	76	83	91	135	145	100	145	93	86
Food	93	81	121	93	112	178	69	106	98	90	107	80	78	75	83	93	136	149	100	146	93	86
Bread and cereals	101	91	118	90	114	169	71	119	100	91	108	96	87	76	83	105	155	155	92	159	98	89
Meat and Fish	90	71	103	92	107	166	72	85	91	82	64	58	70	83	72	71	117	151	87	132	79	78
Fruits and Vegetables	76	95	181	105	117	202	64	131	105	110	206	149	81	66	83	114	135	171	111	178	112	94
Other food and nonalcoholic beverages	98	80	114	92	119	176	75	103	102	85	113	89	79	79	88	88	147	121	107	123	92	88
Alcoholic beverages, tobacco and narcotics	81	61	95	50	137	136	113	77	65	146	127	55	46	90	40	54	120	245	190	100	63	50
Clothing and footwear	71	59	141	72	96	128	48	80	63	77	91	75	58	55	67	97	191	125	58	85	62	62
Clothing	71	55	135	76	93	133	48	84	63	76	90	72	58	56	68	89	195	121	58	85	62	62
Housing, water, electricity, gas and other fuels[a]	65	43	87	125	84	264	88	74	81	64	278	105	59	59	60	113	114	273	44	143	52	80
Furnishings, household equipment and routine household maintenance	73	71	77	71	104	129	60	76	71	65	111	83	55	55	65	64	132	135	66	107	80	71
Health and Education[a]	71	41	103	48	106	258	51	67	35	100	100	46	38	38	55	71	142	227	34	106	76	51
Health[a]	72	43	142	66	102	301	50	74	54	112	100	56	46	46	69	98	124	293	50	98	88	66
Education[a]	70	40	78	36	104	226	53	62	26	92	100	39	33	33	46	57	166	184	24	122	67	41
Transportation and Communication	86	93	162	103	99	176	78	95	117	101	174	93	89	88	78	103	112	210	91	112	100	81
Transportation	89	87	143	108	107	179	84	94	120	92	163	88	85	111	85	98	108	219	96	119	99	101
Communication	73	112	251	84	79	161	56	101	108	122	193	111	103	48	63	124	122	187	72	91	109	53
Recreation and culture[a]	71	70	122	79	87	117	63	79	80	83	135	75	58	48	68	73	120	98	77	98	87	67
Restaurants and hotels	72	59	89	73	111	155	74	71	103	69	89	81	65	52	73	85	131	123	85	98	70	62
Miscellaneous goods and services[a]	72	57	85	72	93	138	65	73	72	74	96	66	57	63	70	74	127	142	60	99	72	63
Individual Consumption Expenditure by Government	67	31	65	48	76	175	67	55	30	68	69	29	31	47	64	70	127	150	33	84	60	39
Collective Consumption Expenditure by Government	66	32	51	66	73	152	69	54	39	63	67	37	37	62	66	70	124	106	40	86	64	43
Gross fixed capital formation	82	75	95	73	86	138	65	67	74	72	90	73	56	73	72	82	116	113	75	104	74	72
Machinery and equipment	115	105	107	93	93	93	79	90	96	84	107	87	73	80	86	93	107	110	90	103	89	86
Construction	66	59	87	60	83	189	57	55	59	65	79	65	46	69	63	76	124	128	65	114	63	64
Other products	114	108	111	93	92	95	73	91	96	84	109	88	71	84	87	93	108	105	90	102	89	87
Changes in inventories and Acquisitions less disposals of valuables	92	83	122	89	112	138	76	94	92	93	114	82	72	76	80	92	129	142	94	115	94	83
Balance of Exports and Imports	100	100	100	100	100	100	100	100	100	100	100	100	100	100	100	100	100	100	100	100	100	100
Individual Consumption Expenditure by Households[b]	79	68	107	84	106	181	68	85	85	85	143	80	65	64	68	87	129	174	74	119	81	73
Individual Consumption Expenditure by Households without Housing[b]	82	70	101	82	111	169	66	87	85	89	129	77	65	64	67	87	131	164	78	114	88	73
Government Final Consumption Expenditure	66	32	56	55	74	161	68	55	37	65	68	34	35	55	65	70	125	121	37	84	62	41
Domestic Absorption	76	63	94	75	94	162	65	74	71	77	110	68	57	63	66	81	125	143	68	108	75	67
Total Consumption	75	57	92	77	98	174	66	77	70	80	121	67	57	60	67	82	130	161	64	111	77	65

BAN = Bangladesh; BHU = Bhutan; BRU = Brunei Darussalam; CAM = Cambodia; FIJ = Fiji; HKG = Hong Kong, China; IND = India; INO = Indonesia; LAO = Lao People's Democratic Republic; MAL = Malaysia; MLD = Maldives; MON = Mongolia; MYA = Myanmar; NEP = Nepal; PAK = Pakistan; PHI = Philippines; PRC = People's Republic of China; SIN = Singapore; SRI = Sri Lanka; TAP = Taipei,China; THA = Thailand; VIE = Viet Nam.

Note: For Myanmar, exchange rate was obtained from publicly available source: International Monetary Fund. International Financial Statistics. http://data.imf.org/ (accessed 26 January 2024).

[a] Includes individual consumption expenditure by households, nonprofit institutions serving households, and government.

[b] Includes expenditure by nonprofit institutions serving households.

Source: Asian Development Bank estimates based on data supplied by the participating economies.

Table A2.4: Real Expenditure, 2017 Revised

(HK$ billion)

Expenditure Category	BAN	BHU	BRU	CAM	FIJ	HKG	IND	INO	LAO	MAL	MLD	MON	MYA	NEP	PAK	PHI	PRC	SIN	SRI	TAP	THA	VIE	AP
Gross Domestic Product	5,132.8	53.5	162.0	372.3	71.5	2,659.6	49,345.7	17,345.0	304.2	5,188.3	55.0	212.1	1,423.4	647.9	6,823.6	5,102.2	125,018.0	3,257.9	1,772.5	7,009.1	7,591.2	5,297.9	244,845.4
Actual Individual Consumption by Households[a]	3,825.7	31.0	44.4	300.3	51.5	1,886.0	34,209.2	10,552.7	181.0	3,318.7	26.5	135.7	842.4	571.9	6,382.1	4,121.2	59,542.9	1,097.2	1,206.5	4,246.0	4,583.6	3,405.8	140,562.4
Food and nonalcoholic beverages	1,595.4	8.7	3.5	121.0	13.9	191.9	9,684.0	2,336.4	60.9	610.4	5.0	34.8	346.0	263.7	1,662.7	1,205.9	9,714.1	77.2	218.5	371.7	887.7	657.4	30,070.6
Food	1,599.6	8.1	3.1	117.3	13.4	180.0	9,733.5	2,095.8	52.1	587.5	4.4	31.9	340.6	264.7	1,605.3	1,096.4	9,463.0	67.7	206.5	351.6	786.0	637.1	29,245.8
Bread and cereals	623.5	1.9	0.7	36.0	2.6	18.7	2,463.2	479.9	13.9	78.8	0.8	3.9	64.4	88.3	341.9	348.4	1,228.6	10.9	66.2	68.1	152.2	174.3	6,267.2
Meat and Fish	297.9	1.0	1.2	34.2	2.9	91.6	842.5	701.9	21.2	205.8	2.0	16.4	115.4	37.1	216.0	446.7	3,803.1	22.4	30.6	115.9	210.6	271.6	7,488.1
Fruits and Vegetables	299.4	2.1	0.4	18.4	3.9	26.3	3,146.2	334.9	9.4	136.4	0.6	1.2	91.4	68.6	277.2	117.4	2,830.8	14.4	24.4	105.4	272.1	96.0	7,877.0
Other food and nonalcoholic beverages	345.5	3.5	1.3	31.2	4.4	55.3	3,349.6	835.2	16.3	194.5	1.8	14.5	78.1	73.3	815.9	296.5	2,108.9	30.8	97.1	81.1	249.5	112.1	8,796.4
Alcoholic beverages, tobacco and narcotics	55.3	0.7	0.0	12.9	4.1	15.2	317.5	598.7	14.0	24.5	0.4	9.3	18.5	11.4	80.7	108.0	1,562.8	9.3	5.5	71.5	87.4	77.2	2,684.9
Clothing and footwear	177.2	1.8	0.4	5.1	1.7	90.4	2,056.4	256.1	3.4	73.6	0.9	5.0	24.9	13.4	364.9	50.5	1,547.8	29.1	75.4	166.5	54.1	68.9	5,067.4
Clothing	163.2	1.4	0.4	2.9	1.5	59.5	1,689.3	215.6	2.8	68.5	0.7	4.2	22.1	11.5	311.3	38.8	1,223.0	26.4	74.9	151.5	56.2	51.6	4,177.2
Housing, water, electricity, gas and other fuels[a]	1,086.1	6.6	13.0	39.1	6.0	294.0	5,013.7	1,711.4	28.4	899.5	4.6	19.8	179.9	107.4	2,133.3	494.2	15,856.4	148.8	246.4	804.2	894.1	552.5	30,539.1
Furnishings, household equipment and routine household maintenance	94.0	0.9	2.5	4.4	2.1	94.4	760.1	331.4	7.5	144.8	1.3	1.8	9.9	8.5	178.6	114.8	1,858.8	40.4	19.8	138.5	125.0	117.1	4,056.6
Health and Education[a]	508.2	9.5	15.1	91.4	11.3	278.8	8,466.3	2,106.5	46.4	539.9	9.5	49.2	207.0	125.4	1,361.7	882.7	15,388.7	217.6	307.8	1,126.5	1,297.1	1,063.0	34,110.4
Health[a]	219.5	4.9	3.7	42.9	3.6	157.4	4,102.4	738.6	13.4	224.4	6.0	18.1	107.3	54.7	702.6	278.2	10,277.5	102.2	129.7	802.0	635.7	422.6	19,047.6
Education[a]	279.6	4.6	12.3	46.7	7.4	121.4	4,259.1	1,346.7	34.1	310.7	3.8	31.3	97.5	68.4	638.4	610.0	5,775.4	112.8	175.7	372.9	654.8	636.7	15,600.4
Transportation and Communication	156.1	2.2	3.1	17.0	6.6	170.2	4,867.8	1,511.4	9.1	518.9	2.5	13.4	30.9	16.4	390.3	437.9	7,844.8	145.7	234.4	587.4	491.3	491.2	17,948.5
Transportation	137.2	1.7	2.7	16.0	4.3	125.7	4,019.4	1,217.9	6.9	368.1	1.4	10.8	23.1	9.5	269.4	376.0	5,896.1	111.2	217.1	444.4	435.4	241.9	13,936.1
Communication	17.3	0.5	0.4	0.6	2.3	44.5	790.5	288.0	2.1	144.3	1.0	2.5	7.5	8.0	120.9	66.4	1,919.3	33.3	10.8	141.4	59.0	273.6	3,934.3
Recreation and culture[a]	44.3	0.7	1.2	5.0	0.6	194.4	210.6	295.6	1.9	136.2	0.7	2.6	7.2	15.9	171.1	68.0	1,587.1	128.1	55.2	218.5	131.1	140.0	3,415.8
Restaurants and hotels	81.9	0.8	1.8	13.2	0.5	166.7	494.2	959.6	12.7	331.5	2.6	2.3	33.8	10.3	140.5	317.9	2,452.7	123.6	31.4	383.5	406.8	300.7	6,269.2
Miscellaneous goods and services[a]	123.9	1.6	7.6	7.2	3.6	390.0	3,809.4	421.7	12.0	318.3	1.8	8.4	23.6	12.4	364.5	491.6	6,823.7	169.4	114.1	588.0	491.7	204.4	14,389.0
Individual Consumption Expenditure by Government	44.9	6.9	16.0	21.9	5.8	101.7	1,887.8	882.5	19.0	406.8	5.7	29.2	71.7	27.6	333.2	256.6	8,089.9	117.4	153.2	705.0	838.1	467.9	14,488.6
Collective Consumption Expenditure by Government	290.0	11.7	56.5	6.5	11.5	159.8	3,137.4	1,238.3	63.6	350.3	7.3	31.4	316.7	31.1	409.3	406.3	12,085.9	249.2	110.5	529.1	686.3	414.9	20,603.6
Government Final Consumption Expenditure	353.9	18.7	72.0	25.9	17.6	261.4	5,096.2	2,126.4	86.7	750.0	12.9	60.1	412.4	58.7	744.8	670.2	20,324.8	366.3	253.8	1,224.5	1,494.4	867.0	35,298.9
Gross fixed capital formation	1,280.9	20.3	47.8	71.4	12.8	576.0	11,766.8	5,291.4	83.5	1,194.1	23.7	37.6	398.1	144.5	795.9	1,104.3	48,179.5	830.8	431.2	1,293.1	1,530.1	1,284.1	76,397.9
Machinery and equipment	143.8	3.4	14.2	22.0	10.8	161.4	2,301.0	417.1	12.2	197.7	5.7	8.3	87.5	31.1	182.6	214.7	9,851.3	176.1	59.7	338.0	498.9	181.5	14,911.0
Construction	1,569.8	22.4	28.7	49.0	10.8	360.4	9,631.2	6,598.8	63.0	1,055.0	18.9	27.9	325.6	115.9	523.5	937.7	37,661.5	400.0	468.2	610.4	750.1	1,413.1	62,641.8
Other products	26.5	0.1	2.8	0.3	0.5	54.2	854.3	240.7	12.0	93.1	0.9	2.9	19.3	8.6	78.9	67.6	3,776.7	181.7	13.1	214.0	95.4	27.2	5,770.8
Changes in inventories and Acquisitions less disposals of valuables	42.8	-0.0	4.8	5.5	1.1	11.0	1,278.9	51.7	0.0	17.9	0.7	7.6	12.2	58.8	81.7	-3.2	1,187.6	53.6	87.8	-7.5	-9.0	64.2	2,948.0
Balance of Exports and Imports	-140.7	-4.0	13.2	-5.9	-2.1	26.8	-516.2	79.1	-6.7	170.8	-1.4	2.1	-41.4	-74.9	-270.5	-232.0	1,689.1	718.0	-49.2	614.5	443.0	55.8	2,467.2
Individual Consumption Expenditure by Households[b]	3,703.7	25.6	32.7	275.1	45.9	1,784.4	32,155.9	9,629.2	161.4	2,937.8	22.0	113.2	764.3	536.8	6,026.7	3,825.5	52,262.2	983.8	1,064.1	3,626.2	3,859.4	2,983.2	126,819.1
Individual Consumption Expenditure by Households without Housing[b]	3,061.6	21.4	26.7	240.6	39.0	1,536.9	27,997.4	8,117.9	136.9	2,414.7	19.0	97.2	670.1	450.6	4,969.6	3,350.1	42,551.4	838.5	873.8	2,986.8	3,105.0	2,607.2	106,112.4
Government Final Consumption Expenditure	353.9	18.7	72.0	25.9	17.6	261.4	5,096.2	2,126.4	86.7	750.0	12.9	60.1	412.4	58.7	744.8	670.2	20,324.8	366.3	253.8	1,224.5	1,494.4	867.0	35,298.9
Domestic Absorption	5,436.1	62.7	140.1	385.8	75.7	2,632.8	50,670.7	17,275.2	319.6	4,881.7	57.6	208.8	1,529.3	817.2	7,431.3	5,579.9	122,909.3	2,227.8	1,886.3	6,017.5	6,732.9	5,204.4	242,482.5
Total Consumption	4,111.5	40.9	83.8	310.4	62.1	2,045.8	37,216.2	11,807.1	235.4	3,670.3	32.9	163.2	1,112.2	603.6	6,729.1	4,531.2	70,927.6	1,321.6	1,330.4	4,763.6	5,238.5	3,832.8	160,170.3

0.0 = magnitude is less than half of the unit employed.

AP = Asia and the Pacific; BAN = Bangladesh; BHU = Bhutan; BRU = Brunei Darussalam; CAM = Cambodia; FIJ = Fiji; HKG = Hong Kong, China; IND = India; INO = Indonesia; LAO = Lao People's Democratic Republic; MAL = Malaysia; MLD = Maldives; MON = Mongolia; MYA = Myanmar; NEP = Nepal; PAK = Pakistan; PHI = Philippines; PRC = People's Republic of China; SIN = Singapore; SRI = Sri Lanka; TAP = Taipei,China; THA = Thailand; VIE = Viet Nam.

Notes:

1. Each real aggregate value is derived by using a purchasing power parity that is specific to that aggregate, so real aggregates may not sum up to the total of their real components for an economy.
2. For Myanmar, total gross domestic product in local currency units were obtained from publicly available source: Central Statistical Organization. https://www.csostat.gov.mm (accessed 20 February 2024).

[a] Includes individual consumption expenditure by households, nonprofit institutions serving households, and government.

[b] Includes expenditure by nonprofit institutions serving households.

Source: Asian Development Bank estimates based on data supplied by the participating economies.

Table A2.5: Economy Shares of Real Expenditure to Asia and the Pacific, 2017 Revised

(%)

Expenditure Category	BAN	BHU	BRU	CAM	FIJ	HKG	IND	INO	LAO	MAL	MLD	MON	MYA	NEP	PAK	PHI	PRC	SIN	SRI	TAP	THA	VIE	AP
Gross Domestic Product	2.10	0.02	0.07	0.15	0.03	1.09	20.15	7.08	0.12	2.12	0.02	0.09	0.58	0.26	2.79	2.08	51.06	1.33	0.72	2.86	3.10	2.16	100.00
Actual Individual Consumption by Households[a]	2.72	0.02	0.03	0.21	0.04	1.34	24.34	7.51	0.13	2.36	0.02	0.10	0.60	0.41	4.54	2.93	42.36	0.78	0.86	3.02	3.26	2.42	100.00
Food and nonalcoholic beverages	5.31	0.03	0.01	0.40	0.05	0.64	32.20	7.77	0.20	2.03	0.02	0.12	1.15	0.88	5.53	4.01	32.30	0.26	0.73	1.24	2.95	2.19	100.00
Food	5.47	0.03	0.01	0.40	0.05	0.62	33.28	7.17	0.18	2.01	0.01	0.11	1.16	0.91	5.49	3.75	32.36	0.23	0.71	1.20	2.69	2.18	100.00
Bread and cereals	9.95	0.03	0.01	0.57	0.04	0.30	39.30	7.66	0.22	1.26	0.01	0.06	1.03	1.41	5.46	5.56	19.60	0.17	1.06	1.09	2.43	2.78	100.00
Meat and Fish	3.98	0.01	0.02	0.46	0.04	1.22	11.25	9.37	0.28	2.75	0.03	0.22	1.54	0.50	2.88	5.97	50.79	0.30	0.41	1.55	2.81	3.63	100.00
Fruits and Vegetables	3.80	0.03	0.01	0.23	0.05	0.33	39.94	4.25	0.12	1.73	0.01	0.02	1.16	0.87	3.52	1.49	35.94	0.18	0.31	1.34	3.45	1.22	100.00
Other food and nonalcoholic beverages	3.93	0.04	0.02	0.35	0.05	0.63	38.08	9.49	0.19	2.21	0.02	0.16	0.89	0.83	3.37	3.37	23.97	0.35	1.10	0.92	2.84	1.27	100.00
Alcoholic beverages, tobacco and narcotics	2.06	0.03	0.00	0.48	0.15	0.57	11.82	22.30	0.52	0.91	0.02	0.34	0.69	0.42	3.00	4.02	43.31	0.35	0.20	2.66	3.25	2.88	100.00
Clothing and footwear	3.50	0.04	0.01	0.10	0.03	1.78	40.58	5.05	0.07	1.45	0.02	0.10	0.49	0.26	7.20	1.00	30.54	0.57	1.49	3.29	1.07	1.36	100.00
Clothing	3.91	0.03	0.01	0.07	0.04	1.42	40.44	5.16	0.07	1.64	0.02	0.10	0.53	0.28	7.45	0.93	29.28	0.63	1.79	3.63	1.34	1.24	100.00
Housing, water, electricity, gas and other fuels[a]	3.56	0.02	0.04	0.13	0.02	0.96	16.42	5.60	0.09	2.95	0.01	0.06	0.59	0.35	6.99	1.62	51.92	0.49	0.81	2.63	2.93	1.81	100.00
Furnishings, household equipment and routine household maintenance	2.32	0.02	0.06	0.11	0.05	2.33	18.74	8.17	0.18	3.57	0.03	0.04	0.25	0.21	4.40	2.83	45.82	1.00	0.49	3.41	3.08	2.89	100.00
Health and Education[a]	1.49	0.03	0.04	0.27	0.03	0.82	24.82	6.18	0.14	1.58	0.03	0.14	0.61	0.37	3.99	2.59	45.11	0.64	0.90	3.30	3.80	3.12	100.00
Health[a]	1.15	0.03	0.02	0.23	0.02	0.83	21.54	3.88	0.07	1.18	0.03	0.10	0.56	0.29	3.69	1.46	53.96	0.54	0.68	4.21	3.34	2.22	100.00
Education[a]	1.79	0.03	0.08	0.30	0.05	0.78	27.30	8.63	0.22	1.99	0.02	0.20	0.63	0.44	3.91	3.91	37.02	0.72	1.13	2.39	4.20	4.08	100.00
Transportation and Communication	0.87	0.01	0.02	0.09	0.04	0.95	27.12	8.42	0.05	2.89	0.01	0.07	0.17	0.09	2.17	2.44	43.71	0.81	1.31	3.27	2.74	2.74	100.00
Transportation	0.98	0.01	0.02	0.11	0.03	0.90	28.84	8.74	0.05	2.64	0.01	0.08	0.17	0.07	1.93	2.70	42.31	0.80	1.56	3.19	3.12	1.74	100.00
Communication	0.44	0.01	0.01	0.02	0.06	1.13	20.09	7.32	0.05	3.67	0.03	0.06	0.19	0.20	3.07	1.69	48.78	0.85	0.27	3.59	1.50	6.95	100.00
Recreation and culture[a]	1.30	0.02	0.03	0.15	0.02	5.69	6.17	8.66	0.06	3.99	0.02	0.07	0.21	0.47	5.01	1.99	46.46	3.75	1.62	6.40	3.84	4.10	100.00
Restaurants and hotels	1.31	0.01	0.05	0.21	0.01	2.66	7.88	15.31	0.20	5.29	0.04	0.04	0.54	0.16	2.24	5.07	39.12	1.97	0.50	6.12	6.49	4.80	100.00
Miscellaneous goods and services[a]	0.86	0.01	0.05	0.05	0.02	2.71	26.47	2.93	0.08	2.21	0.01	0.06	0.16	0.09	2.53	3.42	47.42	1.18	0.79	4.09	3.42	1.42	100.00
Individual Consumption Expenditure by Government	0.31	0.05	0.11	0.15	0.04	0.70	13.03	6.09	0.13	2.81	0.04	0.20	0.49	0.19	2.30	1.77	55.84	0.81	1.06	4.87	5.78	3.23	100.00
Collective Consumption Expenditure by Government	1.41	0.06	0.27	0.03	0.06	0.78	15.23	6.01	0.31	1.70	0.04	0.15	1.54	0.15	1.99	1.97	58.66	1.21	0.54	2.57	3.33	2.01	100.00
Gross fixed capital formation	1.68	0.03	0.06	0.09	0.02	0.75	15.40	6.93	0.11	1.56	0.03	0.05	0.52	0.19	1.04	1.45	63.06	1.09	0.56	1.69	2.00	1.68	100.00
Machinery and equipment	0.96	0.02	0.10	0.15	0.02	1.08	15.43	2.80	0.08	1.33	0.04	0.06	0.59	0.21	1.22	1.44	66.07	1.18	0.40	2.27	3.35	1.22	100.00
Construction	2.51	0.04	0.05	0.08	0.02	0.58	15.38	10.53	0.10	1.68	0.03	0.04	0.52	0.19	0.84	1.50	60.12	0.64	0.75	0.97	1.20	2.26	100.00
Other products	0.46	0.00	0.05	0.01	0.01	0.94	14.80	4.17	0.21	1.61	0.02	0.05	0.33	0.15	1.37	1.17	65.45	3.15	0.23	3.71	1.65	0.47	100.00
Changes in inventories and Acquisitions less disposals of valuables	1.45	-0.00	0.16	0.19	0.04	0.37	43.38	1.75	0.00	0.61	0.03	0.26	0.41	1.99	2.77	-0.11	40.28	1.82	2.98	-0.26	-0.31	2.18	100.00
Balance of Exports and Imports	-5.70	-0.16	0.54	-0.24	-0.08	1.09	-20.92	3.21	-0.27	6.92	-0.06	0.09	-1.68	-3.04	-10.96	-9.41	68.46	29.10	-1.99	24.91	17.96	2.26	100.00
Individual Consumption Expenditure by Households[b]	2.92	0.02	0.03	0.22	0.04	1.41	25.36	7.59	0.13	2.32	0.02	0.09	0.60	0.42	4.75	3.02	41.21	0.78	0.84	2.86	3.04	2.35	100.00
Individual Consumption Expenditure by Households without Housing[b]	2.89	0.02	0.03	0.23	0.04	1.45	26.38	7.65	0.13	2.28	0.02	0.09	0.63	0.42	4.68	3.16	40.10	0.79	0.82	2.81	2.93	2.46	100.00
Government Final Consumption Expenditure	1.00	0.05	0.20	0.07	0.05	0.74	14.44	6.02	0.25	2.12	0.04	0.17	1.17	0.17	2.11	1.90	57.58	1.04	0.72	3.47	4.23	2.46	100.00
Domestic Absorption	2.24	0.03	0.06	0.16	0.03	1.09	20.90	7.12	0.13	2.01	0.02	0.09	0.63	0.34	3.06	2.30	50.69	0.92	0.78	2.48	2.78	2.15	100.00
Total Consumption	2.57	0.03	0.05	0.19	0.04	1.28	23.24	7.37	0.15	2.29	0.02	0.10	0.69	0.38	4.20	2.83	44.28	0.83	0.83	2.97	3.27	2.39	100.00

0.00 = magnitude is less than half of the unit employed.

AP = Asia and the Pacific; BAN = Bangladesh; BHU = Bhutan; BRU = Brunei Darussalam; CAM = Cambodia; FIJ = Fiji; HKG = Hong Kong, China; IND = India; INO = Indonesia; LAO = Lao People's Democratic Republic; MAL = Malaysia; MLD = Maldives; MON = Mongolia; MYA = Myanmar; NEP = Nepal; PAK = Pakistan; PHI = Philippines; PRC = People's Republic of China; SIN = Singapore; SRI = Sri Lanka; TAP = Taipei,China; THA = Thailand; VIE = Viet Nam.

Notes:

1. Each real aggregate value is derived by using a purchasing power parity that is specific to that aggregate; so real aggregates may not sum up to the total of their real components for an economy.

2. For Myanmar, total gross domestic product in local currency units were obtained from publicly available source: Central Statistical Organization. https://www.csostat.gov.mm (accessed 20 February 2024).

[a] Includes individual consumption expenditure by households, nonprofit institutions serving households, and government.

[b] Includes expenditure by nonprofit institutions serving households.

Source: Asian Development Bank estimates based on data supplied by the participating economies.

Table A2.6: Per Capita Real Expenditure, 2017 Revised
(HK$)

Expenditure Category	BAN	BHU	BRU	CAM	FIJ	HKG	IND	INO	LAO	MAL	MLD	MON	MYA	NEP	PAK	PHI	PRC	SIN	SRI	TAP	THA	VIE	AP
Gross Domestic Product	31,547	73,537	379,880	23,633	80,799	359,737	37,662	66,365	44,075	162,021	111,870	68,472	26,660	23,132	32,856	48,980	89,541	580,502	82,656	297,557	110,200	56,190	64,345
Actual Individual Consumption by Households[a]	23,514	42,649	104,013	19,064	58,156	255,105	26,109	40,377	26,226	103,635	54,008	43,792	15,778	20,420	30,730	39,563	42,646	195,501	56,265	180,253	66,540	36,122	36,939
Food and nonalcoholic beverages	9,806	11,899	8,229	7,684	15,714	25,954	7,391	8,940	8,827	19,060	10,162	11,232	6,480	9,415	8,006	11,576	6,957	13,761	10,188	15,781	12,887	6,972	7,902
Food	9,832	11,206	7,323	7,448	15,183	24,349	7,429	8,019	7,554	18,348	8,919	10,288	6,380	9,450	7,730	10,526	6,778	12,056	9,630	14,925	11,411	6,757	7,686
Bread and cereals	3,832	2,653	1,571	2,286	2,939	2,525	1,880	1,836	2,017	2,461	1,541	1,261	1,207	3,153	1,646	3,345	880	1,939	3,089	2,889	2,210	1,848	1,647
Meat and Fish	1,831	1,432	2,768	2,172	3,309	12,390	643	2,686	3,070	6,428	4,143	5,308	2,161	1,324	1,040	4,288	2,724	3,999	1,426	4,922	3,058	2,880	1,968
Fruits and Vegetables	1,840	2,918	942	1,166	4,415	3,556	2,401	1,281	1,363	4,260	1,310	383	1,712	2,448	1,335	1,127	2,027	2,565	1,136	4,473	3,951	1,018	2,070
Other food and nonalcoholic beverages	2,124	4,800	3,126	1,982	5,014	7,483	2,556	3,196	2,367	6,073	3,668	4,684	1,462	2,616	3,929	2,846	1,510	5,490	4,527	3,441	3,622	1,189	2,312
Alcoholic beverages, tobacco and narcotics	340	928	104	820	4,589	2,062	242	2,291	2,025	766	862	2,987	347	406	388	1,037	1,109	1,654	254	3,035	785	819	706
Clothing and footwear	1,089	2,483	1,042	321	1,942	12,227	1,570	980	490	2,298	1,762	1,603	467	478	1,757	485	833	5,192	3,515	7,068	1,268	730	1,332
Clothing	1,003	1,991	948	183	1,736	8,041	1,289	825	403	2,139	1,364	1,352	414	411	1,499	372	876	4,703	3,492	6,433	785	548	1,098
Housing, water, electricity, gas and other fuels[a]	6,676	9,033	30,479	2,480	6,794	39,764	3,827	6,548	4,122	28,089	9,283	6,388	3,369	3,833	10,272	4,744	11,357	26,507	11,491	34,140	12,980	5,859	8,026
Furnishings, household equipment and routine household maintenance	578	1,265	5,921	278	2,333	12,771	580	1,268	1,082	4,522	2,548	576	186	305	860	1,102	1,331	7,195	923	5,878	1,814	1,241	1,066
Health and Education[a]	3,124	12,997	35,446	5,800	12,750	37,711	6,462	8,060	6,722	16,859	19,355	15,896	3,878	4,478	6,557	8,474	11,022	38,774	14,352	47,825	18,839	11,275	8,964
Health[a]	1,349	6,741	8,767	2,722	4,041	21,284	3,131	2,826	1,942	7,007	12,301	5,859	2,009	1,954	3,383	2,671	7,361	18,219	6,047	34,049	9,228	4,483	5,006
Education[a]	1,718	6,354	28,859	2,963	8,414	16,427	3,251	5,153	4,942	9,702	7,725	10,090	1,827	2,442	3,074	5,856	4,136	20,101	8,193	15,832	9,506	6,753	4,100
Transportation and Communication	960	3,021	7,177	1,078	7,449	23,020	3,715	5,783	1,312	16,205	5,137	4,313	578	586	1,879	4,204	5,619	25,956	10,932	24,936	7,133	5,210	4,717
Transportation	843	2,296	6,417	1,013	4,833	17,002	3,068	4,660	1,000	11,496	2,872	3,500	433	339	1,297	3,609	4,223	19,820	10,124	18,866	6,321	2,565	3,662
Communication	107	699	946	39	2,633	6,019	603	1,102	300	4,507	2,061	814	140	287	582	638	1,375	5,937	503	6,003	856	2,902	1,034
Recreation and culture[a]	272	975	2,698	320	630	26,290	161	1,131	273	4,252	1,381	825	136	569	824	653	1,137	22,830	2,575	9,278	1,903	1,484	898
Restaurants and hotels	503	1,066	4,284	841	565	22,551	377	3,672	1,834	10,352	5,223	747	633	367	677	3,052	1,757	22,030	1,466	16,283	5,905	3,189	1,648
Miscellaneous goods and services[a]	762	2,151	17,923	457	4,056	52,754	2,907	1,613	1,741	9,940	3,679	2,707	442	444	1,755	4,719	4,887	30,185	5,320	24,961	7,137	2,168	3,781
Individual Consumption Expenditure by Government	276	9,447	37,631	1,391	6,584	13,751	1,441	3,376	2,752	12,703	11,558	9,433	1,342	985	1,604	2,464	5,794	20,916	7,146	29,928	12,167	4,962	3,808
Collective Consumption Expenditure by Government	1,782	16,066	132,484	410	12,996	21,612	2,395	4,738	9,217	10,938	14,756	10,146	5,933	1,110	1,971	3,900	8,656	44,400	5,151	22,462	9,963	4,401	5,415
Gross fixed capital formation	7,873	27,849	111,984	4,533	14,512	77,906	8,981	20,246	12,105	37,290	48,299	12,154	7,456	5,160	3,832	10,601	34,507	148,025	20,109	54,898	22,212	13,619	20,077
Machinery and equipment	884	4,718	33,247	1,396	3,136	21,834	1,756	1,596	1,763	6,175	11,591	2,691	1,639	1,110	879	2,061	7,056	31,370	2,783	14,350	7,242	1,925	3,919
Construction	9,648	30,827	67,210	3,111	12,204	48,747	7,351	25,248	9,134	32,946	38,348	9,001	6,099	4,138	2,520	9,001	26,974	71,266	21,834	25,915	10,888	14,987	16,462
Other products	163	101	6,499	22	600	7,325	652	921	1,738	2,908	1,813	921	362	306	380	649	2,705	32,381	610	9,087	1,385	288	1,517
Changes in inventories and Acquisitions less disposals of valuables	263	−45	11,283	350	1,282	1,484	976	198	0	559	1,524	2,453	228	2,099	393	−31	851	9,542	4,095	−320	−131	681	775
Balance of Exports and Imports	−865	−5,528	30,973	−376	−2,353	3,630	−394	303	−978	5,334	−2,897	693	−776	−2,675	−1,302	−2,228	1,210	127,933	−2,295	26,087	6,431	592	648
Individual Consumption Expenditure by Households[b]	22,764	35,243	76,756	17,464	51,823	241,354	24,542	36,843	23,383	91,743	44,776	36,540	14,316	19,165	29,019	36,724	37,431	175,295	49,620	153,944	56,027	31,640	33,328
Individual Consumption Expenditure by Households without Housing[b]	18,817	29,421	62,651	15,273	44,028	207,885	21,368	31,061	19,843	75,405	38,635	31,371	12,551	16,086	23,928	32,160	30,476	149,414	40,746	126,798	45,076	27,652	27,886
Government Final Consumption Expenditure	2,175	25,773	168,951	1,644	19,839	35,363	3,890	8,136	12,569	23,421	26,252	19,391	7,725	2,096	3,586	6,434	14,557	65,268	11,836	51,985	21,694	9,196	9,276
Domestic Absorption	33,412	86,268	328,484	24,492	85,544	356,107	38,673	66,098	46,315	152,446	117,129	67,420	28,643	29,178	35,782	53,566	88,030	396,948	87,963	255,459	97,740	55,198	63,724
Total Consumption	25,270	56,192	196,567	19,708	70,197	276,717	28,405	45,176	34,115	114,616	66,881	52,689	20,831	21,549	32,401	43,498	50,800	235,485	62,042	202,229	76,047	40,651	42,092

0 = magnitude is less than half of the unit employed.

AP = Asia and the Pacific; BAN = Bangladesh; BHU = Bhutan; BRU = Brunei Darussalam; CAM = Cambodia; FIJ = Fiji; HKG = Hong Kong, China; IND = India; INO = Indonesia; LAO = Lao People's Democratic Republic; MAL = Malaysia; MLD = Maldives; MON = Mongolia; MYA = Myanmar; NEP = Nepal; PAK = Pakistan; PHI = Philippines; PRC = People's Republic of China; SIN = Singapore; SRI = Sri Lanka; TAP = Taipei,China; THA = Thailand; VIE = Viet Nam.

Notes:

1. Each real aggregate value is derived by using a purchasing power parity that is specific to that aggregate, so real aggregates may not sum up to the total of their real components for an economy.

2. For Myanmar, total gross domestic product in local currency units and population (as of 1 October) were obtained from publicly available source: Central Statistical Organization. https://www.csostat.gov.mm (accessed 20 February 2024).

[a] Includes individual consumption expenditure by households, nonprofit institutions serving households, and government.

[b] Includes expenditure by nonprofit institutions serving households.

Source: Asian Development Bank estimates based on data supplied by the participating economies.

Table A2.7: Per Capita Real Expenditure Index, 2017 Revised

(Hong Kong, China = 100)

Expenditure Category	BAN	BHU	BRU	CAM	FIJ	HKG	IND	INO	LAO	MAL	MLD	MON	MYA	NEP	PAK	PHI	PRC	SIN	SRI	TAP	THA	VIE	AP
Gross Domestic Product	9	20	106	7	22	100	10	18	12	45	31	19	7	6	9	14	25	161	23	83	31	16	18
Actual Individual Consumption by Households[a]	9	17	41	7	23	100	10	16	10	41	21	17	6	8	12	16	17	77	22	71	26	14	14
Food and nonalcoholic beverages	38	46	32	30	61	100	28	34	34	73	39	43	25	36	31	45	27	53	39	61	50	27	30
Food	40	46	30	31	62	100	31	33	31	75	37	42	26	39	32	43	28	50	40	61	47	28	32
Bread and cereals	152	105	62	91	116	100	74	73	80	97	61	50	48	125	65	132	35	77	122	114	88	73	65
Meat and Fish	15	12	22	18	27	100	5	22	25	52	33	43	17	11	8	35	22	32	12	40	25	23	16
Fruits and Vegetables	52	82	26	33	124	100	68	36	38	120	43	37	48	69	38	32	57	72	32	126	111	29	58
Other food and nonalcoholic beverages	28	64	42	26	67	100	34	43	32	81	49	63	20	35	53	38	20	73	60	46	62	16	31
Alcoholic beverages, tobacco and narcotics	16	45	5	40	223	100	12	111	98	37	42	145	17	20	19	50	40	80	12	147	62	40	34
Clothing and footwear	9	20	9	3	16	100	13	8	4	19	14	13	4	4	14	4	9	42	29	58	6	6	11
Clothing	12	25	12	2	22	100	16	10	5	27	17	17	5	5	19	5	11	58	43	80	10	7	14
Housing, water, electricity, gas and other fuels[a]	17	23	77	6	17	100	10	16	10	71	23	16	8	10	26	12	29	67	29	86	33	15	20
Furnishings, household equipment and routine household maintenance	5	10	46	2	18	100	5	10	8	35	20	5	1	2	7	9	10	56	7	46	14	10	8
Health and Education[a]	8	34	94	15	34	100	17	21	18	45	51	42	10	12	17	22	29	103	38	127	50	30	24
Health[a]	6	32	41	13	19	100	15	13	9	33	58	28	9	9	16	13	35	86	28	160	43	21	24
Education[a]	10	39	176	18	51	100	20	31	30	59	47	61	11	15	19	36	25	122	58	96	58	41	25
Transportation and Communication	4	13	31	5	32	100	16	25	6	70	22	19	3	3	8	18	24	113	47	108	31	23	20
Transportation	5	14	38	6	28	100	18	27	6	68	17	21	3	2	8	21	25	117	60	111	37	15	22
Communication	2	12	16	1	44	100	10	18	5	75	34	14	2	5	10	11	23	99	8	100	14	48	17
Recreation and culture[a]	1	4	10	1	2	100	1	4	1	16	5	3	1	2	3	2	4	87	10	35	7	6	3
Restaurants and hotels	2	5	19	4	3	100	2	16	8	46	23	3	3	2	3	14	8	98	7	72	26	14	7
Miscellaneous goods and services[a]	1	4	34	1	8	100	6	3	3	19	7	5	1	1	3	9	9	57	10	47	14	4	7
Individual Consumption Expenditure by Government	2	69	274	10	48	100	10	25	20	92	84	69	10	7	12	18	42	152	52	218	88	36	28
Collective Consumption Expenditure by Government	8	74	613	2	60	100	11	22	43	51	68	47	27	5	9	18	40	205	24	104	46	20	25
Gross fixed capital formation	10	36	144	6	19	100	12	26	16	48	62	16	10	7	5	14	44	190	26	70	29	17	26
Machinery and equipment	4	22	152	6	14	100	8	7	8	28	53	12	8	5	4	9	32	144	13	66	33	9	18
Construction	20	63	138	6	25	100	15	52	19	68	79	18	13	8	5	18	55	146	45	53	22	31	34
Other products	2	1	89	0	8	100	9	13	24	40	25	13	5	4	5	9	37	442	8	124	19	4	21
Changes in inventories and Acquisitions less disposals of valuables	18	-3	760	24	86	100	66	13	0	38	103	165	15	141	26	-2	57	643	276	-22	-9	46	52
Balance of Exports and Imports	-24	-152	853	-10	-65	100	-11	8	-27	147	-80	19	-21	-74	-36	-61	33	3,524	-63	719	177	16	18
Individual Consumption Expenditure by Households[b]	9	15	32	7	21	100	10	15	10	38	19	15	6	8	12	15	16	73	21	64	23	13	14
Individual Consumption Expenditure by Households without Housing[b]	9	14	30	7	21	100	10	15	10	36	19	15	6	8	12	15	15	72	20	61	22	13	13
Government Final Consumption Expenditure	6	73	478	5	56	100	11	23	36	66	74	55	22	6	10	18	41	185	33	147	61	26	26
Domestic Absorption	9	24	92	7	24	100	11	19	13	43	33	19	8	8	10	15	25	111	25	72	27	16	18
Total Consumption	9	20	71	7	25	100	10	16	12	41	24	19	8	8	12	16	18	85	22	73	27	15	15

0 = magnitude is less than half of the unit employed.

AP = Asia and the Pacific; BAN = Bangladesh; BHU = Bhutan; BRU = Brunei Darussalam; CAM = Cambodia; FIJ = Fiji; HKG = Hong Kong, China; IND = India; INO = Indonesia; LAO = Lao People's Democratic Republic; MAL = Malaysia; MLD = Maldives; MON = Mongolia; MYA = Myanmar; NEP = Nepal; PAK = Pakistan; PHI = Philippines; PRC = People's Republic of China; SIN = Singapore; SRI = Sri Lanka; TAP = Taipei,China; THA = Thailand; VIE = Viet Nam.

Notes:

1. Each real aggregate value is derived by using a purchasing power parity that is specific to that aggregate, so real aggregates may not sum up to the total of their real components for an economy.

2. For Myanmar, total gross domestic product in local currency units and population (as of 1 October) were obtained from publicly available source: Central Statistical Organization. https://www.csostat.gov.mm (accessed 20 February 2024).

[a] Includes individual consumption expenditure by households, nonprofit institutions serving households, and government.

[b] Includes expenditure by nonprofit institutions serving households.

Source: Asian Development Bank estimates based on data supplied by the participating economies.

Table A2.8: Per Capita Real Expenditure Index, 2017 Revised
(Asia and the Pacific = 100)

Expenditure Category	BAN	BHU	BRU	CAM	FIJ	HKG	IND	INO	LAO	MAL	MLD	MON	MYA	NEP	PAK	PHI	PRC	SIN	SRI	TAP	THA	VIE	AP
Gross Domestic Product	49	114	590	37	126	559	59	103	68	252	174	106	41	36	51	76	139	902	128	462	171	87	100
Actual Individual Consumption by Households[a]	64	115	282	52	157	691	71	109	71	281	146	119	43	55	83	107	115	529	152	488	180	98	100
Food and nonalcoholic beverages	124	151	104	97	199	328	94	113	112	241	129	142	82	119	101	146	88	174	129	200	163	88	100
Food	128	146	95	97	198	317	97	104	98	239	116	134	83	123	101	137	88	157	125	194	148	88	100
Bread and cereals	233	161	95	139	178	153	114	111	122	149	94	77	73	191	100	203	53	118	188	175	134	112	100
Meat and Fish	93	73	141	110	168	630	33	136	156	327	211	270	110	67	53	218	138	203	72	250	155	146	100
Fruits and Vegetables	89	141	46	56	213	172	116	62	66	206	63	19	83	118	64	54	98	124	55	216	191	49	100
Other food and nonalcoholic beverages	92	208	135	86	217	324	111	138	102	263	159	203	63	113	170	123	65	238	196	149	157	51	100
Alcoholic beverages, tobacco and narcotics	48	132	15	116	650	292	34	325	287	109	122	423	49	58	55	147	118	234	36	430	180	116	100
Clothing and footwear	82	186	78	24	146	918	118	74	37	173	132	120	35	36	132	36	83	390	264	531	59	55	100
Clothing	91	181	86	17	158	733	117	75	37	195	124	123	38	37	137	34	80	428	318	586	74	50	100
Housing, water, electricity, gas and other fuels[a]	83	113	380	31	85	495	48	82	51	350	116	80	42	48	128	59	142	330	143	425	162	73	100
Furnishings, household equipment and routine household maintenance	54	119	555	26	219	1,198	54	119	102	424	239	54	17	29	81	103	125	675	87	551	170	116	100
Health and Education[a]	35	145	395	65	142	421	72	90	75	188	216	177	43	50	73	95	123	433	160	534	210	126	100
Health[a]	27	135	175	54	81	425	63	56	39	140	246	117	40	39	68	53	147	364	121	680	184	90	100
Education[a]	42	155	704	72	205	401	79	126	121	237	188	246	45	60	75	143	101	490	200	386	232	165	100
Transportation and Communication	20	64	152	23	158	488	79	123	28	344	109	91	12	12	40	89	119	550	232	529	151	110	100
Transportation	23	63	175	28	132	464	84	127	27	314	78	96	12	9	35	99	115	541	276	515	173	70	100
Communication	10	68	92	4	255	582	58	107	29	436	199	79	14	28	56	62	133	574	49	581	83	281	100
Recreation and culture[a]	30	109	301	36	70	2,929	18	126	30	474	154	92	15	63	92	73	127	2,543	287	1,034	212	165	100
Restaurants and hotels	31	65	260	51	34	1,369	23	223	111	628	317	45	38	22	41	185	107	1,337	89	988	358	194	100
Miscellaneous goods and services[a]	20	57	474	12	107	1,395	77	43	46	263	97	72	12	12	46	125	129	798	141	660	189	57	100
Individual Consumption Expenditure by Government	7	248	988	37	173	361	38	89	72	334	304	248	35	26	42	65	152	549	188	786	320	130	100
Collective Consumption Expenditure by Government	33	297	2,447	8	240	399	44	88	170	202	273	187	110	21	36	72	160	820	95	415	184	81	100
Gross fixed capital formation	39	139	558	23	72	388	45	101	60	186	241	61	37	26	19	53	172	737	100	273	111	68	100
Machinery and equipment	23	120	848	36	80	557	45	41	55	158	296	69	42	28	22	53	180	801	71	366	185	49	100
Construction	59	187	408	19	74	296	45	153	55	200	233	55	37	25	15	55	164	433	133	157	66	91	100
Other products	11	7	429	1	40	483	43	61	115	192	120	61	24	20	25	43	178	2,135	40	599	91	19	100
Changes in inventories and Acquisitions less disposals of valuables	34	-6	1,456	45	166	192	126	26	0	72	197	317	29	271	51	-4	110	1,232	529	-41	-17	88	100
Balance of Exports and Imports	-133	-853	4,777	-58	-363	560	-61	47	-151	823	-447	107	-120	-413	-201	-344	187	19,731	-354	4,023	992	91	100
Individual Consumption Expenditure by Households[b]	68	106	230	52	155	724	74	111	70	275	134	110	43	58	87	110	112	526	149	462	168	95	100
Individual Consumption Expenditure by Households without Housing[b]	67	106	225	55	158	745	77	111	71	270	139	112	45	58	86	115	109	536	146	455	162	99	100
Government Final Consumption Expenditure	23	278	1,821	18	214	381	42	88	135	252	283	209	83	23	39	69	157	704	128	560	234	99	100
Domestic Absorption	52	135	515	38	134	559	61	104	73	239	184	106	45	46	56	84	138	623	138	401	153	87	100
Total Consumption	60	133	467	47	167	657	67	107	81	272	159	125	49	51	77	103	121	559	147	480	181	97	100

0 = magnitude is less than half of the unit employed.

AP = Asia and the Pacific; BAN = Bangladesh; BHU = Bhutan; BRU = Brunei Darussalam; CAM = Cambodia; FIJ = Fiji; HKG = Hong Kong, China; IND = India; INO = Indonesia; LAO = Lao People's Democratic Republic; MAL = Malaysia; MLD = Maldives; MON = Mongolia; MYA = Myanmar; NEP = Nepal; PAK = Pakistan; PHI = Philippines; PRC = People's Republic of China; SIN = Singapore; SRI = Sri Lanka; TAP = Taipei,China; THA = Thailand; VIE = Viet Nam.

Notes:
1. Each real aggregate value is derived by using a purchasing power parity that is specific to that aggregate, so real aggregates may not sum up to the total of their real components for an economy.
2. For Myanmar, total gross domestic product in local currency units and population (as of 1 October) were obtained from publicly available source: Central Statistical Organization. https://www.csostat.gov.mm (accessed 20 February 2024).
a Includes individual consumption expenditure by households, nonprofit institutions serving households, and government.
b Includes expenditure by nonprofit institutions serving households.
Source: Asian Development Bank estimates based on data supplied by the participating economies.

Table A2.9: Nominal Expenditure, 2017 Revised

(HK$ billion)

Expenditure Category	BAN	BHU	BRU	CAM	FIJ	HKG	IND	INO	LAO	MAL	MLD	MON	MYA	NEP	PAK	PHI	PRC	SIN	SRI	TAP	THA	VIE	AP
Gross Domestic Product	2,404.6	20.2	94.5	172.8	41.7	2,659.6	19,901.2	7,915.7	133.0	2,487.1	37.5	89.5	492.5	242.6	2,765.5	2,560.2	96,046.8	2,675.8	735.5	4,604.7	3,557.0	2,192.7	151,830.8
Actual Individual Consumption by Households[a]	1,634.8	10.8	25.3	134.5	29.4	1,886.0	12,775.5	4,812.3	78.8	1,536.3	19.7	55.2	288.5	196.1	2,394.9	1,950.6	43,024.2	1,049.3	463.5	2,725.7	2,014.4	1,314.3	78,420.4
Food and nonalcoholic beverages	838.1	4.1	2.4	64.0	8.9	191.9	3,819.3	1,401.2	34.2	312.4	3.1	16.1	153.5	113.8	785.1	623.1	7,462.7	63.7	124.5	305.8	470.0	320.5	17,118.5
Food	834.7	3.7	2.1	61.2	8.4	180.0	3,766.8	1,246.9	28.6	298.8	2.6	14.4	149.3	112.2	747.1	571.3	7,234.0	56.8	116.2	289.1	411.5	307.9	16,443.8
Bread and cereals	372.3	1.0	0.5	19.2	1.8	18.7	1,033.7	338.1	8.3	42.5	0.5	2.2	33.1	39.9	168.2	216.0	1,126.3	10.0	36.1	64.1	88.0	91.8	3,712.1
Meat and Fish	160.5	0.4	0.7	19.0	1.9	91.6	363.9	359.6	11.6	101.3	0.8	5.7	48.7	18.6	93.5	191.9	2,679.9	20.4	16.0	92.2	99.8	127.6	4,505.6
Fruits and Vegetables	113.1	1.0	0.4	9.5	2.3	26.3	998.2	216.9	4.9	74.4	0.7	0.9	36.7	22.3	113.8	66.4	1,898.6	12.2	13.4	92.9	151.5	44.9	3,901.2
Other food and nonalcoholic beverages	192.3	1.6	0.9	16.3	3.0	55.3	1,423.5	486.6	9.5	94.2	1.2	7.3	34.9	33.0	409.6	148.8	1,757.9	21.2	59.0	56.7	130.6	56.2	4,999.5
Alcoholic beverages, tobacco and narcotics	32.8	0.3	0.0	4.7	4.1	15.2	264.2	338.6	6.6	26.3	0.4	3.8	6.2	7.5	23.6	42.5	1,023.1	16.7	7.6	52.7	65.5	28.2	1,970.8
Clothing and footwear	98.3	0.8	0.5	2.8	1.3	90.4	770.8	159.4	1.7	44.5	0.6	2.9	11.2	5.7	191.8	38.1	2,306.1	28.4	34.0	110.5	26.6	33.6	3,959.9
Clothing	87.6	0.6	0.4	1.6	1.1	59.5	614.5	136.8	1.3	38.9	0.5	2.3	9.6	4.8	158.0	25.9	1,792.7	24.0	32.4	96.7	26.2	24.1	3,139.5
Housing, water, electricity, gas and other fuels[a]	268.0	1.1	4.3	18.5	1.9	294.0	1,670.5	482.1	8.7	216.6	4.8	7.9	39.9	24.0	488.7	211.0	6,858.8	154.0	40.8	435.5	174.8	167.7	11,573.6
Furnishings, household equipment and routine household maintenance	52.9	0.5	1.5	2.4	1.7	94.4	349.6	194.2	4.1	72.5	1.1	1.1	4.2	3.6	89.4	57.0	1,896.6	42.1	10.2	114.8	77.1	64.4	3,135.4
Health and Education[a]	139.2	1.5	6.0	16.9	4.6	278.8	1,663.4	550.8	6.3	209.9	3.7	8.8	30.5	18.3	291.1	244.3	8,461.6	191.0	40.3	462.7	381.7	208.5	13,220.1
Health[a]	52.5	0.7	1.8	9.4	1.2	157.4	676.0	182.3	2.4	83.3	2.0	3.4	16.4	8.3	161.4	90.2	4,220.6	99.5	21.6	261.7	186.8	92.7	6,331.7
Education[a]	86.7	0.8	4.2	7.5	3.4	121.4	987.4	368.5	3.9	126.6	1.7	5.4	14.1	10.0	129.7	154.1	4,241.0	91.6	18.8	201.0	194.9	115.7	6,888.4
Transportation and Communication	76.2	1.2	2.8	9.9	3.7	170.2	2,166.0	820.2	6.0	298.0	2.5	7.1	15.7	8.2	174.2	256.4	5,026.2	174.5	121.2	374.3	280.7	227.4	10,222.7
Transportation	68.3	0.8	2.2	9.6	2.6	125.7	1,888.9	640.2	4.6	188.9	1.3	5.3	11.0	5.9	127.1	205.0	3,569.0	135.7	116.3	294.4	240.7	136.8	7,780.3
Communication	7.9	0.4	0.6	0.3	1.1	44.5	277.1	180.0	1.4	109.1	1.2	1.7	4.8	2.4	47.1	51.3	1,457.2	38.7	4.8	80.0	40.0	90.6	2,442.4
Recreation and culture[a]	26.9	0.4	1.2	3.4	0.4	194.4	113.8	201.5	1.3	97.3	0.8	1.6	3.6	6.5	100.0	42.5	1,629.2	108.1	36.4	182.8	97.4	80.7	2,930.3
Restaurants and hotels	37.7	0.3	1.0	6.2	0.4	166.7	235.5	440.1	8.4	147.0	1.5	1.2	14.0	3.4	66.4	174.0	2,067.3	98.0	17.1	242.8	183.6	119.3	4,032.1
Miscellaneous goods and services[a]	64.6	0.6	4.7	3.7	2.4	390.0	1,792.3	224.2	6.3	171.4	1.3	4.0	9.7	5.7	184.6	261.7	6,292.6	173.6	49.3	422.9	257.0	94.0	10,416.6
Individual Consumption Expenditure by Government	17.1	1.2	6.0	6.1	2.5	101.7	725.9	278.5	3.3	158.7	2.3	4.8	12.5	7.4	122.2	102.6	5,868.8	101.0	28.7	337.9	286.2	105.6	8,280.8
Collective Consumption Expenditure by Government	126.9	2.5	19.1	2.8	5.5	159.8	1,418.3	443.4	16.5	144.6	3.2	7.7	77.2	12.8	178.7	187.3	9,868.4	173.6	29.0	298.8	289.5	116.6	13,582.1
Gross fixed capital formation	755.3	11.0	32.7	37.9	8.0	576.0	5,521.3	2,545.8	44.4	623.4	15.5	20.0	161.8	76.3	415.1	656.5	40,354.4	680.0	232.4	971.9	816.2	667.4	55,223.1
Machinery and equipment	177.4	3.9	16.3	22.1	2.8	161.4	1,943.7	402.2	12.5	179.2	6.5	7.8	68.7	26.7	167.8	215.6	11,328.8	208.2	58.0	373.8	475.3	168.2	16,027.0
Construction	545.9	7.0	13.1	15.5	4.7	360.4	2,915.5	1,912.5	19.7	361.1	7.9	9.5	78.6	42.0	174.7	374.5	24,735.0	271.2	162.1	367.0	251.4	474.2	33,103.5
Other products	32.0	0.1	3.3	0.3	0.5	54.2	662.1	231.0	12.2	83.1	1.0	2.6	14.5	7.6	72.5	66.5	4,290.6	200.6	12.4	231.2	89.4	25.0	6,092.7
Changes in inventories and Acquisitions less disposals of valuables	28.4	-0.0	4.2	3.6	0.9	11.0	702.2	35.2	0.0	12.0	0.6	4.5	6.4	32.2	47.3	-2.2	1,110.6	55.0	59.8	-6.3	-6.1	38.6	2,138.0
Balance of Exports and Imports	-140.7	-4.0	13.2	-5.9	-2.1	26.8	-516.2	79.1	-6.7	170.8	-1.4	2.1	-41.4	-74.9	-270.5	-232.0	1,689.1	718.0	-49.2	614.5	443.0	55.8	2,467.2
Individual Consumption Expenditure by Households[b]	1,617.7	9.6	19.4	128.5	26.8	1,784.4	12,049.6	4,533.8	75.5	1,377.7	17.4	50.3	276.0	188.8	2,272.7	1,848.0	37,155.4	948.3	434.8	2,387.9	1,728.3	1,208.7	70,139.5
Individual Consumption Expenditure by Households without Housing[b]	1,482.2	8.9	16.0	116.2	25.6	1,536.9	10,902.3	4,177.5	68.8	1,268.4	14.6	44.5	258.1	170.0	1,973.5	1,720.8	33,103.1	816.2	406.3	2,015.6	1,616.5	1,131.5	62,873.6
Government Final Consumption Expenditure	144.0	3.7	25.0	8.9	8.0	261.4	2,144.2	722.0	19.8	303.2	5.5	12.5	89.7	20.1	300.9	289.9	15,737.3	274.5	57.8	636.7	575.7	222.2	21,863.0
Domestic Absorption	2,545.4	24.2	81.3	178.8	43.8	2,632.8	20,417.4	7,836.6	139.8	2,316.3	39.0	87.3	534.0	317.5	3,035.9	2,792.2	94,357.7	1,957.8	784.7	3,990.2	3,114.0	2,136.9	149,363.6
Total Consumption	1,761.7	13.3	44.4	137.3	34.9	2,045.8	14,193.8	5,255.7	95.3	1,680.9	22.9	62.8	365.8	208.9	2,573.6	2,137.9	52,892.7	1,222.9	492.5	3,024.5	2,303.9	1,430.9	92,002.5

0.0 = magnitude is less than half of the unit employed.

AP = Asia and the Pacific; BAN = Bangladesh; BHU = Bhutan; BRU = Brunei Darussalam; CAM = Cambodia; FIJ = Fiji; HKG = Hong Kong, China; IND = India; INO = Indonesia; LAO = Lao People's Democratic Republic; MAL = Malaysia; MLD = Maldives; MON = Mongolia; MYA = Myanmar; NEP = Nepal; PAK = Pakistan; PHI = Philippines; PRC = People's Republic of China; SIN = Singapore; SRI = Sri Lanka; TAP = Taipei,China; THA = Thailand; VIE = Viet Nam.

Note: For Myanmar, total gross domestic product in local currency units were obtained from publicly available source: Central Statistical Organization. https://www.csostat.gov.mm (accessed 20 February 2024).

[a] Includes individual consumption expenditure by households, nonprofit institutions serving households, and government.

[b] Includes expenditure by nonprofit institutions serving households.

Source: Asian Development Bank estimates based on data supplied by the participating economies.

Table A2.10: Economy Shares of Nominal Expenditure to Asia and the Pacific, 2017 Revised
(%)

Expenditure Category	BAN	BHU	BRU	CAM	FIJ	HKG	IND	INO	LAO	MAL	MLD	MON	MYA	NEP	PAK	PHI	PRC	SIN	SRI	TAP	THA	VIE	AP
Gross Domestic Product	1.58	0.01	0.06	0.11	0.03	1.75	13.11	5.21	0.09	1.64	0.02	0.06	0.32	0.16	1.82	1.69	63.26	1.76	0.48	3.03	2.34	1.44	100.00
Actual Individual Consumption by Households[a]	2.08	0.01	0.03	0.17	0.04	2.41	16.29	6.14	0.10	1.96	0.03	0.07	0.37	0.25	3.05	2.49	54.86	1.34	0.59	3.48	2.57	1.68	100.00
Food and nonalcoholic beverages	4.90	0.02	0.01	0.37	0.05	1.12	22.31	8.19	0.20	1.82	0.02	0.09	0.90	0.66	4.59	3.64	43.59	0.37	0.73	1.79	2.75	1.87	100.00
Food	5.08	0.02	0.01	0.37	0.05	1.09	22.91	7.58	0.17	1.82	0.02	0.09	0.91	0.68	4.54	3.47	43.99	0.35	0.71	1.76	2.50	1.87	100.00
Bread and cereals	10.03	0.03	0.01	0.52	0.05	0.50	27.85	9.11	0.22	1.15	0.01	0.06	0.89	1.07	4.53	5.82	30.34	0.27	0.97	1.73	2.37	2.47	100.00
Meat and Fish	3.56	0.01	0.02	0.42	0.04	2.03	8.08	7.98	0.26	2.25	0.02	0.13	1.08	0.41	2.08	4.26	59.48	0.45	0.36	2.05	2.22	2.83	100.00
Fruits and Vegetables	2.90	0.03	0.01	0.24	0.06	0.67	25.59	5.56	0.13	1.91	0.02	0.02	0.94	0.57	2.92	1.70	48.67	0.31	0.34	2.38	3.88	1.15	100.00
Other food and nonalcoholic beverages	3.85	0.03	0.02	0.33	0.06	1.11	28.47	9.73	0.19	1.88	0.02	0.15	0.70	0.66	8.19	2.98	35.16	0.42	1.18	1.13	2.61	1.12	100.00
Alcoholic beverages, tobacco and narcotics	1.66	0.02	0.00	0.24	0.21	0.77	13.40	17.18	0.34	1.33	0.02	0.19	0.32	0.57	1.20	2.16	51.92	0.85	0.39	2.68	3.32	1.43	100.00
Clothing and footwear	2.48	0.02	0.01	0.07	0.03	2.28	19.47	4.02	0.04	1.12	0.02	0.07	0.28	0.38	4.84	0.96	58.24	0.72	0.86	2.79	0.67	0.85	100.00
Clothing	2.79	0.02	0.01	0.05	0.03	1.89	19.57	4.36	0.04	1.24	0.01	0.07	0.30	0.15	5.03	0.82	57.10	0.76	1.03	3.08	0.83	0.77	100.00
Housing, water, electricity, gas and other fuels[a]	2.32	0.01	0.04	0.16	0.02	2.54	14.43	4.17	0.08	1.87	0.04	0.07	0.34	0.21	4.22	1.82	59.26	1.33	0.35	3.76	1.51	1.45	100.00
Furnishings, household equipment and routine household maintenance	1.69	0.02	0.05	0.08	0.05	3.01	11.15	6.19	0.13	2.31	0.03	0.04	0.13	0.12	2.85	1.82	60.49	1.34	0.32	3.66	2.46	2.06	100.00
Health and Education[a]	1.05	0.01	0.05	0.13	0.03	2.11	12.58	4.17	0.05	1.59	0.03	0.07	0.23	0.14	2.20	1.85	64.01	1.44	0.31	3.50	2.89	1.58	100.00
Health[a]	0.83	0.01	0.03	0.15	0.02	2.49	10.68	2.88	0.04	1.32	0.03	0.05	0.26	0.13	2.55	1.43	66.66	1.57	0.34	4.13	2.95	1.46	100.00
Education[a]	1.26	0.01	0.06	0.11	0.05	1.76	14.33	5.35	0.06	1.84	0.02	0.08	0.20	0.14	1.88	2.24	61.57	1.33	0.27	2.92	2.83	1.68	100.00
Transportation and Communication	0.75	0.01	0.03	0.10	0.04	1.66	21.19	8.02	0.06	2.91	0.02	0.07	0.15	0.08	1.70	2.51	49.17	1.71	1.19	3.66	2.75	2.22	100.00
Transportation	0.88	0.01	0.03	0.12	0.03	1.62	24.28	8.23	0.06	2.43	0.02	0.07	0.14	0.08	1.63	2.64	45.87	1.74	1.50	3.78	3.09	1.76	100.00
Communication	0.32	0.01	0.03	0.01	0.05	1.82	11.34	7.37	0.06	4.47	0.05	0.07	0.20	0.10	1.93	2.10	59.66	1.59	0.20	3.27	1.64	3.71	100.00
Recreation and culture[a]	0.92	0.01	0.04	0.12	0.01	6.63	3.88	6.88	0.04	3.32	0.03	0.06	0.12	0.22	3.41	1.45	55.60	3.69	1.24	6.24	3.32	2.75	100.00
Restaurants and hotels	0.94	0.01	0.03	0.15	0.01	4.13	5.84	10.91	0.21	3.64	0.04	0.03	0.35	0.09	1.65	4.32	51.27	2.43	0.42	6.02	4.55	2.96	100.00
Miscellaneous goods and services[a]	0.62	0.01	0.05	0.04	0.02	3.74	17.21	2.15	0.06	1.65	0.01	0.04	0.09	0.05	1.77	2.51	60.41	1.67	0.47	4.06	2.47	0.90	100.00
Individual Consumption Expenditure by Government	0.21	0.01	0.07	0.07	0.03	1.23	8.77	3.36	0.04	1.92	0.03	0.06	0.15	0.09	1.48	1.24	70.87	1.22	0.35	4.08	3.46	1.28	100.00
Collective Consumption Expenditure by Government	0.93	0.02	0.14	0.02	0.04	1.18	10.44	3.26	0.12	1.06	0.02	0.06	0.57	0.09	1.32	1.38	72.66	1.28	0.21	2.20	2.13	0.86	100.00
Gross fixed capital formation	1.37	0.02	0.06	0.07	0.01	1.04	10.00	4.61	0.08	1.13	0.03	0.04	0.29	0.14	0.75	1.19	73.08	1.23	0.42	1.76	1.48	1.21	100.00
Machinery and equipment	1.11	0.02	0.10	0.14	0.02	1.01	12.13	2.51	0.08	1.12	0.04	0.05	0.43	0.17	1.05	1.34	70.69	1.30	0.36	2.33	2.97	1.05	100.00
Construction	1.65	0.02	0.04	0.05	0.01	1.09	8.81	5.78	0.06	1.09	0.02	0.03	0.24	0.13	0.53	1.13	74.72	0.82	0.49	1.11	0.76	1.43	100.00
Other products	0.52	0.00	0.05	0.01	0.01	0.89	10.87	3.79	0.20	1.36	0.02	0.04	0.24	0.13	1.19	1.09	70.42	3.29	0.20	3.79	1.47	0.41	100.00
Changes in inventories and Acquisitions less disposals of valuables	1.33	-0.00	0.20	0.17	0.04	0.51	32.85	1.64	0.00	0.56	0.03	0.21	0.30	1.51	2.21	-0.10	51.95	2.57	2.80	-0.29	-0.29	1.81	100.00
Balance of Exports and Imports	-5.70	-0.16	0.54	-0.24	-0.08	1.09	-20.92	3.21	-0.27	6.92	-0.06	0.09	-1.68	-3.04	-10.96	-9.41	68.46	29.10	-1.99	24.91	17.96	2.26	100.00
Individual Consumption Expenditure by Households[b]	2.31	0.01	0.03	0.18	0.04	2.54	17.18	6.46	0.11	1.96	0.02	0.07	0.39	0.27	3.24	2.63	52.97	1.35	0.62	3.40	2.46	1.72	100.00
Individual Consumption Expenditure by Households without Housing[b]	2.36	0.01	0.03	0.18	0.04	2.44	17.34	6.64	0.11	2.02	0.02	0.07	0.41	0.27	3.14	2.74	52.65	1.30	0.65	3.21	2.57	1.80	100.00
Government Final Consumption Expenditure	0.66	0.02	0.11	0.04	0.04	1.20	9.81	3.30	0.09	1.39	0.02	0.06	0.41	0.09	1.38	1.33	71.98	1.26	0.26	2.91	2.63	1.02	100.00
Domestic Absorption	1.70	0.02	0.05	0.12	0.03	1.76	13.67	5.25	0.09	1.55	0.03	0.06	0.36	0.21	2.03	1.87	63.17	1.31	0.53	2.67	2.08	1.43	100.00
Total Consumption	1.91	0.01	0.05	0.15	0.04	2.22	15.43	5.71	0.10	1.83	0.02	0.07	0.40	0.23	2.80	2.32	57.49	1.33	0.54	3.29	2.50	1.56	100.00

0.00 = magnitude is less than half of the unit employed.

AP = Asia and the Pacific; BAN = Bangladesh; BHU = Bhutan; BRU = Brunei Darussalam; CAM = Cambodia; FIJ = Fiji; HKG = Hong Kong, China; IND = India; INO = Indonesia; LAO = Lao People's Democratic Republic; MAL = Malaysia; MLD = Maldives; MON = Mongolia; MYA = Myanmar; NEP = Nepal; PAK = Pakistan; PHI = Philippines; PRC = People's Republic of China; SIN = Singapore; SRI = Sri Lanka; TAP = Taipei,China; THA = Thailand; VIE = Viet Nam.

Note: For Myanmar, total gross domestic product in local currency units were obtained from publicly available source: Central Statistical Organization. https://www.csostat.gov.mm (accessed 20 February 2024).

a Includes individual consumption expenditure by households, nonprofit institutions serving households, and government.

b Includes expenditure by nonprofit institutions serving households.

Source: Asian Development Bank estimates based on data supplied by the participating economies.

Table A2.11: Per Capita Nominal Expenditure, 2017 Revised
(HK$)

Expenditure Category	BAN	BHU	BRU	CAM	FIJ	HKG	IND	INO	LAO	MAL	MLD	MON	MYA	NEP	PAK	PHI	PRC	SIN	SRI	TAP	THA	VIE	AP
Gross Domestic Product	14,780	27,786	221,717	10,974	47,152	359,737	15,189	30,287	19,274	77,668	76,360	28,887	9,225	8,660	13,316	24,577	68,791	476,775	34,299	195,482	51,636	23,256	39,901
Actual Individual Consumption by Households[a]	10,048	14,883	59,353	8,542	33,189	255,105	9,751	18,413	11,422	47,977	40,044	17,806	5,404	7,003	11,532	18,725	30,815	186,964	21,614	115,716	29,243	13,940	20,609
Food and nonalcoholic beverages	5,151	5,587	5,681	4,061	10,067	25,954	2,915	5,361	4,963	9,755	6,269	5,213	2,874	4,063	3,780	5,981	5,345	11,357	5,807	12,984	6,823	3,400	4,499
Food	5,130	5,134	4,967	3,885	9,535	24,349	2,875	4,771	4,151	9,330	5,361	4,640	2,797	4,005	3,597	5,485	5,181	10,118	5,420	12,273	5,974	3,265	4,321
Bread and cereals	2,288	1,430	1,095	1,220	1,990	2,525	789	1,294	1,199	1,328	982	714	620	1,424	810	2,074	807	1,778	1,683	2,721	1,278	974	976
Meat and Fish	986	1,370	1,711	1,205	2,129	12,390	278	1,376	1,677	3,165	1,596	1,843	913	664	450	1,842	1,919	3,636	747	3,913	1,449	1,353	1,184
Fruits and Vegetables	695	844	2,030	604	2,550	3,556	762	830	712	2,322	1,339	283	688	798	548	637	1,360	2,167	625	3,942	2,200	476	1,025
Other food and nonalcoholic beverages	1,182	1,943	845	1,032	3,397	7,483	1,086	1,862	1,375	2,940	2,352	2,373	654	1,177	1,972	1,428	1,259	3,777	2,752	2,408	1,896	597	1,314
Alcoholic beverages, tobacco and narcotics	202	414	72	301	4,615	2,062	202	1,295	963	821	806	1,215	117	269	113	408	733	2,979	355	2,238	951	299	518
Clothing and footwear	604	1,153	1,145	179	1,461	12,227	588	610	240	1,388	1,253	937	209	204	924	366	1,652	5,063	1,584	4,690	386	356	1,041
Clothing	539	829	958	104	1,216	8,041	469	523	191	1,216	918	735	179	172	761	248	1,284	4,279	1,511	4,107	380	256	825
Housing, water, electricity, gas and other fuels[a]	1,647	1,473	10,057	1,175	2,172	39,764	1,275	1,845	1,261	6,762	9,779	2,548	747	855	2,353	2,026	4,912	27,447	1,902	18,489	2,538	1,779	3,042
Furnishings, household equipment and routine household maintenance	325	692	3,527	153	1,884	12,771	267	743	592	2,265	2,189	370	79	130	430	547	1,358	7,502	474	4,874	1,119	683	824
Health and Education[a]	856	2,085	14,083	1,076	5,223	37,711	1,270	2,108	914	6,555	7,533	2,828	571	653	1,402	2,345	6,060	34,038	1,881	19,643	5,541	2,211	3,474
Health[a]	323	962	4,149	599	1,374	21,284	516	698	351	2,602	4,108	1,086	306	298	777	866	3,023	17,722	1,006	11,110	2,712	984	1,664
Education[a]	533	1,123	9,934	477	3,849	16,427	754	1,410	563	3,953	3,425	1,743	264	356	624	1,479	3,038	16,316	875	8,533	2,830	1,228	1,810
Transportation and Communication	468	1,597	6,610	631	4,179	23,020	1,653	3,138	872	9,305	5,086	2,284	295	294	839	2,461	3,600	31,085	5,651	15,892	4,075	2,412	2,686
Transportation	420	1,109	5,138	611	2,894	17,002	1,442	2,449	670	5,899	2,618	1,723	205	209	612	1,968	2,556	24,184	5,425	12,497	3,495	1,451	2,045
Communication	48	488	1,472	20	1,285	6,019	211	689	201	3,406	2,467	561	90	85	227	493	1,044	6,901	226	3,395	580	961	642
Recreation and culture[a]	165	586	2,830	216	468	26,290	87	771	189	3,039	1,596	532	67	233	481	408	1,167	19,270	1,695	7,762	1,414	855	770
Restaurants and hotels	232	405	2,461	393	403	22,551	180	1,684	1,220	4,589	2,978	392	263	123	320	1,671	1,481	17,468	798	10,309	2,666	1,266	1,060
Miscellaneous goods and services[a]	397	891	11,053	238	2,718	52,754	1,368	858	907	5,354	2,556	1,287	182	202	889	2,512	4,507	30,925	2,299	17,953	3,731	997	2,737
Individual Consumption Expenditure by Government	105	1,673	13,955	385	2,876	13,751	554	1,066	477	4,955	4,584	1,553	234	263	588	985	4,203	17,990	1,339	14,344	4,154	1,120	2,176
Collective Consumption Expenditure by Government	780	3,380	44,749	177	6,215	21,612	1,082	1,697	2,392	4,515	6,515	2,471	1,447	456	860	1,798	7,068	30,926	1,355	12,685	4,203	1,237	3,569
Gross fixed capital formation	4,642	15,078	76,686	2,403	9,062	77,906	4,214	9,741	6,438	19,466	31,435	6,456	3,031	2,726	1,998	6,302	28,903	121,156	10,838	41,262	11,849	7,078	14,512
Machinery and equipment	1,091	5,342	38,254	1,400	3,134	21,834	1,484	1,539	1,817	5,596	13,290	2,524	1,287	953	808	2,069	8,114	37,095	2,703	15,867	6,900	1,784	4,212
Construction	3,355	9,621	30,805	981	5,345	48,747	2,225	7,318	2,851	11,276	16,052	3,079	1,472	1,500	841	3,595	17,716	48,315	7,557	15,580	3,650	5,030	8,699
Other products	196	114	7,627	22	583	7,325	505	884	1,770	2,594	2,093	854	271	273	349	638	3,073	35,745	578	9,815	1,298	265	1,601
Changes in inventories and Acquisitions less disposals of valuables	175	-27	9,955	227	1,040	1,484	536	135	0	376	1,262	1,461	120	1,150	228	-21	795	9,796	2,787	-267	-89	409	562
Balance of Exports and Imports	-865	-5,528	30,973	-376	-2,353	3,630	-394	303	-978	5,334	-2,897	693	-776	-2,675	-1,302	-2,228	1,210	127,933	-2,295	26,087	6,431	592	648
Individual Consumption Expenditure by Households[b]	9,943	13,210	45,398	8,157	30,313	241,354	9,197	17,347	10,945	43,022	35,460	16,253	5,170	6,741	10,943	17,740	26,612	168,974	20,275	101,372	25,089	12,819	18,432
Individual Consumption Expenditure by Households without Housing[b]	9,110	12,238	37,560	7,376	28,879	207,885	8,321	15,984	9,977	39,610	29,632	14,360	4,834	6,071	9,502	16,519	23,709	145,435	18,949	85,567	23,466	12,001	16,523
Government Final Consumption Expenditure	885	5,053	58,704	562	9,091	35,363	1,637	2,762	2,869	9,470	11,099	4,024	1,681	718	1,449	2,783	11,271	48,916	2,694	27,029	8,357	2,357	5,746
Domestic Absorption	15,644	33,314	190,743	11,349	49,506	356,107	15,583	29,985	20,251	72,334	79,257	28,193	10,001	11,335	14,618	26,805	67,581	348,842	36,594	169,395	45,205	22,664	39,252
Total Consumption	10,828	18,263	104,102	8,720	39,404	276,717	10,833	20,110	13,814	52,492	46,560	20,277	6,851	7,459	12,392	20,523	37,883	217,890	22,968	128,401	33,446	15,176	24,178

0 = magnitude is less than half of the unit employed.

AP = Asia and the Pacific; BAN = Bangladesh; BHU = Bhutan; BRU = Brunei Darussalam; CAM = Cambodia; FIJ = Fiji; HKG = Hong Kong, China; IND = India; INO = Indonesia; LAO = Lao People's Democratic Republic; MAL = Malaysia; MLD = Maldives; MON = Mongolia; MYA = Myanmar; NEP = Nepal; PAK = Pakistan; PHI = Philippines; PRC = People's Republic of China; SIN = Singapore; SRI = Sri Lanka; TAP = Taipei,China; THA = Thailand; VIE = Viet Nam.

Note: For Myanmar, total gross domestic product in local currency units and population (as of 1 October) were obtained from publicly available source: Central Statistical Organization. https://www.csostat.gov.mm (accessed 20 February 2024).

a Includes individual consumption expenditure by households, nonprofit institutions serving households, and government.

b Includes expenditure by nonprofit institutions serving households.

Source: Asian Development Bank estimates based on data supplied by the participating economies.

Table A2.12: Per Capita Nominal Expenditure Index, 2017 Revised
(Hong Kong, China = 100)

Expenditure Category	BAN	BHU	BRU	CAM	FIJ	HKG	IND	INO	LAO	MAL	MLD	MON	MYA	NEP	PAK	PHI	PRC	SIN	SRI	TAP	THA	VIE	AP
Gross Domestic Product	4	8	62	3	13	100	4	8	5	22	21	8	3	2	4	7	19	133	10	54	14	6	11
Actual Individual Consumption by Households[a]	4	6	23	3	13	100	4	7	4	19	16	7	2	3	5	7	12	73	8	45	11	5	8
Food and nonalcoholic beverages	20	22	22	16	39	100	11	21	19	38	24	20	11	16	15	23	21	44	22	50	26	13	17
Food	21	21	20	16	39	100	12	20	17	38	22	19	11	16	15	23	21	42	22	50	25	13	18
Bread and cereals	91	57	43	48	79	100	31	51	48	53	39	28	25	56	32	82	32	70	67	108	51	39	39
Meat and Fish	8	5	14	10	17	100	2	11	14	26	13	15	7	5	4	15	15	29	6	32	12	11	10
Fruits and Vegetables	20	39	24	17	72	100	21	23	20	65	38	8	19	22	15	18	38	61	18	111	62	13	29
Other food and nonalcoholic beverages	16	29	27	14	45	100	15	25	18	39	31	32	9	16	26	19	17	50	37	32	25	8	18
Alcoholic beverages, tobacco and narcotics	10	20	4	15	224	100	10	63	47	40	39	59	6	13	6	20	36	144	17	109	46	15	25
Clothing and footwear	5	9	9	1	12	100	5	7	2	11	11	9	2	2	8	3	14	41	13	38	3	3	9
Clothing	7	10	12	1	15	100	6	5	2	15	25	6	2	2	9	3	16	53	19	51	5	3	10
Housing, water, electricity, gas and other fuels[a]	4	4	25	3	5	100	3	5	3	17	25	6	2	2	6	5	12	69	5	46	6	4	8
Furnishings, household equipment and routine household maintenance	3	5	28	1	15	100	2	6	5	18	17	3	1	1	3	4	11	59	4	38	9	5	6
Health and Education[a]	2	6	37	3	14	100	3	6	2	17	20	7	2	2	4	6	16	90	5	52	15	6	9
Health[a]	2	5	19	3	6	100	2	3	2	12	19	5	1	1	4	4	14	83	5	52	13	5	8
Education[a]	3	7	60	3	23	100	5	9	3	24	21	11	2	2	4	9	18	99	5	52	17	7	11
Transportation and Communication	2	7	29	3	18	100	7	14	4	40	22	10	1	1	4	11	16	135	25	69	18	10	12
Transportation	2	7	30	4	17	100	8	14	4	35	15	10	1	1	4	12	15	142	32	74	21	9	12
Communication	1	8	24	0	21	100	4	11	3	57	41	9	1	1	4	8	17	115	4	56	10	16	11
Recreation and culture[a]	1	2	11	1	2	100	0	3	1	12	6	2	0	1	2	2	4	73	6	30	5	3	3
Restaurants and hotels	1	2	11	2	2	100	1	7	5	20	13	2	1	1	1	7	7	77	4	46	12	6	5
Miscellaneous goods and services[a]	1	2	21	0	5	100	3	2	2	10	5	2	0	0	2	5	9	59	4	34	7	2	5
Individual Consumption Expenditure by Government	1	12	101	3	21	100	4	8	3	36	33	11	2	2	4	7	31	131	10	104	30	8	16
Collective Consumption Expenditure by Government	4	16	207	1	29	100	5	8	11	21	30	11	7	2	4	8	33	143	6	59	19	6	17
Gross fixed capital formation	6	19	98	3	12	100	5	13	8	25	40	12	4	3	3	8	37	156	14	53	15	9	19
Machinery and equipment	5	24	175	6	14	100	7	7	7	26	61	12	6	3	4	9	37	170	12	73	32	8	19
Construction	7	20	63	2	11	100	5	15	6	23	33	6	3	3	3	7	36	99	16	32	7	10	18
Other products	3	2	104	0	8	100	7	12	24	35	29	12	4	4	5	9	42	488	8	134	18	4	22
Changes in inventories and Acquisitions less disposals of valuables	12	-2	671	15	70	100	36	9	0	25	85	98	8	78	15	-1	54	660	188	-18	-6	28	38
Balance of Exports and Imports	-24	-152	853	-10	-65	100	-11	8	-27	147	-80	19	-21	-74	-36	-61	33	3,524	-63	719	177	16	18
Individual Consumption Expenditure by Households[b]	4	5	19	3	13	100	4	7	5	18	15	7	2	3	5	7	11	70	8	42	10	5	8
Individual Consumption Expenditure by Households without Housing[b]	4	6	18	4	14	100	4	8	5	19	14	7	2	3	5	8	11	70	9	41	11	6	8
Government Final Consumption Expenditure	3	14	166	2	26	100	5	8	8	27	31	11	5	2	4	8	32	138	8	76	24	7	16
Domestic Absorption	4	9	54	3	14	100	4	8	6	20	22	8	3	3	4	8	19	98	10	48	13	6	11
Total Consumption	4	7	38	3	14	100	4	7	5	19	17	7	2	3	4	7	14	79	8	46	12	5	9

0 = magnitude is less than half of the unit employed.

AP = Asia and the Pacific; BAN = Bangladesh; BHU = Bhutan; BRU = Brunei Darussalam; CAM = Cambodia; FIJ = Fiji; HKG = Hong Kong, China; IND = India; INO = Indonesia; LAO = Lao People's Democratic Republic; MAL = Malaysia; MLD = Maldives; MON = Mongolia; MYA = Myanmar; NEP = Nepal; PAK = Pakistan; PHI = Philippines; PRC = People's Republic of China; SIN = Singapore; SRI = Sri Lanka; TAP = Taipei,China; THA = Thailand; VIE = Viet Nam.

Note: For Myanmar, total gross domestic product in local currency units and population (as of 1 October) were obtained from publicly available source: Central Statistical Organization. https://www.csostat.gov.mm (accessed 20 February 2024).

a Includes individual consumption expenditure by households, nonprofit institutions serving households, and government.

b Includes expenditure by nonprofit institutions serving households.

Source: Asian Development Bank estimates based on data supplied by the participating economies.

Table A2.13: Per Capita Nominal Expenditure Index, 2017 Revised
(Asia and the Pacific = 100)

Expenditure Category	BAN	BHU	BRU	CAM	FIJ	HKG	IND	INO	LAO	MAL	MLD	MON	MYA	NEP	PAK	PHI	PRC	SIN	SRI	TAP	THA	VIE	AP
Gross Domestic Product	37	70	556	28	118	902	38	76	48	195	191	72	23	22	33	62	172	1,195	86	490	129	58	100
Actual Individual Consumption by Households^a	49	72	288	41	161	1,238	47	89	55	233	194	86	26	34	56	91	150	907	105	561	142	68	100
Food and nonalcoholic beverages	115	124	126	90	224	577	65	119	110	217	139	116	64	90	84	133	119	252	129	289	152	76	100
Food	119	119	115	90	221	563	67	110	96	216	124	107	65	93	83	127	120	234	125	284	138	76	100
Bread and cereals	235	147	112	125	204	259	81	133	123	136	101	73	64	146	83	213	83	182	173	279	131	100	100
Meat and Fish	83	52	145	102	180	1,046	23	116	142	267	135	156	77	56	38	156	162	307	63	330	122	114	100
Fruits and Vegetables	68	134	82	59	249	347	74	81	69	226	131	28	67	78	53	62	133	211	61	385	215	46	100
Other food and nonalcoholic beverages	90	166	155	79	259	570	83	142	105	224	179	181	50	90	150	109	96	287	209	183	144	45	100
Alcoholic beverages, tobacco and narcotics	39	80	14	58	891	398	39	250	186	159	156	235	23	52	22	79	141	575	69	432	184	58	100
Clothing and footwear	58	111	110	17	140	1,175	57	59	23	133	120	90	20	20	89	35	159	487	152	451	37	34	100
Clothing	65	100	116	13	147	975	57	63	23	147	111	89	22	21	92	30	156	519	183	498	46	31	100
Housing, water, electricity, gas and other fuels^a	54	48	331	39	71	1,307	42	61	41	222	322	84	25	28	77	67	162	902	63	608	83	58	100
Furnishings, household equipment and routine household maintenance	39	84	428	19	229	1,550	32	90	72	275	266	45	10	16	52	66	165	910	58	592	136	83	100
Health and Education^a	25	60	405	31	150	1,085	37	61	26	189	217	81	16	19	40	67	174	980	54	565	160	64	100
Health^a	19	58	249	36	83	1,279	31	42	21	156	247	65	18	18	47	52	182	1,065	60	668	163	59	100
Education^a	29	62	549	26	213	907	42	78	31	218	189	96	15	20	34	82	168	901	48	471	156	68	100
Transportation and Communication	17	59	246	23	156	857	62	117	32	346	189	85	11	11	31	92	134	1,157	210	592	152	90	100
Transportation	21	54	251	30	142	832	71	120	33	289	128	84	10	10	30	96	125	1,183	265	611	171	71	100
Communication	8	76	229	3	200	938	33	107	31	531	384	87	14	13	35	77	163	1,075	35	529	90	150	100
Recreation and culture^a	21	76	368	28	61	3,414	11	100	24	395	207	69	9	30	63	53	152	2,502	220	1,008	184	111	100
Restaurants and hotels	22	38	232	37	38	2,128	17	159	115	433	281	37	25	12	30	158	140	1,649	75	973	252	119	100
Miscellaneous goods and services^a	14	33	404	9	99	1,927	50	31	33	196	93	47	7	7	32	92	165	1,130	84	656	136	36	100
Individual Consumption Expenditure by Government	5	77	641	18	132	632	25	49	22	228	211	71	11	12	27	45	193	827	62	659	191	51	100
Collective Consumption Expenditure by Government	22	95	1,254	5	174	605	30	48	67	126	183	69	41	13	24	50	198	866	38	355	118	35	100
Gross fixed capital formation	32	104	528	17	62	537	29	67	44	134	217	44	21	19	14	43	199	835	75	284	82	49	100
Machinery and equipment	26	127	908	33	74	518	35	37	43	133	316	60	31	23	19	49	193	881	64	377	164	42	100
Construction	39	111	354	11	61	560	26	84	33	130	185	35	17	17	10	41	204	555	87	179	42	58	100
Other products	12	7	476	1	36	457	32	55	111	162	131	53	17	17	22	40	192	2,232	36	613	81	17	100
Changes in inventories and Acquisitions less disposals of valuables	31	-5	1,772	40	185	264	95	24	0	67	225	260	21	205	41	-4	142	1,744	496	-48	-16	73	100
Balance of Exports and Imports	-133	-853	4,777	-58	-363	560	-61	47	-151	823	-447	107	-120	-413	-201	-344	187	19,731	-354	4,023	992	91	100
Individual Consumption Expenditure by Households^b	54	72	246	44	164	1,309	50	94	59	233	192	88	28	37	59	96	144	917	110	550	136	70	100
Individual Consumption Expenditure by Households without Housing^b	55	74	227	45	175	1,258	50	97	60	240	179	87	29	37	58	100	143	880	115	518	142	73	100
Government Final Consumption Expenditure	15	88	1,022	10	158	615	28	48	50	165	193	70	29	13	25	48	196	851	47	470	145	41	100
Domestic Absorption	40	85	486	29	126	907	40	76	52	184	202	72	25	29	37	68	172	889	93	432	115	58	100
Total Consumption	45	76	431	36	163	1,145	45	83	57	217	193	84	28	31	51	85	157	901	95	531	138	63	100

0 = magnitude is less than half of the unit employed.

AP = Asia and the Pacific; BAN = Bangladesh; BHU = Bhutan; BRU = Brunei Darussalam; CAM = Cambodia; FIJ = Fiji; HKG = Hong Kong, China; IND = India; INO = Indonesia; LAO = Lao People's Democratic Republic; MAL = Malaysia; MLD = Maldives; MON = Mongolia; MYA = Myanmar; NEP = Nepal; PAK = Pakistan; PHI = Philippines; PRC = People's Republic of China; SIN = Singapore; SRI = Sri Lanka; TAP = Taipei,China; THA = Thailand; VIE = Viet Nam.

Note: For Myanmar, total gross domestic product in local currency units and population (as of 1 October) were obtained from publicly available source: Central Statistical Organization. https://www.csostat.gov.mm (accessed 20 February 2024).

^a Includes individual consumption expenditure by households, nonprofit institutions serving households, and government.

^b Includes expenditure by nonprofit institutions serving households.

Source: Asian Development Bank estimates based on data supplied by the participating economies.

Table A2.14: Shares of Nominal Expenditure, 2017 Revised

(%)

Expenditure Category	BAN	BHU	BRU	CAM	FIJ	HKG	IND	INO	LAO	MAL	MLD	MON	MYA	NEP	PAK	PHI	PRC	SIN	SRI	TAP	THA	VIE	AP
Gross Domestic Product	100.00	100.00	100.00	100.00	100.00	100.00	100.00	100.00	100.00	100.00	100.00	100.00	100.00	100.00	100.00	100.00	100.00	100.00	100.00	100.00	100.00	100.00	100.00
Actual Individual Consumption by Households[a]	67.98	53.56	26.77	77.84	70.39	70.91	64.19	60.79	59.26	61.77	52.44	61.64	58.58	80.86	86.60	76.19	44.80	39.21	63.02	59.20	56.63	59.94	51.65
Food and nonalcoholic beverages	34.85	20.11	2.56	37.00	21.35	7.21	19.19	17.70	25.75	12.56	8.21	18.05	31.16	46.92	28.39	24.34	7.77	2.38	16.93	6.64	13.21	14.62	11.27
Food	34.71	18.48	2.24	35.40	20.22	6.77	18.93	15.75	21.54	12.01	7.02	16.06	30.32	46.24	27.02	22.32	7.53	2.12	15.80	6.28	11.57	14.04	10.83
Bread and cereals	15.48	5.15	0.49	11.12	4.22	0.70	5.19	4.27	6.22	1.71	1.29	2.47	6.72	16.44	6.08	8.44	1.17	0.37	4.91	1.39	2.47	4.19	2.44
Meat and Fish	6.67	2.20	0.77	10.98	4.52	3.44	1.83	4.54	8.70	4.07	2.09	6.38	9.89	7.67	3.38	7.49	2.79	0.76	2.18	2.00	2.81	5.82	2.97
Fruits and Vegetables	4.70	4.93	0.38	5.50	5.41	0.99	5.02	2.74	3.69	2.99	1.75	0.98	7.45	9.21	4.12	2.59	1.98	0.45	1.82	2.02	4.26	2.05	2.57
Other food and nonalcoholic beverages	8.00	7.83	0.92	9.41	7.20	2.08	7.15	6.15	7.14	3.79	3.08	8.21	7.09	13.59	14.81	5.81	1.83	0.79	8.02	1.23	3.67	2.56	3.29
Alcoholic beverages, tobacco and narcotics	1.36	1.49	0.03	2.74	9.79	0.57	1.33	4.28	1.06	1.06	3.24	4.21	1.27	3.10	0.85	1.66	1.07	0.62	1.04	1.15	1.84	1.29	1.30
Clothing and footwear	4.09	4.15	0.52	1.64	3.10	3.40	3.87	2.01	1.25	1.79	1.64	3.24	2.27	2.36	6.94	1.49	2.40	1.06	4.62	2.40	0.75	1.53	2.61
Clothing	3.64	2.98	0.43	0.95	2.58	2.24	3.09	1.73	0.99	1.57	1.20	2.55	1.94	1.99	5.71	1.01	1.87	0.90	4.41	2.10	0.74	1.10	2.07
Housing, water, electricity, gas and other fuels[a]	11.15	5.30	4.54	10.71	4.61	11.05	8.39	6.09	6.54	8.71	12.81	8.82	8.10	9.88	17.67	8.24	7.14	5.76	5.54	9.46	4.91	7.65	7.62
Furnishings, household equipment and routine household maintenance	2.20	2.49	1.59	1.40	4.00	3.55	1.76	2.45	3.07	2.92	2.87	1.28	0.86	1.50	3.23	2.22	1.97	1.57	1.38	2.49	2.17	2.94	2.07
Health and Education[a]	5.79	7.50	6.35	9.80	11.08	10.48	8.36	6.96	4.74	8.44	9.87	9.79	6.19	7.54	10.53	9.54	8.81	7.14	5.48	10.05	10.73	9.51	8.71
Health[a]	2.19	3.46	1.87	5.46	2.91	5.92	3.40	2.30	1.82	3.35	5.38	3.76	3.32	3.44	5.84	3.52	4.39	3.72	2.93	5.68	5.25	4.23	4.17
Education[a]	3.61	4.04	4.48	4.34	8.16	4.57	4.96	4.66	2.92	5.09	4.49	6.03	2.87	4.11	4.69	6.02	4.42	3.42	2.55	4.36	5.48	5.28	4.54
Transportation and Communication	3.17	5.75	2.98	5.75	8.86	6.40	10.88	10.36	4.52	7.60	6.66	7.91	3.19	3.40	6.30	10.01	5.23	6.52	16.47	8.13	7.89	10.37	6.73
Transportation	2.84	3.99	2.32	5.56	6.14	4.73	9.49	8.09	3.48	4.39	3.43	5.96	2.22	2.41	4.60	8.01	3.72	5.07	15.82	6.39	6.77	6.24	5.12
Communication	0.33	1.76	0.66	0.19	2.73	1.67	1.39	2.27	1.05	3.21	3.23	1.94	0.97	0.98	1.70	2.01	1.52	1.45	0.66	1.74	1.12	4.13	1.61
Recreation and culture[a]	1.12	2.11	1.28	1.97	0.99	7.31	0.57	2.55	0.98	3.91	2.09	1.84	0.73	2.69	3.62	1.66	1.70	4.04	4.94	4.43	2.74	3.68	1.82
Restaurants and hotels	1.57	1.46	1.93	3.58	0.85	6.27	1.18	5.56	5.56	5.91	1.70	1.36	2.85	1.42	2.40	6.80	2.15	3.66	2.33	5.27	5.16	4.29	2.66
Miscellaneous goods and services[a]	2.68	3.21	4.99	3.25	5.76	14.66	8.66	2.83	5.79	8.87	3.35	5.14	1.97	2.05	6.67	10.22	6.55	6.46	4.29	9.18	7.23	4.06	6.86
Individual Consumption Expenditure by Government	0.71	6.02	6.29	3.51	6.10	3.82	3.65	3.52	2.47	6.38	6.00	5.37	2.54	3.03	4.42	4.01	6.11	3.77	3.90	7.34	8.04	4.82	5.45
Collective Consumption Expenditure by Government	5.28	12.17	20.18	1.62	13.18	6.01	7.13	5.60	12.41	5.81	8.53	8.55	15.68	5.26	6.46	7.32	10.27	6.49	3.95	6.49	8.14	5.32	8.95
Gross fixed capital formation	31.41	54.26	34.59	21.90	19.22	21.66	27.74	32.16	33.40	25.06	41.17	22.35	32.85	31.48	15.01	25.64	42.02	25.41	31.60	21.11	22.95	30.44	36.37
Machinery and equipment	7.38	19.23	17.25	12.76	6.65	6.07	9.77	5.08	9.43	7.21	17.40	8.74	13.96	11.01	6.07	8.42	11.80	7.78	7.88	8.12	13.36	7.67	10.56
Construction	22.70	34.63	13.89	8.94	11.34	13.55	14.65	24.16	14.79	14.52	21.02	10.66	15.96	17.32	6.32	14.63	25.75	10.13	22.03	7.97	7.07	21.63	21.80
Other products	1.33	0.41	3.44	0.20	1.24	2.04	3.33	2.92	9.18	3.34	2.74	2.96	2.94	3.15	2.62	2.60	4.47	7.50	1.69	5.02	2.51	1.14	4.01
Changes in inventories and Acquisitions less disposals of valuables	1.18	-0.10	4.49	2.07	2.21	0.41	3.53	0.44	0.00	0.48	1.65	5.06	1.30	13.28	1.71	-0.08	1.16	2.05	8.13	-0.14	-0.17	1.76	1.41
Balance of Exports and Imports	-5.85	-19.90	13.97	-3.42	-4.99	1.01	-2.59	1.00	-5.07	6.87	-3.79	2.40	-8.41	-30.89	-9.78	-9.06	1.76	26.83	-6.69	13.34	12.45	2.54	1.62
Individual Consumption Expenditure by Households[b]	67.27	47.54	20.48	74.34	64.29	67.09	60.55	57.28	56.79	55.39	46.44	56.26	56.04	77.83	82.18	72.18	38.68	35.44	59.11	51.86	48.59	55.12	46.20
Individual Consumption Expenditure by Households without Housing[b]	61.64	44.04	16.94	67.22	61.25	57.79	54.78	52.77	51.76	51.00	38.81	49.71	52.40	70.10	71.36	67.21	34.47	30.50	55.25	43.77	45.45	51.60	41.41
Government Final Consumption Expenditure	5.99	18.19	26.48	5.12	19.28	9.83	10.77	9.12	14.88	12.19	14.54	13.93	18.22	8.29	10.88	11.32	16.38	10.26	7.85	13.83	16.18	10.13	14.40
Domestic Absorption	105.85	119.90	86.03	103.42	104.99	98.99	102.59	99.00	105.07	93.13	103.79	97.60	108.41	130.89	109.78	109.06	98.24	73.17	106.69	86.66	87.55	97.46	98.38
Total Consumption	73.26	65.73	46.95	79.46	83.57	76.92	71.32	66.40	71.67	67.58	60.97	70.19	74.26	86.13	93.06	83.51	55.07	45.70	66.97	65.68	64.77	65.26	60.60

0.00 = magnitude is less than half of the unit employed.

AP = Asia and the Pacific; BAN = Bangladesh; BHU = Bhutan; BRU = Brunei Darussalam; CAM = Cambodia; FIJ = Fiji; HKG = Hong Kong, China; IND = India; INO = Indonesia; LAO = Lao People's Democratic Republic; MAL = Malaysia; MLD = Maldives; MON = Mongolia; MYA = Myanmar; NEP = Nepal; PAK = Pakistan; PHI = Philippines; PRC = People's Republic of China; SIN = Singapore; SRI = Sri Lanka; TAP = Taipei,China; THA = Thailand; VIE = Viet Nam.

Note: For Myanmar, total gross domestic product in local currency units were obtained from publicly available source: Central Statistical Organization. https://www.csostat.gov.mm (accessed 20 February 2024).

a Includes individual consumption expenditure by households, nonprofit institutions serving households, and government.

b Includes expenditure by nonprofit institutions serving households.

Source: Asian Development Bank estimates based on data supplied by the participating economies.

Table A2.15: Gross Domestic Product, 2017 Revised

(billion local currency units)

Expenditure Category	BAN	BHU	BRU	CAM	FIJ	HKG	IND	INO	LAO	MAL	MLD	MON	MYA	NEP	PAK	PHI	PRC	SIN	SRI	TAP	THA	VIE
Gross Domestic Product	24,818	169	17	89,831	11	2,660	166,281	13,589,826	140,698	1,372	74	28,011	85,969	3,253	37,371	16,557	83,204	474	14,387	17,983	15,489	6,293,905
Actual Individual Consumption by Households[a]	16,872	90	4	69,926	8	1,886	106,744	8,261,823	83,378	848	39	17,266	50,359	2,630	32,364	12,614	37,271	186	9,066	10,645	8,772	3,772,574
Food and nonalcoholic beverages	8,650	34	0	33,240	2	192	31,911	2,405,595	36,227	172	6	5,055	26,785	1,526	10,610	4,029	6,465	11	2,436	1,194	2,047	920,085
Food	8,614	31	0	31,803	2	180	31,473	2,140,705	30,302	165	5	4,499	26,063	1,504	10,096	3,695	6,267	10	2,274	1,129	1,792	883,745
Bread and cereals	3,842	9	0	9,986	0	19	8,637	580,410	8,754	23	1	692	5,776	535	2,272	1,397	976	2	706	250	383	263,601
Meat and Fish	1,656	4	0	9,863	0	92	3,040	617,451	12,242	56	2	1,787	8,504	250	1,264	1,241	2,322	4	313	360	435	366,216
Fruits and Vegetables	1,167	8	0	4,942	1	26	8,340	372,395	5,194	41	1	274	6,408	300	1,539	429	1,645	2	262	363	660	128,831
Other food and nonalcoholic beverages	1,984	13	0	8,449	1	55	11,894	835,338	10,036	52	2	2,301	6,097	442	5,535	962	1,523	4	1,154	222	569	161,436
Alcoholic beverages, tobacco and narcotics	338	3	0	2,463	1	15	2,207	581,287	7,032	15	1	1,178	1,089	101	319	275	886	3	149	206	285	80,967
Clothing and footwear	1,015	7	0	1,469	0	90	6,440	273,621	1,752	25	1	909	1,947	77	2,592	247	1,998	5	664	431	116	96,303
Clothing	904	5	0	851	0	59	5,135	234,787	1,397	21	1	713	1,670	65	2,135	167	1,553	4	634	378	114	69,249
Housing, water, electricity, gas and other fuels[a]	2,766	9	1	9,618	1	294	13,958	827,663	9,206	119	9	2,471	6,963	321	6,604	1,365	5,942	27	798	1,701	761	481,350
Furnishings, household equipment and routine household maintenance	546	4	0	1,254	1	94	2,921	333,415	4,320	40	2	359	738	49	1,208	368	1,643	7	199	448	336	184,979
Health and Education[a]	1,437	13	1	8,807	1	279	13,899	945,695	6,671	116	7	2,742	5,320	245	3,934	1,580	7,330	34	789	1,807	1,662	598,441
Health[a]	542	6	0	4,906	0	157	5,648	313,022	2,562	46	4	1,053	2,855	112	2,181	584	3,656	18	422	1,022	813	266,227
Education[a]	895	7	1	3,901	1	121	8,250	632,673	4,109	70	3	1,690	2,465	134	1,752	996	3,674	16	367	785	849	332,214
Transportation and Communication	786	10	0	5,165	1	170	18,098	1,408,143	6,363	164	5	2,214	2,745	111	2,354	1,658	4,354	31	2,370	1,462	1,222	652,809
Transportation	705	7	0	4,998	1	126	15,782	1,099,050	4,892	104	3	1,671	1,911	79	1,717	1,326	3,092	24	2,275	1,150	1,048	392,629
Communication	81	3	0	167	0	44	2,315	309,093	1,471	60	2	544	834	32	637	332	1,262	7	95	312	174	260,180
Recreation and culture[a]	278	4	0	1,766	0	194	951	345,987	1,377	54	2	516	625	87	1,351	275	1,411	19	711	714	424	231,526
Restaurants and hotels	389	2	0	3,216	1	167	1,967	755,577	8,904	81	3	380	2,451	46	898	1,125	1,791	17	335	948	800	342,539
Miscellaneous goods and services[a]	666	5	1	1,947	1	390	14,976	384,839	6,623	95	2	1,248	1,695	76	2,494	1,692	5,451	31	964	1,652	1,119	269,716
Individual Consumption Expenditure by Government	177	10	1	3,150	1	102	6,065	478,172	3,480	88	4	1,506	2,182	99	1,651	664	5,084	18	562	1,320	1,246	303,170
Collective Consumption Expenditure by Government	1,310	21	3	1,452	1	160	11,850	761,297	17,462	80	6	2,396	13,481	171	2,414	1,211	8,549	31	568	1,167	1,261	334,713
Gross fixed capital formation	7,795	92	6	19,671	2	576	46,133	4,370,575	46,996	344	31	6,260	28,242	1,024	5,609	4,246	34,958	120	4,546	3,796	3,554	1,915,634
Machinery and equipment	1,831	32	3	11,460	1	161	16,240	690,539	13,262	99	13	2,447	11,997	358	2,268	1,394	9,814	37	1,134	1,460	2,070	482,740
Construction	5,634	58	2	8,034	1	360	24,360	3,283,436	20,811	199	16	2,985	13,718	563	2,361	2,422	21,428	48	3,170	1,433	1,095	1,361,250
Other products	330	1	1	176	0	54	5,532	396,600	12,923	46	2	828	2,527	102	980	430	3,717	36	243	903	389	71,645
Changes in inventories and Acquisitions less disposals of valuables	293	-0	1	1,857	0	11	5,867	60,353	0	7	1	1,417	1,116	432	639	-14	962	10	1,169	-25	-27	110,806
Balance of Exports and Imports	-1,452	-34	2	-3,076	-1	27	-4,313	135,778	-7,138	94	-3	672	-7,230	-1,005	-3,655	-1,501	1,463	127	-963	2,400	1,929	160,177
Individual Consumption Expenditure by Households[b]	16,695	80	3	66,776	7	1,784	100,679	7,783,651	79,898	760	34	15,760	48,177	2,532	30,713	11,951	32,187	168	8,505	9,326	7,526	3,469,404
Individual Consumption Expenditure by Households without Housing[b]	15,297	74	3	60,380	7	1,537	91,093	7,172,016	72,832	700	29	13,924	45,049	2,280	26,668	11,128	28,677	145	7,949	7,872	7,039	3,247,948
Government Final Consumption Expenditure	1,486	31	4	4,602	2	261	17,916	1,239,470	20,941	167	11	3,902	15,663	270	4,066	1,875	13,633	49	1,130	2,487	2,507	637,883
Domestic Absorption	26,270	202	14	92,906	12	2,633	170,595	13,454,048	147,836	1,278	77	27,338	93,198	4,257	41,026	18,057	81,740	347	15,350	15,584	13,560	6,133,727
Total Consumption	18,182	111	8	71,378	9	2,046	118,594	9,023,120	100,840	927	45	19,662	63,840	2,801	34,779	13,826	45,820	217	9,635	11,812	10,032	4,107,287

0 = magnitude is less than half of the unit employed.

BAN = Bangladesh; BHU = Bhutan; BRU = Brunei Darussalam; CAM = Cambodia; FIJ = Fiji; HKG = Hong Kong, China; IND = India; INO = Indonesia; LAO = Lao People's Democratic Republic; MAL = Malaysia; MLD = Maldives; MON = Mongolia; MYA = Myanmar; NEP = Nepal; PAK = Pakistan; PHI = Philippines; PRC = People's Republic of China; SIN = Singapore; SRI = Sri Lanka; TAP = Taipei,China; THA = Thailand; VIE = Viet Nam.

Notes:

1. Expenditure aggregates in local currency units presented are the best possible estimates provided by the participating economies, using most recent available data sources, and some of these aggregates may be different from the published expenditure estimates by the economies.

2. For Myanmar, total gross domestic product in local currency units were obtained from publicly available source: Central Statistical Organization. https://www.csostat.gov.mm (accessed 20 February 2024).

[a] Includes individual consumption expenditure by households, nonprofit institutions serving households, and government.

[b] Includes expenditure by nonprofit institutions serving households.

Source: Expenditures in local currency units were supplied by the participating economies for the International Comparison Program.

Appendix 3: Scope and Coverage of Main Gross Domestic Product Aggregates— 2017 and 2021 Cycles

Price Survey	2017	2021
Individual consumption expenditure by households	• The 2017 ICP list was based on the 2011 product list, with obsolete items dropped and new items added based on regional updates and the 2017 ICP global list. • Price collection covered 887 items in the list for Asia and the Pacific.	• The 2021 ICP list was based on the 2017 product list, with obsolete items dropped and new items added based on regional updates and from the 2021 ICP global list. • Price collection covered 992 items in the list for the 2021 ICP in Asia and the Pacific. Two items were dropped after rigorous validation and 990 items were finally used for regional and global comparisons. • Out of 990 items, 857 items were used in the regional comparisons, and 563 items were used for global linking. • There were 430 overlapping items in the 2021 ICP Asia and the Pacific and the ICP global lists.
	• Price collection was conducted monthly, quarterly, semiannually, or annually, depending on the volatility of the items, with some prices collected weekly for fruits, vegetables, and fresh meat products depending on each economy's survey framework. • Prices of durable and less volatile products were collected quarterly, semiannually, and annually.	• No change; same as in 2017.
	• Price collection was conducted nationwide or throughout the economy.	• Price collection was conducted nationwide except for the Philippines where price collection was only in the National Capital Region.
Government final consumption expenditure	• Price collection included annual average compensation for 35 government occupations, with 34 occupations included in the list prepared by the ICP global office, and one additional occupation priced only in Asia and the Pacific. • One item was excluded in the comparison after validation.	• No change; same as in 2017.
Gross fixed capital formation in construction	• Price collection included annual average prices for 58 construction input items of materials, equipment rental, and labor. • Economy relevance indicators were also collected but the regional relevance indicators were used instead.	• Price collection included annual average prices for 52 construction inputs of materials, equipment rental, and labor but after thorough validation, one item was dropped. • Regional relevance indicators were also used even though economy relevance indicators were collected.
Gross fixed capital formation in machinery and equipment	• Price collection included annual average prices for a total of 196 items, including other products.	• Price collection included annual average prices for 182 items. • After data validation, some unspecified items were split; two items dropped; and one item was not priced, resulting in a total of 203 items.

ICP = International Comparison Program.
Source: Asian Development Bank (Economic Research and Development Impact Department).

Appendix 4: List of Reference Purchasing Power Parities

Table A4: List of Reference Purchasing Power Parities

2017 International Comparison Program[a]			2021 International Comparison Program		
Code	Description	Reference	Code	Description	Reference
1100000	**INDIVIDUAL CONSUMPTION EXPENDITURE BY HOUSEHOLDS**				
1102311	Narcotics	Tobacco	1102311	Narcotics	Tobacco
1104A	Actual and imputed rentals for housing	Volume relatives of individual consumption expenditures by households and NPISHs without housing	1104A	Actual and imputed rentals for housing	Not a reference BH in 2021 ICP, used the New Hybrid Approach for Housing
1104421	Miscellaneous services relating to the dwelling	Maintenance and repair of dwelling Water supply	1104421	Miscellaneous services relating to the dwelling	Maintenance and repair of dwelling Water supply
1105131	Repair of furniture, furnishings and floor coverings	Maintenance and repair of dwelling	1105131	Repair of furniture, furnishings and floor coverings	Maintenance and repair of dwelling
1105331	Repair of household appliances	Maintenance and repair of dwelling	1105331	Repair of household appliances	Maintenance and repair of dwelling
1106311	Hospital services	Medical services Dental services Paramedical services	1106311	Hospital services	Medical services Dental services Paramedical services
1107141	Animal drawn vehicles	Bicycles	1107141	Animal drawn vehicles	Bicycles
1107351	Combined passenger transport	Fuels and lubricants for personal transport equipment Maintenance and repair of personal transport equipment Other services in respect of personal transport equipment Passenger transport by railway Passenger transport by road Passenger transport by air Passenger transport by sea and inland waterway	1107351	Combined passenger transport	Fuels and lubricants for personal transport equipment Maintenance and repair of personal transport equipment Other services in respect of personal transport equipment Passenger transport by railway Passenger transport by road Passenger transport by air Passenger transport by sea and inland waterway
1109211	Major durables for outdoor and indoor recreation	Bicycles Audio-visual, photographic and information processing equipment Recording media Repair of audio-visual, photographic and information processing equipment	1109211	Major durables for outdoor and indoor recreation	Furniture and furnishings Carpets and other floor coverings Major household appliances whether electric or not Major tools and equipment Therapeutic appliances and equipment Motor cars Motor cycles Bicycles Telephone and telefax equipment Audio-visual, photographic and information processing equipment Jewellery, clocks and watches
1109231	Maintenance and repair of other major durables for recreation and culture	Maintenance and repair of personal transport equipment Repair of audio-visual, photographic and information processing equipment	1109231	Maintenance and repair of other major durables for recreation and culture	Maintenance and repair of personal transport equipment Repair of audio-visual, photographic and information processing equipment
1109431	Games of chance	Recreational and sporting services	1109431	Games of chance	Recreational and sporting services
1112211	Prostitution	PPP for individual consumption expenditure by households (110000), excluding health and education BHs and BHs with reference PPPs	1112211	Prostitution	PPP for individual consumption expenditure by households (110000), excluding health and education BHs and BHs with reference PPPs
1112411	Social protection	Compensation of employees from health and education services	1112411	Social protection	PPP for Production of Health and Education services: Compensation of employees Intermediate consumption Gross operating surplus
1112511	Insurance	PPP for individual consumption expenditure by households (110000), excluding health and education BHs and BHs with reference PPPs	1112511	Insurance	PPP for individual consumption expenditure by households (110000), excluding health and education BHs and BHs with reference PPPs
1112611	Financial intermediation services indirectly measured (FISIM)	PPP for individual consumption expenditure by households (110000), excluding health and education BHs and BHs with reference PPPs	1112611	Financial intermediation services indirectly measured (FISIM)	PPP for individual consumption expenditure by households (110000), excluding health and education BHs and BHs with reference PPPs
1112621	Other financial services n.e.c.	PPP for individual consumption expenditure by households (110000), excluding health and education BHs and BHs with reference PPPs	1112621	Other financial services n.e.c.	PPP for individual consumption expenditure by households (110000), excluding health and education BHs and BHs with reference PPPs
1112711	Other services n.e.c.	PPP for individual consumption expenditure by households (110000), excluding health and education BHs and BHs with reference PPPs	1112711	Other services n.e.c.	PPP for individual consumption expenditure by households (110000), excluding health and education BHs and BHs with reference PPPs
1113111	Net purchases abroad	Exchange rates	1113111	Net purchases abroad	Exchange rates

continued on next page

Table A4: *continued*

2017 International Comparison Program[a]			2021 International Comparison Program		
Code	Description	Reference	Code	Description	Reference
1200000	**INDIVIDUAL CONSUMPTION EXPENDITURE BY NPISHs**				
1201111	Housing NPISH	Actual and Imputed rentals for housing (ICEH)	1201111	Housing NPISH	Actual and Imputed rentals for housing (ICEH)
1202111	Health – NPISH	Compensation of employees from production of health services	1202111	Health – NPISH	PPP for Production of Health services: Compensation of employees Intermediate consumption Gross operating surplus
1203111	Recreation and culture NPISH	Cultural services (ICEH) Recreational and sporting services (ICEH)	1203111	Recreation and culture NPISH	Cultural services (ICEH) Recreational and sporting services (ICEH)
1204111	Education – NPISH	Compensation of employees from production of education services	1204111	Education – NPISH	PPP for Production of Education services: Compensation of employees Intermediate consumption Gross operating surplus
1205111	Social protection and other services – NPISH	Compensation of employees from production of health and education services	1205111	Social protection and other services – NPISH	PPP for Production of Health and Education services: Compensation of employees Intermediate consumption Gross operating surplus
1300000	**INDIVIDUAL CONSUMPTION EXPENDITURE BY GOVERNMENT**				
1301111	Housing	Actual and Imputed rentals for housing (ICEH)	1301111	Housing	Actual and Imputed rentals for housing (ICEH)
1302111	Pharmaceutical products	Pharmaceutical products (ICEH)	1302111	Pharmaceutical products	Pharmaceutical products (ICEH)
1302112	Other medical products	Other medical products (ICEH)	1302112	Other medical products	Other medical products (ICEH)
1302113	Therapeutic appliances and equipment	Therapeutic appliances and equipment (ICEH)	1302113	Therapeutic appliances and equipment	Therapeutic appliances and equipment (ICEH)
1302121	Out-patient medical services	Medical services (ICEH)	1302121	Out-patient medical services	Medical services (ICEH)
1302122	Out-patient dental services	Dental services (ICEH)	1302122	Out-patient dental services	Dental services (ICEH)
1302123	Out-patient paramedical services	Paramedical services (ICEH)	1302123	Out-patient paramedical services	Paramedical services (ICEH)
1302124	Hospital services	Hospital services (ICEH)	1302124	Hospital services	Hospital services (ICEH)
1302221	Intermediate consumption	PPP for individual consumption expenditure by households (110000), excluding BHs with reference PPPs	1302221	Intermediate consumption	PPP for individual consumption expenditure by households (110000), excluding health and education BHs and BHs with reference PPPs
1302231	Gross operating surplus	PPP for gross fixed capital formation (150000), excluding BHs with reference PPPs	1302231	Gross operating surplus	PPP for gross fixed capital formation (150000), excluding BHs with reference PPPs
1302241	Net taxes on production	Compensation of employees from production of health services	1302241	Net taxes on production	PPP for Production of Health services: Compensation of employees Intermediate consumption Gross operating surplus
1302251	Receipts from sales	Compensation of employees from production of health services	1302251	Receipts from sales	PPP for Production of Health services: Compensation of employees Intermediate consumption Gross operating surplus
1303111	Recreation and culture	Cultural services (ICEH) Recreational and sporting services (ICEH)	1303111	Recreation and culture	Cultural services (ICEH) Recreational and sporting services (ICEH)
1304111	Education benefits and reimbursements	Education (1110000)	1304111	Education benefits and reimbursements	Education (1110000)
1304221	Intermediate consumption	PPP for individual consumption expenditure by households (110000), excluding BHs with reference PPPs	1304221	Intermediate consumption	PPP for individual consumption expenditure by households (110000), excluding health and education BHs and BHs with reference PPPs
1304231	Gross operating surplus	PPP for gross fixed capital formation (150000), excluding BHs with reference PPPs	1304231	Gross operating surplus	PPP for gross fixed capital formation (150000), excluding BHs with reference PPPs
1304241	Net taxes on production	Compensation of employees from production of education services	1304241	Net taxes on production	PPP for Production of Education services: Compensation of employees Intermediate consumption Gross operating surplus
1304251	Receipt from sales	Compensation of employees from production of education services	1304251	Receipt from sales	PPP for Production of Education services: Compensation of employees Intermediate consumption Gross operating surplus
1305111	Social protection	Compensation of employees from production of health and education services	1305111	Social protection	PPP for Production of Health and Education services: Compensation of employees Intermediate consumption Gross operating surplus

continued on next page

Table A4: *continued*

2017 International Comparison Program[a]			2021 International Comparison Program		
Code	Description	Reference	Code	Description	Reference
1400000	**COLLECTIVE CONSUMPTION EXPENDITURE BY GOVERNMENT**				
1401121	Intermediate consumption	PPP for individual consumption expenditure by households (110000), excluding BHs with reference PPPs	1401121	Intermediate consumption	PPP for individual consumption expenditure by households (110000), excluding BHs with reference PPPs
1401131	Gross operating surplus	PPP for gross fixed capital formation (150000), excluding BHs with reference PPPs	1401131	Gross operating surplus	PPP for gross fixed capital formation (150000), excluding BHs with reference PPPs
1401141	Net taxes on production	Compensation of employees from production of collective services	1401141	Net taxes on production	PPP for Production of Collective services: Compensation of employees Intermediate consumption Gross operating surplus
1401151	Receipts from sales	Compensation of employees from production of collective services	1401151	Receipts from sales	PPP for Production of Collective services: Compensation of employees Intermediate consumption Gross operating surplus
1500000	**GROSS CAPITAL FORMATION**				
1501122	Other transport equipment	Road transport equipment	1501122	Other transport equipment	Road transport equipment
1501311	Other products	Electrical and optical equipment General purpose machinery Special purpose machinery Road transport equipment	1501311	Other products	Electrical and optical equipment General purpose machinery Special purpose machinery Road transport equipment
1502111	Change in inventories	BHs classified as containing predominantly goods, excluding BHs with reference PPPs	1502111	Change in inventories	BHs classified as containing predominantly goods, excluding BHs with reference PPPs
1503111	Acquisitions less disposals of valuables	Exchange rates	1503111	Acquisitions less disposals of valuables	Exchange rates
1600000	**BALANCE OF EXPORTS AND IMPORTS**				
1601111	Exports of goods and services	Exchange rates	1601111	Exports of goods and services	Exchange rates
1601112	Imports of goods and services	Exchange rates	1601112	Imports of goods and services	Exchange rates

BH = basic heading, ICEH = individual consumption expenditure by households, ICP = International Comparison Program, NPISH = nonprofit institutions serving households, PPP = purchasing power parity.

[a] Based on the references used in the 2017 ICP and recommendations from the ICP global office at the World Bank.

Notes:

1. Inclusion of ICEH in parentheses indicates that individual consumption expenditure by households is the main aggregate category of the BH under the ICP classification.

2. The ICP classification is available at International Comparison Program. Classification of Final Expenditure on GDP. https://thedocs.worldbank.org/en/doc/708531575560035925-0050022019/original/ICPClassificationdescription20191205.pdf.

Source: The ICP global office at the World Bank.

Appendix 5: Deriving Price Level Indexes and Per Capita Real Expenditure Indexes with Asia and the Pacific = 100

The methodology to measure price level indexes (PLIs) and indexes of per capita real and nominal expenditures is explained in this appendix.

The results of these measures are presented relative to Hong Kong, China as the reference economy, and relative to the Asia and Pacific region as the base. When Hong Kong, China is the base, its PLI and per capita indexes are equal to 100 and indexes of the rest of the economies are expressed relative to the base economy. When the entire region is used as reference with PLI for example of 100, each participating economy (including Hong Kong, China) is compared to the region as the reference.

Appendix Table A5 demonstrates how to calculate the indexes with the region as the base. For each of the 21 economies, the gross domestic product (GDP) in local currency units; purchasing power parities with Hong Kong, China equal to 1; exchange rates; and population are provided in columns 1 to 4. The total real GDP (column 5), divided by total nominal GDP (column 6) gives the conversion factor μ to express indexes with Hong Kong, China as reference economy to the Asia and Pacific region. In this case, μ for GDP is obtained as 317,918/204,629 = 1.554. The conversion varies for each expenditure category and can be calculated in a similar manner.

Per capita real GDP with the Hong Kong dollar as the reference currency is presented in column 7, with the average real per capita income set at HK$82,030 for the region. In column 8, the indexes for per capita real GDP with Asia and the Pacific = 100 are obtained by dividing the real per capita GDP of each economy by the regional average HK$82,030 and multiplying by 100 to convert it as an index. An index above 100 implies higher per capita real GDP for that economy when compared to the regional average and vice versa.

Again, PLI with Asia and the Pacific as reference implies that the PLI for the region = 100. To convert the PLI for each economy expressed with Hong Kong, China's PLI = 100 (column 9) into PLI with Asia and the Pacific =100, the PLI values in column 9 are multiplied by the conversion factor 1.554 to obtain PLIs with Asia and the Pacific as the reference presented in column 10. It can be seen that the PLI for Hong Kong, China has changed from 100 to 155 with respect to region = 100. As noted in the previous paragraph, a PLI greater than 100 implies higher prices in that economy than the regional average. Note that the relativities between economies do not change irrespective of whether the indexes are expressed with Hong Kong, China or the region as the base.

This methodology is applied at each level of analysis.

Table A5: Deriving Price Level Indexes and Per Capita Real Expenditure Indexes (Asia and the Pacific = 100)

Economy	Gross Domestic Product in LCU (billion) (1)	PPPs (HK$ = 1.00) (2)	Exchange Rates (HK$ = 1.00) (3)	Population (million) (4)	Gross Domestic Product: Real (HK$ billion) (1)/(2) (5)	Gross Domestic Product: Nominal (HK$ billion) (1)/(3) (6)	Per Capita Real Expenditure (HK$) (5)/(4)*1000 (7)	Per Capita Real Expenditure (Asia and the Pacific = 100) (7)/82,030*100[a] (8)	Price Level Index (Hong Kong, China = 100) (2)/(3)*100 (9)	Price Level Index (Asia and the Pacific = 100) (9)*μ[a] (10)
Bangladesh	37,510	4.82	10.95	170.26	7,784	3,427	45,717	56	44	68
Bhutan	205	3.34	9.51	0.76	61	22	81,049	99	35	55
Brunei Darussalam	19	0.09	0.17	0.44	208	109	470,955	574	52	82
Cambodia	110,506	243.01	527.23	16.59	455	210	27,407	33	46	72
China, People's Republic of	114,924	0.68	0.83	1,412.36	169,242	138,482	119,829	146	82	127
Fiji	9	0.15	0.27	0.89	58	33	64,376	78	58	90
Hong Kong, China	2,868	1.00	1.00	7.41	2,868	2,868	386,832	472	100	155
India	227,243	3.53	9.51	1,367.17	64,376	23,899	47,087	57	37	58
Indonesia	16,976,751	818.87	1,840.51	272.68	20,732	9,224	76,030	93	44	69
Lao People's Democratic Republic	184,982	516.29	1,247.48	7.34	358	148	48,828	60	41	64
Malaysia	1,549	0.26	0.53	32.58	6,004	2,906	184,316	225	48	75
Maldives	81	1.40	1.98	0.57	58	41	101,638	124	71	110
Mongolia	43,555	148.19	366.52	3.28	294	119	89,532	109	40	63
Nepal	4,543	5.53	15.20	29.06	821	299	28,263	34	36	57
Pakistan	61,230	7.40	20.92	224.78	8,277	2,927	36,821	45	35	55
Philippines	19,411	3.30	6.34	110.20	5,883	3,064	53,383	65	52	81
Singapore	583	0.14	0.17	5.45	4,223	3,373	774,311	944	80	124
Sri Lanka	17,600	9.46	25.58	22.16	1,861	688	84,007	102	37	57
Taipei,China	21,663	2.45	3.60	23.47	8,836	6,010	376,515	459	68	106
Thailand	16,189	1.90	4.11	69.69	8,527	3,935	122,360	149	46	72
Viet Nam	8,479,667	1,212.53	2,979.15	98.51	6,993	2,846	70,994	87	41	63
Asia and the Pacific[b]	n.a.	n.a.	n.a.	3,876	317,918	204,629	82,030[c]	100	n.a.	100[d]

GDP = gross domestic product, HK$ = Hong Kong dollar, LCU = local currency unit, n.a. = not applicable, PPP = purchasing power parity.
[a] The conversion factor μ, in this case 1.554, is obtained by dividing total real GDP (column 5) by total nominal GDP (column 6) for Asia and the Pacific: 317,918/204,629 = 1.554.
[b] The results for Asia and the Pacific, where applicable, are the sum of the values in that column for all 21 participating economies.
[c] The value HK$82,030 (column 7) is the per capita real expenditure for Asia and the Pacific.
[d] The value 100 (column 10) is the real-GDP–weighted average of price level indexes (Asia and the Pacific = 100).
Source: Asian Development Bank estimates based on data supplied by the participating economies.

Appendix 6: Participating Economies—Implementing Agencies and Local Currency Units

Economy	Implementing Agency	Local Currency Units
Bangladesh	Bangladesh Bureau of Statistics	taka (Tk)
Bhutan	National Statistics Bureau	ngultrum (Nu)
Brunei Darussalam	Department of Economic Planning and Statistics	Brunei dollar(s) (B$)
Cambodia	National Institute of Statistics	riel(s) (KR)
China, People's Republic of	National Bureau of Statistics of China	yuan (CNY)
Fiji	Fiji Bureau of Statistics	Fiji dollar(s) (F$)
Hong Kong, China	Census and Statistics Department	Hong Kong dollar(s) (HK$)
India	Ministry of Statistics and Programme Implementation	Indian rupee(s) (₹)
Indonesia	Badan Pusat Statistik	rupiah (Rp)
Lao People's Democratic Republic	Lao Statistics Bureau	kip (KN)
Malaysia	Department of Statistics Malaysia	ringgit (RM)
Maldives	Maldives Bureau of Statistics	rufiyaa (Rf)
Mongolia	National Statistics Office of Mongolia	togrog (MNT)
Nepal	National Statistics Office	Nepalese rupee(s) (NRe/NRs)
Pakistan	Pakistan Bureau of Statistics	Pakistan rupee(s) (PRe/PRs)
Philippines	Philippine Statistics Authority	peso(s) (₱)
Singapore	Department of Statistics	Singapore dollar(s) (S$)
Sri Lanka	Department of Census and Statistics	Sri Lanka rupee(s) (SLRe/SLRS)
Taipei, China	Directorate-General of Budget, Accounting and Statistics	NT dollar(s) (NT$)
Thailand	Trade Policy and Strategy Office | National Economic and Social Development Council	baht (B)
Viet Nam	General Statistics Office	dong (D)

Source: International Comparison Program in Asia and the Pacific. History of ICP and the Involvement of Asia and the Pacific. Asian Development Bank. https://icp.adb.org/about-icp.

Appendix 7: Membership of the Regional Advisory Board in the International Comparison Program for Asia and the Pacific

Members from Implementing Agencies	
	Commissioner, Census and Statistics Department, Hong Kong, China
	Chief Statistician of India and Secretary, Ministry of Statistics and Programme Implementation
	Chief Statistician, Department of Statistics Malaysia
	Chief Statistician, Maldives Bureau of Statistics
	Director General, International Statistical Information Center, National Bureau of Statistics of China, People's Republic of China
	Director General, National Institute of Statistics, Cambodia
	Director General, Trade Policy and Strategy Office, Thailand
Institutional Members	
	Chief Economist and Director General, Economic Research and Development Impact Department, Asian Development Bank
	General Manager, Prices and Transformation Division, Australian Bureau of Statistics
	Chief, Economic and Environment Statistics Section, Statistics Division, United Nations Economic and Social Commission for Asia and the Pacific
Ex-Officio Members	
	Director, Data Division, Economic Research and Development Impact Department, Asian Development Bank
	Director, Development Data Group, World Bank
Member Secretary	Regional Coordinator, International Comparison Program (ICP) Asia and the Pacific, Asian Development Bank
Secretariat	Asian Development Bank ICP Team

Source: International Comparison Program in Asia and the Pacific. 2021 ICP Regional Advisory Board. Asian Development Bank. https://icp.adb.org/regional-advisory-board.

Glossary

Term	Definition
Actual individual consumption by households	The actual individual consumption by households is the sum of individual consumption expenditures by households, expenditures by nonprofit institutions serving households (NPISH), and individual consumption expenditure by government at purchasers' prices.
Additivity	Additivity is a concept in which the real expenditures for higher-level aggregates can be obtained simply by adding the real expenditures of the sub-aggregates of which they are composed. Real expenditures obtained using Gini–Èltetö–Köves–Szulc-based purchasing power parities are not additive, so the sum of the real expenditures for the components of gross domestic product does not equal the real expenditure on gross domestic product. See also *Real expenditure; Gini–Èltetö–Köves–Szulc method*
Base economy invariance	The property whereby the relativities between the purchasing power parities, price level indexes, and volume indexes of economies are not affected by either the choice of currency as numeraire or the choice of reference economy.
Basic heading	The basic heading, in principle, is a group of similar well-defined goods or services for which a sample of products can be selected that are both representative of their type and of the purchases made in economies. In practice, a basic heading is defined as the smallest aggregate for which expenditure data is available.
Benchmark	The benchmark is a standard or point of reference against which an estimate can be compared, assessed, measured, or judged. In the International Comparison Program, the reference year is often referred to as the "benchmark year" or simply as the "benchmark." Purchasing power parities are computed using price data from a full list of household and nonhousehold products and weights derived from the expenditures on gross domestic product for a specified reference year.
Big Mac index	The Big Mac index was developed and used by *The Economist* to illustrate the use of purchasing power parities. It is based on the price of a McDonald's Big Mac hamburger compared across economies.

Term	Definition
Binary comparison	Also referred to as a "bilateral comparison," binary comparison is a price or volume comparison between two economies that draws on data only for those two economies. Also referred to as a "bilateral comparison."
Change in inventories	These are variations in (i) stocks of outputs that are still held by the units that produced them prior to their being further processed, sold, delivered to other units, or used in other ways; and (ii) stocks of products acquired from other units that are intended to be used for intermediate consumption or for resale without further processing. They are measured by the value of the entries into inventories less the value of withdrawals and the value of any recurrent losses of goods held in inventories.
Characteristicity	Characteristicity is the property that requires transitive multilateral comparisons between members of a group of economies to retain the essential features of the intransitive binary comparisons that existed between them before transitivity. A transitive multilateral comparison between a pair of economies is influenced by the price and quantity data of all other economies. Characteristicity requires that the impact of these influences be kept to a minimum when they are introduced into the intransitive binary comparison. In other words, the multilateral purchasing power parity between two economies should deviate as little as possible from their binary purchasing power parity.
Classification of individual consumption according to purpose	This classification is used to identify the objectives of both individual consumption expenditure and actual individual consumption.
Collective consumption expenditure by government	The collective consumption expenditure by government is final consumption expenditure provided by general government on collective services. The collective services are provided simultaneously to all members of the community or to all members of a particular section of the community, such as all households living in a particular region.
Comparability	Comparability is a requirement for economies to price products that are identical or, if not identical, equivalent. Pricing comparable products ensures that differences in prices between economies for a product reflect actual price differences and are not influenced by differences in quality. Two or more products are said to be comparable either if their physical and economic characteristics are identical, or if they are sufficiently similar that consumers are indifferent between them.

Term	Definition
Comparison-resistant	This term was first used to describe nonmarket services that are difficult to compare across economies because (i) they have no economically significant prices with which to value outputs; (ii) their units of output cannot be otherwise defined and measured, or the institutional arrangements for their provision and the conditions of payment differ from economy to economy; and (iii) their quality varies between economies but the differences cannot be identified and quantified. Increasingly, the term is being used to describe capital goods and many market services whose complexity, variation, and economy specificity make it difficult for them to be priced comparably across economies.
Compensation of employees	This refers to total remuneration, in cash or in kind, payable by enterprises to employees in return for work done by the employees during the accounting period.
Component	A component is a subset of goods or services, or both, which make up some defined aggregate.
Consumer price index	The consumer price index is an index of price changes within an economy across time.
Country–product–dummy method	This is a multilateral method used to obtain transitive purchasing power parities (PPPs) at the basic heading level through regression analysis. This method is anchored on the "law of one price" which simply states that the observed price of a commodity in an economy is the product of the international average price of the commodity, general price level in the economy and a random disturbance term. This method regresses log price on country and product dummy variables and hence the label. The method produces measures of reliability for the estimated PPPs.
Domestic absorption	Domestic absorption is the sum of individual consumption by households (individual consumption expenditure by households [ICEH] plus nonprofit institutions serving households [NPISH]), government final consumption expenditure (GFCE), gross fixed capital formation (GFCF), and changes in inventories and acquisitions less disposals of valuables.
Dwellings	Dwellings are buildings that are used entirely or primarily as residences, including any associated structures, such as garages, and all permanent fixtures customarily installed in residences. Movable structures, such as caravans, used as principal residences of households are included.

Term	Definition
Expenditures	Expenditures are values of the amounts that buyers pay, or agree to pay, to sellers in exchange for goods or services that sellers provide to them or to other institutional units designated by the buyers.
Final consumption	Final consumption comprises all goods and services used up by individual households or the community during a given period to satisfy their individual or collective needs or wants.
Fixity	Fixity is a principle that purchasing power parities between economies in a region (and therefore the volume relativities based on purchasing power parities) do not change when the results from that region are combined with those from another region (or regions).
Gini–Eltetö–Köves–Szulc method (GEKS)	The GEKS method is a procedure that enables transformation of nontransitive binary purchasing power parities into transitive purchasing power parities, so that comparisons made between any pair of economies are mutually consistent. The GEKS method produces transitive purchasing power parities that are as close as possible to the nontransitive purchasing power parities originally calculated in the binary comparisons of two or more economies. In practice, the GEKS method is relevant only to the second part of this process (i.e., making the purchasing power parities transitive). Real expenditures obtained using GEKS-based purchasing power parities are not additive, so the sum of the real expenditures for the components of gross domestic product does not equal the real expenditure on gross domestic product.
Goods	Goods are physical objects for which a demand exists, over which ownership rights can be established, and whose ownership can be transferred from one institutional unit to another by engaging in transactions on the market. They are in demand because they may be used to satisfy the needs or wants of households or the community, or used to produce other goods or services
Government final consumption expenditure (GFCE)	The GFCE is the final consumption expenditure by government consisting of expenditure, including imputed expenditure, incurred by general government on both individual consumption goods and services and on collective consumption services.
Gross capital formation	The gross capital formation is a measure of the total value of gross fixed capital formation, changes in inventories, and acquisitions less disposals of valuables for a unit or sector.
Gross domestic product (GDP)—expenditure-based	When estimated from the expenditure side, GDP is a measure of the total value of the final consumption expenditures of households, and general government, gross capital formation plus the balance of exports and imports.

Term	Definition
Gross fixed capital formation	The gross fixed capital formation measures the total value of a producer's acquisitions, less disposals, of fixed assets during the accounting period. It includes certain additions to the value of nonproduced assets (such as subsoil assets or major improvements in the quantity, quality, or productivity of land) realized by the productive activity of institutional units.
Household products	Household products refer to the consumption of households for the following components: • Food and nonalcoholic beverages • Alcoholic beverages, tobacco and narcotics • Clothing and footwear • Housing, water, electricity, gas, and other fuels • Furnishings, household equipment, and routine maintenance of the house • Health • Transport • Communication • Recreation and culture • Education • Restaurant and hotels • Miscellaneous goods and services (personal grooming, personal care, personal effects, financial services, and other services).
Individual consumption expenditure by households (ICEH)	The ICEH is the total value of actual and imputed final consumption expenditures incurred by households for goods and services consumed by the households. In the context of the International Comparison Program in Asia and the Pacific, ICEH also includes the individual consumption expenditure by NPISH.
Local currency unit	The local currency unit is a monetary unit in which economic values are expressed in an economy.
Lorenz curve	Developed by Max Lorenz in 1905, the Lorenz curve is a graphical representation of the distribution of income or wealth. The horizontal axis of the graph represents the percentiles of population, while the vertical axis represents the cumulative income or wealth.
Multilateral comparison	A multilateral comparison is a simultaneous price or volume comparison of more than two economies that produces consistent relations among all pairs of economies, i.e., one that satisfies the transitivity requirement. See also *Transitivity*.

Term	Definition
National annual average price	National annual average price is a price that has been averaged over all localities of an economy to account for regional variations in prices and over the days, weeks, months, or quarters of the reference year to allow for seasonal variations in prices, as well as general inflation and changes in price structures.
Net purchases abroad	Purchases by residential households in the rest of the world (as tourists, travelling businessmen and government officials, crews, border and seasonal workers, diplomatic and military personal stationed abroad) less purchases by nonresidential households in the economic territory of the country (as tourists, travelling businessmen, and government officials, crews, border and seasonal workers, diplomatic and military personal stationed abroad). See also *Resident; Rest of the world.*
Nominal expenditure	The term nominal expenditure is used when expenditures in local currency units is converted to a common currency using market exchange rates. Nominal expenditure may be presented either in terms of a common currency or as an index number relative to the region's total nominal expenditure.
Nonprofit institutions serving households (NPISH)	The NPISH are entities not predominantly financed and controlled by government and that provide goods or services to households free or at prices that are not economically significant.
Per capita expenditure	Per capita expenditure is obtained by dividing the total expenditure by the total population of a given economy or the reference geography.
Price	The monetary value of one unit of a particular good or service.
Price level index (PLI)	Also referred to as "comparative price levels", the PLI is the ratio of a purchasing power parity to the corresponding exchange rate. It shows how the price levels of an economy compare with each other. It is expressed as an index on a base of 100. A PLI greater than 100 means that when the national average prices are converted at exchange rates, the resulting prices tend to be higher on average than prices in the base economy. At the level of gross domestic product, PLIs provide a measure of the differences in the general price levels of economies.
Productivity adjustment	This is an adjustment made to wages and salaries of employees in different economies so that they reflect the same level of labor productivity.

Term	Definition
Purchasing power parity (PPP)	A relative price that measures the number of units of economy B's currency that are needed in economy B to purchase the same quantity and quality of an individual good or service, which one unit of economy A's currency can purchase in economy A.
Real expenditure	Real expenditures are measures obtained by using PPPs to convert final expenditures on product groups, major aggregates, and GDP of different economies into a common currency, by valuing them at a uniform price level. They are the spatial equivalent of a time series of GDP for a single economy expressed at constant prices. Expenditures so converted reflect only volume differences, providing a measure of the relative magnitudes of the product groups or aggregates being compared across economies. At the level of GDP, real expenditure is used to compare the sizes of economies. They may be presented either in terms of a particular currency or as an index number.
Reference purchasing power parities	Reference purchasing power parities are used for basic headings, which are based on prices collected for other basic headings. See also *Basic heading*.
Relative price levels	Relative price levels are ratios of PPPs for components of GDP to the overall PPP for GDP for an economy. They indicate whether the price level for a given basic heading or aggregate is higher or lower in relation to the general price level in the economy.
Resident	An institutional unit is resident in an economy when it has a center of economic interest in the economic territory.
Rest of the world	The rest of the world consists of all nonresident institutional units that enter into transactions with resident units, or that have other economic links with resident units.
Services	Services are the result of a production activity that changes the conditions of the consuming units or facilitates the exchange of products or financial assets.
Structured product descriptions	These are generic descriptions that list the characteristics relevant to a particular narrow cluster of products.
Total consumption	This is the total value of ICEH, NPISH, and GFCE at purchasers' prices.

Term	Definition
Transitivity	Sometimes referred to as "circularity", transitivity is a property whereby the direct purchasing power parities between any two economies (or regions) yields the same result as an indirect comparison via a third economy (or region).
Volume measure	Also referred to as real expenditures. See also *Real expenditure*.

References

Asian Development Bank (ADB). International Comparison Program in Asia and the Pacific. https://icp.adb.org/about-icp.

——. 2019. *Corporate Results Framework, 2019–2024: Policy Paper.*

——. 2020. *2017 International Comparison Program for Asia and the Pacific: Purchasing Power Parities and Real Expenditures: Results and Methodology.* https://www.adb.org/sites/default/files/publication/639696/icp-2017-results-methodology.pdf.

——. 2021. Key Indicators for Asia and the Pacific 2021. 52nd edition. https://www.adb.org/publications/key-indicators-asia-and-pacific-2021.

——. 2023. Key Indicators for Asia and the Pacific 2023. 54th edition. https://www.adb.org/publications/key-indicators-asia-andpacific-2023.

B. Balassa. 1964. The Purchasing-Power Parity Doctrine: A Reappraisal. *Journal of Political Economy.* 72 (6, December). pp. 584–596. https://www.jstor.org/stable/1829464.

B. Balk, A. Rambaldi, and D. S. P. Rao. 2020. Macroeconomic Measures for a Globalized World: Global Growth and Inflation. *Macroeconomic Dynamics.* 1–47. https://doi.org/10.1017/S1365100520000152.

Central Statistical Organization. https://www.csostat.gov.mm (accessed 20 February 2024).

W. E. Diewert. 2013. Methods of Aggregation Above the Basic Heading Level Within Regions. In *Measuring the Real Size of the World Economy.* World Bank.

Food and Agriculture Organization of the United Nations (FAO) et al. 2023. *The State of Food Security and Nutrition in the World 2023. Urbanization, Agrifood Systems Transformation and Healthy Diets Across the Rural–Urban Continuum.* Rome: FAO. https://openknowledge.fao.org/items/445c9d27-b396-4126-96c9-50b335364d01.

A. Heston. 2013. Dwelling Services. In *Measuring the Real Size of the World Economy.* World Bank.

R. C. Inklaar. 2019. Productivity Adjustment in ICP. Paper presented at the 4th Technical Advisory Group Meeting, International Comparison Program. 28–29 October 2019. Washington, DC. World Bank.

R. C. Inklaar and D. S. P. Rao. 2017. Cross-Country Income Levels over Time: Did the Developing World Suddenly Become Much Richer? *American Economic Journal: Macroeconomics.* 9 (1, January). pp. 265–290. https://www.aeaweb.org/articles?id=10.1257/mac.20150155.

International Comparison Program in Asia and the Pacific. History of ICP and the Involvement of Asia and the Pacific. Asian Development Bank. https://icp.adb.org/about-icp.

International Comparison Program in Asia and the Pacific. 2021 ICP Regional Advisory Board. Asian Development Bank. https://icp.adb.org/regional-advisory-board.

International Monetary Fund. International Financial Statistics. http://data.imf.org/ (accessed 26 January 2024).

P. McCarthy. 2013. Extrapolating PPPs and Comparing ICP Benchmark Results. In *Measuring the Real Size of the World Economy.* World Bank.

D. S. P. Rao. 2013. The Framework of the International Comparison Program. In *Measuring the Real Size of the World Economy.* World Bank.

P. Samuelson. 1964. Theoretical Notes on Trade Problems. *Review of Economics and Statistics*. 46 (2). pp. 145–154. https://www.jstor.org/stable/1928178.

J. E. Stiglitz, A. Sen, and J. Fitoussi. 2009. *Report by the Commission on the Measurement of Economic Performance and Social Progress*. Government of France.

The Economist. 2024. Burgernomics—The Big Mac Index. https://www.economist.com/big-mac-index (accessed 6 May 2024).

United Nations. 2009. *System of National Accounts 2008*. https://unstats.un.org/unsd/nationalaccount/docs/sna2008.pdf.

United Nations Economic and Social Council (ECOSOC). 2016a. *Final Report of the Friends of the Chair Group on the Evaluation of the 2011 Round of the International Comparison Programme*.

——. 2016b. *Statistical Commission: Report of the Forty-Seventh Session*. 8–11 March 2016.

——. 2020. *Report of the World Bank on the International Comparison Programme*. https://unstats.un.org/UNSDWebsite/statcom/session_52/documents/2021-22-ICP-E.pdf.

World Bank. International Comparison Program—History. https://www.worldbank.org/en/programs/icp/history.

——. 2013. *Measuring the Real Size of the World Economy: The Framework, Methodology, and Results of the International Comparison Program—ICP*. World Bank. https://thedocs.worldbank.org/en/doc/927971487091799574-0050022017/original/ICPBookeBookFINAL.pdf.

——. 2016. *International Comparison Program: Classification of Final Expenditure on GDP*. World Bank. http://pubdocs.worldbank.org/en/708531575560035925/pdf/ICP-Classification-description-2019-1205.pdf.

——. 2020. *Purchasing Power Parities and the Size of World Economies: Results from the 2017 International Comparison Program*. https://openknowledge.worldbank.org/handle/10986/33623.

——. 2021. *Purchasing Power Parities for Policy Making: A Visual Guide to Using Data from the International Comparison Program*. http://hdl.handle.net/10986/35736.

——. World Development Indicators. https://databank.worldbank.org/source/world-development-indicators (accessed 7 May 2024).

——. DataBank: ICP 2021. https://databank.worldbank.org/source/icp-2021 (accessed 31 May 2024).